Getting There

Tasks for Academic Writing

Getting There
Tasks for Academic Writing

Jessica Williams
University of Illinois at Chicago

Jacqueline R. Evans

HARCOURT COLLEGE PUBLISHERS

Fort Worth   Philadelphia   San Diego   New York   Orlando   Austin   San Antonio
Toronto   Montreal   London   Sydney   Tokyo

Publisher	Phyllis Dobbins
Market Strategist	Kenneth S. Kasee
Developmental Editor	Mary K. Coman
Project Editor	Laura Therese Miley
Art Director	Susan Journey
Production Manager	Angela Williams Urquhart

Photo credit: ©Photopia
Cartoons provided by Rachel Scheiner

ISBN: 0-03-031096-2
Library of Congress Catalog Card Number: 99–67206

Address for Domestic Orders
Harcourt College Publishers, 6277 Sea Harbor Drive, Orlando, FL 32887-6777
800-782-4479

Address for International Orders
International Customer Service
Harcourt, Inc., 6277 Sea Harbor Drive, Orlando, FL 32887-6777
407-345-3800
(fax) 407-345-4060
(e-mail) hbintl@harcourt.com

Address for Editorial Correspondence
Harcourt College Publishers, 301 Commerce Street, Suite 3700, Fort Worth, TX 76102

Web Site Address
http://www.harcourtcollege.com

Harcourt College Publishers will provide complimentary supplements or supplement packages to those adopters qualified under our adoption policy. Please contact your sales representative to learn how you qualify. If as an adopter or potential user you receive supplements you do not need, please return them to your sales representative or send them to: Attn: Returns Department, Troy Warehouse, 465 South Lincoln Drive, Troy, MO 63379.

Printed in the United States of America

9 0 1 2 3 4 5 6 7 8 048 9 8 7 6 5 4 3 2 1

Harcourt College Publishers

Getting There: Tasks for Academic Writing is an intermediate writing text for college or college-bound students who are not native speakers of English. It prepares these students for typical academic writing tasks that involve the collection, organization, and analysis of information. It also teaches some of the conventions of academic written expression.

We have designed this textbook with a specific group of students in mind: second language writers who may have had limited experience writing in *any* language. These same students are now, or soon will be, confronted with academic writing tasks. The goal of this text is to prepare them for these tasks. To this end, we believe it is important that they begin multi-paragraph writing immediately.

The five units revolve around tasks. By *task*, we mean that the students have to do something, not just write something although, of course, each task culminates in a writing assignment. We have tried to make these tasks as *authentic* as possible, approximating the kinds of analytic and writing activities that are typical outside the composition classroom. These include relatively simple tasks, such as listing and relating personal experiences, as well as more complex problem-solving tasks that involve critical thinking skills such as interpretation, evaluation, and synthesis.

The text begins with a task that requires writers to draw on their personal experience. This is a comfortable place to begin the writing process because it is an area in which each writer is automatically "an expert." Subsequent tasks, however, require students to gather and analyze information from other sources so that they gain expertise on, and write about, more academic topics.

The tasks increase in *cognitive complexity* as the text progresses, but they do not require increasing language proficiency. The object is to engage students in academic tasks and academic writing without frustrating them with material that is linguistically too complex. The tasks build from less demanding activities to ones that begin to approximate academic writing. The first unit presents a familiar and straightforward task: writing a personal narrative. Later, writers collect information from a variety of sources, extract generalizations, and present arguments based on these generalizations, each unit building on previously learned skills. Because the tasks increase in complexity, it is important to work through the text in order, at least through Unit Three.

The success of any materials can be measured by the performance of learners after they have stopped using them. Thus, *learner autonomy* is another major goal of this text. When students finish this course, we hope that they will have a good idea of how to move from a set of data or ideas to a written product. In the beginning, learners are guided through the writing process in a fairly controlled manner. Each activity is supported by material in the text, with instruction on how to collect, organize, and analyze information and later, on how to move effectively through the writing process of drafting, revising, and editing. Gradually, students do more for themselves with less and less guidance from the text. Instruction becomes less directed. For instance, in later units, students are not given step-by-step instruction on how to accomplish a task. Instead they are simply told to use the tools they have learned in previous units. For this reason, units become shorter as students progress through the text. It is not that they are expected to do less work in later units; rather, they are expected to accomplish more of the work on their own.

Peer Response

Peer response is an integral part of the text. The most important thing that students must understand about this part of the process is that by learning to respond to the writing of others, they are in fact learning to critique and improve their own writing. The text shows students how to respond to a peer's writing and how to use a peer's response to improve their own work, step by step. Examples are provided for all phases of the writing process, including a first draft, a peer response, instructor comments, revision plans, and a revised draft. Providing clear examples of how to accomplish each step is especially important in demonstrating peer response and will facilitate this phase of revising that many students, and even many instructors, find a challenge. To incorporate peer response effectively into the writing process, it is also crucial that the instructor both explain the purpose of peer response and demonstrate the process itself. Students do not automatically know how to respond effectively to their classmates' writing; and, they may not necessarily see how the instructor's and peers' comments can be used in revising. Peer response can provide helpful feedback on student writing as well as useful practice for self-evaluation, but it requires a great deal of initial support and modeling.

Sample drafts are based on student essays. These are not essays in the classic sense; they are far from perfect writing. They were written by students but have been edited to reflect the pertinent writing focus and for some grammatical errors. The level of writing competence the essays represent should be within the grasp of students using this text.

Organization of Units

Every unit of *Getting There* features *high interest* topics. Students write best when they are writing about material that interests them. The topics were chosen on the basis of hundreds of survey responses from students in a variety of educational settings. The readings are intended to provide an entry point for the topic, to raise the students' interest, and to help them generate ideas for writing. Students are not expected to respond to the readings in writing or to use them in their writing assignments. Additional readings on each topic are provided in a separate section at the back of the book, for instructors or students who wish to explore certain topics in greater depth. Some of the additional readings are slightly more difficult than the ones within each unit; others explore somewhat different aspects of the topic. The Instructor's Manual also includes suggestions for films on some of the units' topics. Use of the films is optional, however, because not all institutions and/or students have access to films or equipment.

All units follow the same basic plan. They open with an introduction to the topic and readings, followed by questions to stimulate discussion. Students then have an opportunity to generate ideas on the topic. This step is followed by instruction on the information-gathering part of the task, as well as, in early units, guidance on preparing to write. After students have done their own first draft, they look at some sample first drafts and peer responses provided in the text. At this point, the text presents the writing instruction that is the focus of that unit, such as writing an introduction or providing support. Students use this information to respond to a peer's work and then to their own. They use suggestions in the peer response in preparing their second draft. Finally, they reach the editing phase of the writing process. Each unit provides an editing focus appropriate for the unit. Each Editing Practice has brief explanations of the grammar point in question. Samples in the editing practice sections are based on student-generated texts, rather than on single sentences. One section addresses the use of learner dictionaries. We strongly encourage instructors to model the use of such dictionaries and to have students use them when they write. Additional Editing Practice sections are provided at the back of the book to give instructors maximum flexibility.

Grammar

Although most users of *Getting There* have already had quite a bit of grammar instruction, their writing often continues to be plagued by sentence-level errors. The editing portion in this text focuses on errors in aspects of grammar that students have already "learned," and those that significantly affect their writing. This is not a grammar text, and we do not attempt to teach new or very difficult forms, or to provide exhaustive coverage of any area of grammar. Instead, the focus is on increasing learners' awareness of basic errors in their own writing. For example, we concentrate on editing issues such as sentence fragments and tense continuity, rather than providing a thorough treatment of modals or all the uses of the present perfect.

The approach to grammar in *Getting There* is designed to enable learners to make sentence-level improvements independently. The Editing Practice sections contain a step-by-step guide to editing. These guidelines assume that students know what a noun, verb, and adjective are, but little else. Students can practice editing on sample essays that are provided after the guidelines. These samples contain a single type of error in order to focus the students' attention on a particular grammar point. Students then repeat the process on their own writing. Sample essays with multiple problems appear after Editing Practice 6–12 and provide additional practice.

Learning Logs

Learning Logs are introduced in the editing phase of Unit Three. Students use them in deciding what grammar points have caused them difficulty in their writing and in making a plan for improvement. The Learning Logs provide students with a way of tracking their own progress and maintaining control over the accuracy of their writing. As with many other aspects of the writing process, it is important for the instructor to model the use of Learning Logs and to encourage students to use them.

We know that many of our ESL writing students are making an important and difficult transition. Soon they will have to become independent writers in a second language and tackle challenging topics and tasks. It is our hope that this text will help in the process of getting there.

There is an Instructor's Manual available that explains the process unit by unit.

This book is designed to help you to become a more skillful and independent writer and to prepare for college work. You will learn step by step how to gather data about a particular topic from different sources, sort through and organize that data, and then use the data to make and support a claim. This is the core of most academic writing that you will undertake in college.

In addition to understanding and organizing data, a crucial part of writing well is the ability to revise and critique your own work. Most writers write several drafts and make many revisions before they arrive at a finished piece of work. How do they do this? Where should *you* start? You will start by responding to the work of others, and then you will critically examine your own writing. You will learn what the important elements of an essay are, and you will give feedback on essays in the book and then on essays that your classmates write. You will also receive feedback from your classmates and instructor about your own writing. As part of the writing process, you will learn how to use this feedback to improve your writing in later drafts. Most important perhaps, you will be writing about topics that interest you.

One of the basic goals we have set in this text is for you to begin writing independently. In the beginning of the book, you will get lots of support, both from the book and from your instructor and classmates. By the end, you should be writing more successfully on your own because by then, you will have the skills to analyze what you have written and to improve it. This is what you will need to do in your other college courses, so it is important that you begin right now to think of yourself as an independent writer.

Acknowledgments

Many people assisted in the long process of bringing *Getting There* to print. The teaching assistants and students at the University of Illinois at Chicago suffered through many bulky, photocopied drafts of the book. Alissa Cohen was particularly helpful in providing useful suggestions in the early stages of revision.

Our deepest appreciation goes to UIC's Council on Excellence in Teaching and Learning for supporting our initial efforts to come up with appropriate materials for our students. We are also grateful to Ruth Williams, for her assistance and suggestions, to Jacqueline Record, for her careful editorial attention, and to Phyllis Dobbins, for her perseverance.

We would also like to express our thanks to the Harcourt editorial and production teams: Marie Schein, acquisitions editor; Mary K. Coman, developmental editor; Laura Miley, project editor; Susan Journey, art director; and Angela Urquhart, production manager.

TO THE INSTRUCTOR   V

TO THE STUDENT   IX

UNIT ONE   STEREOTYPES AND PREJUDICE   3

UNIT TWO   COMPUTERS AND CHANGE   53

UNIT THREE   STRATEGIES IN ADVERTISING   113

UNIT FOUR   NAVIGATING THE UNIVERSITY   153

UNIT FIVE   ATTITUDES ACROSS GENERATIONS   183

EDITING PRACTICE   218

ADDITIONAL READINGS   255

CREDITS   279

To the Instructor   v

To the Student   ix

Brief Table of Contents   xi

UNIT ONE STEREOTYPES AND PREJUDICE   3

1. **EXPLORING IDEAS   3**
   Readings   5
   About the Readings in this Book   5
   Current Situation: Hate Crimes/Black-Asian Tensions   6
   Blacks Can Be Racist, Too   8
   Little Things Are Big   10
   Thinking about the Topic   11

2. **GENERATING IDEAS AND DRAFTING   12**
   About the Writing Process   12
   Writing Focus: Writing with a Point   13
   Choosing a Topic   16
   Generating and Organizing Ideas   16
   Drafting: Writing Your First Draft   19

3. **REVISING   19**
   Evaluating Essays   19
   Writing Focus: Expressing a Main Point   24
   Responding to a Peer's Writing   29
   Preparing for a Second Draft   33
   Evaluating Your Own Work   40
   Preparing for a Conference   45
   Writing Your Second Draft   45

4. **EDITING   45**
   About the Editing Process   45
   Editing Practice #1: Finding and Correcting Fragments   46
   Editing Your Own Work: The Final Draft   50

UNIT TWO COMPUTERS AND CHANGE   53

1. **EXPLORING IDEAS   53**
   Readings   53
   No Privacy on the Web   54
   Japan's Newest Young Heartthrobs Are Sexy, Talented and Virtual   56

Minefields: MiningCo.com Is Digging for Online Gems So That You Don't Have To 60
Thinking about the Topic 62

2. **GATHERING INFORMATION AND DRAFTING 64**
   Generating Ideas 64
   Preparing a Questionnaire 65
   Identifying Trends 68
   Writing Focus: Linking Body Paragraphs to the Main Point 76
   Drafting: Writing Your First Draft 77

3. **REVISING 78**
   Evaluating Essays 78
   Writing Focus: Making Claims and Providing Support in Body Paragraphs 87
   Analyzing a Revision 89
   Responding to a Peer's Writing 97
   Evaluating Your Own Work 101
   Writing Your Second Draft 105

4. **EDITING 105**
   Editing Practice #2: Comma Splices and run-on Sentences 105
   Editing Your Own Work: The Final Draft 110

UNIT THREE STRATEGIES IN ADVERTISING 113

1. **EXPLORING IDEAS 113**
   Readings 113
      Advertising 114
      Lotion Voyage 116
      Three Advertisements 119
   Thinking about the Topic 120

2. **GATHERING INFORMATION AND DRAFTING 121**
   Identifying Advertising Strategies 121
   Gathering Information 123
   Analyzing Data 124
   Drafting: Body Paragraphs 127
   Drafting: Linking Body Paragraphs to the Main Point 128

3. **REVISING 129**
   Evaluating Essays 129
   Writing Focus: Introductions and Conclusions 137
   Responding to a Peer's Writing 139
   Evaluating Your Own Work 143
   Writing Your Second Draft 144

4. **EDITING 144**
   Editing Practice #3: Using a learner dictionary 144

About Learning Logs   145
Editing Your Own Work: The Final Draft   151

UNIT FOUR NAVIGATING THE UNIVERSITY   153

1. EXPLORING IDEAS   153
Readings   153
   Jean-Baptiste   154
   Shanti   155
   Application Packet: Office of Student Financial Aid   156
   Faculty and Student Perceptions of Irritating Behaviors in the College Classroom   159
Thinking about the Topic   162

2. GATHERING INFORMATION AND DRAFTING   164
Gathering Information   164
Analyzing Your Text   165
Drafting: Writing Your First Draft   169

3. REVISING   171
Evaluating Essays   171
Writing Focus: Body Paragraphs with Different Purposes   173
Evaluating Your Own Work   175
Writing Your Second Draft   177

4. EDITING   178
Editing Practice #4: Verbal adjectives   178
Editing Your Own Work: The Final Draft   180
Learning from Your Final Draft   180

UNIT FIVE ATTITUDES ACROSS GENERATIONS   183

1. EXPLORING IDEAS   183
Readings 183
   A Totally Alien Life Form: Teenagers   184
   Hardship and Dreams   186
   For Many Immigrants, a Cultural Reluctance to Spare the Rod   190
Thinking about the Topic   193

2. GATHERING INFORMATION AND DRAFTING   195
Preparing for an Interview   195
Analyzing the Data   198
Drafting: Writing Your First Draft   199

3. REVISING   200
Evaluating Essays   200
Writing Focus: Taking Risks   206

Evaluating Your Own Work   207
Writing Your Second Draft   208

4. EDITING   208
Editing Practice #5: Present and past tense   208
Editing Your Own Work: The Final Draft   217
Learning from Your Final Draft   217

EDITING PRACTICE   218

- #6: Working with sentence and clause boundaries   218
- #7: Agreement   226
- #8: Present perfect versus past tense   230
- #9: Embedded questions   234
- #10: Word form   236
- #11: Noncount nouns   240
- #12: *Must* and *should*   243

Editing Abbreviation Chart   247
Practice Exercises   248

ADDITIONAL READINGS   255

Unit One
   English Spoken Here   255
   Sexism and Kids' Software   258
Unit Two
   Intimate Strangers   260
   E-mail Smiles and Other Basic Netiquette   262
Unit Three
   Mediaspeak   264
   "Sunday Best" Becoming More of a Daily Ritual   266
Unit Four
   Fresh Air Interview with Anne Matthews   268
   Excerpt: Lives on the Boundary   272
Unit Five
   Excerpt: A Regular Revolution   273
   Excerpt: Dear Diane   276

Credits   279

Getting There

Tasks for Academic Writing

STEREOTYPES AND PREJUDICE

Task
- Writing from personal experience

Writing Focus
- Writing with a point

Editing Focus
- Finding and correcting fragments

In this unit, you will begin to practice the steps of writing an essay. First you will explore ideas and experiences related to *prejudice* and *stereotypes*. Then you will work through the process of **generating ideas, drafting** and **revising**, and, finally, **editing** the essay. Each of these steps is a crucial part of producing a thorough, well-written essay. Prejudice and stereotypes touch almost everyone in one way or another. In this unit, you will read about and discuss different aspects of prejudice and stereotypes and then write about a personal experience. You will use this experience to make a larger point about prejudice or stereotypes in general.

1. EXPLORING IDEAS

Activity 1.1

A. *Look up these words in a dictionary. Write the definitions you find.*

1. prejudice _____

_____

_____

2. stereotype _____

_____

_____

B. *The definitions for "prejudice" that you find may vary somewhat depending on what dictionary you use, but they have one thing in common: the notion of a negative attitude or judgment that someone forms before he or she knows the facts.*

Stereotypes are related to prejudice, but they are not exactly the same thing. A stereotype may or may not be based on facts, but it involves the oversimplified notion that all members of a certain group have essentially the same characteristics or behave in the same way.

1. Give an example of each.

prejudice _____

_____

_____

stereotype _____

_____

_____

2. What is the difference between a stereotype and a prejudice?

_____

_____

_____

C. *The characteristics of a group's stereotype can be good or bad. Did the stereotype you thought of assume negative or positive characteristics?*

1. Make a list of other stereotypes.

Stereotypes that stress positive characteristics

Example:

African-Americans   a good sense of rhythm

_____   _____

_____   _____

_____   _____

Stereotypes that stress negative characteristics

_____   _____

_____   _____

_____   _____

2. With your classmates, discuss why even positive stereotypes might be just as much a problem as negative ones.

D. *Many of you may have had personal experiences involving prejudice or stereotypes. Find out if any of your classmates or someone they know has had an experience similar to yours. Or, perhaps you have been on the other side of the fence and believed* *in a stereotype that you later discovered was not justified. Find out if this has ever happened to any of your classmates.*

READINGS

About the Readings in This Book

In every unit, you will find several readings that deal with the unit topic. In Unit One, the readings deal with the issues of prejudice and stereotypes. Each reading has an introduction and is followed by discussion questions for you to talk about with your classmates. The purpose of these readings is simply to get you thinking and talking about the topic and perhaps to introduce some new ideas or viewpoints for you to consider. There are more readings for each unit in the back of the book.

In the 1970s and 1980s, the U.S. auto industry was having serious economic problems. Many people who had spent their whole lives working in auto plants lost their jobs. In some cases, entire towns were deeply affected because their economy depended on the local plant. Because the workers had no money, many other businesses also closed and people had to move to find work. Although the problem was not a simple one, some people blamed their job losses on the fact that many foreign cars were being sold in the United States for less than American cars. They felt that the agreements the U.S. government made with other nations were not fair and gave special advantages to other countries, especially Japan. This was a difficult time for a lot of people, and many were very angry. Some people saw Asians as the root of their trouble and, as a result, tensions were high between autoworkers and Asian-Americans— even those who were not Japanese. It was during this time that Vincent Chin, whom you will read about in the first segment of this reading, was attacked.

The second segment of this reading deals with the case of Soon Ja Du and Latasha Harlins and the conflicts that often occur between Asian-Americans and African-Americans, especially in large urban areas like Los Angeles. Some Asian-Americans have opened businesses in poor black communities where there have been few businesses or opportunities for employment for a long time. Some of the residents of these neighborhoods feel angry or resentful when they see outsiders come in and open businesses. Often these residents or their neighbors were turned down when they applied for business loans themselves. Some Asian-Americans see violence in the neighborhood and assume that all blacks are dangerous. The result is often miscommunication and problems between the two groups. These are some of the circumstances surrounding the case you will read about.

Current Situation: Hate Crimes/Black–Asian Tensions

"Hate Crimes"

Despite their achievements, and to some extent because of them, Asian-Americans remain vulnerable to violent "**hate crimes**." Reliable figures on such offenses are hard to come by, since reporting criteria vary from **jurisdiction** to jurisdiction, and many Asian-American victims hesitate to approach the police because they fear **retaliation** or feel ashamed. But anecdotal evidence from across the country strongly suggests that attacks on Asian-Americans are on the rise.

Within the Asian-American community, one hate crime stands out above all others: the 1982 slaying in Detroit of Vincent Chin, 27, a U.S.-born draftsman of Chinese ancestry. On June 19, 1982, Chin and three friends visited a topless bar to celebrate an impending marriage. Two white men got into an argument with Chin, using racial **slurs**. A **scuffle** ensued, and the participants were ejected from the bar. Later that night, the two whites spotted Chin at a fast-food restaurant. When he left, one of the assailants held him while the others struck him repeatedly with a baseball bat. Chin died four days later.

Attackers Get Probation

Chin's attackers, who were laid-off autoworkers, apparently believed he was Japanese and blamed him for the U.S. auto industry's troubles. Originally charged with second-degree murder, the two were subsequently allowed to plead guilty to a lesser offense, **manslaughter**. Wayne County Circuit Judge Charles Kaufman placed them on three years' probation and fined them each $3,780.

The Asian-American community reacted with fury to what it viewed as a **miscarriage of justice**. A "Justice for Vincent Chin" committee was formed, petitions were circulated, and pressure was brought to bear on the Justice Department to enter the case. The protests eventually yielded a federal indictment charging Ronald Ebens, the bat-wielding assailant, with depriving Chin of his civil rights. Ebens was tried, found guilty, and sentenced to 25 years in prison, but judicial errors caused the conviction to be **reversed on appeal**.

At the 1987 retrial, Ebens's attorney persuaded the jury that the assault on Chin was not racially motivated. The autoworker went free. A subsequent civil suit was settled by a court-approved agreement under which Ebens agreed to pay, in installments, $1.5 million to Chin's estate.

Though the Chin tragedy occurred nearly a decade ago, it has left an enduring mark on the Asian-American community. Now, as then, it is perceived as evidence that Asian-Americans are still not regarded as U.S. citizens worthy of equal protection under the law. Chin's death also underscored the need to identify and eliminate the causes of hate crimes directed at Asian-Americans and to take vigorous countermeasures whenever such crimes occur.

Stanley Mark, a staff member of the Asian-American Legal Defense and Edu-

hate crime a violent act committed against a person or group because of their race, religion, ethnicity, or sexual orientation

jurisdiction territory or area under judicial or legal control

retaliation an attack in revenge

slur insult

scuffle fight

manslaughter the crime of killing a person but not intentionally; a less serious crime than murder

miscarriage of justice a failure of the legal system to be fair or just

reversed on appeal a higher court changed the decision and set Ebens free

(continued on next page)

(continued from previous page)

cation Fund, a non-profit civil rights organization based in New York, feels hate crimes are caused by "**bias**, just bias, it's not rational." He adds, "There is a stereotype that Asians are foreigners even though they've been here many generations. There is a sense that they are competing for jobs, that there are too many of them even though the number is under 4 percent of the whole population of the United States. Many people feel they are the cause of job layoffs and other economic ills. These stereotypes feed into a biased context, and some people act on it violently."

bias prejudice

Black–Asian Tensions

The violence is by no means one-sided. Soon Ja Du, a Korean-born grocer in Los Angeles, was convicted of voluntary manslaughter Oct. 11 in the shooting death of a 15-year-old black girl the merchant had accused of stealing a $1.79 bottle of orange juice. The incident occurred in Du's store in the south-central section of the city, where **animosity** between Korean shopkeepers and their black customers runs deep. Similar tensions have been noted in other cities with sizable numbers of Asian-Americans and African-Americans.

animosity hostility; resentment

Du's shooting of Latasha Harlins was recorded on videotape, which was shown at the trial. On the tape, Du is seen firing a .38 caliber handgun she has retrieved from under the counter. According to the *Los Angeles Times*' description of the videotape: "At that point, the teenager turns toward the camera, which is mounted over the entrance to the store, and appears to be walking away from Du. Then, the gun in Du's hand is seen firing. The girl falls, a single mortal wound to the back of the head." Although Du's attorneys argued that she acted in self-defense and that the gun fired accidentally, the jury came to a different conclusion. It found Du guilty of voluntary manslaughter. In doing so, it rejected a more serious charge of second-degree murder as well as a lesser charge of involuntary manslaughter.

Du was sentenced to five years' **probation**, creating outrage in the black community. Los Angeles District Attorney Ira Reiner said on Nov. 26 that he would appeal the sentence.

probation the system of allowing a lawbreaker to go free if he or she promises to behave well

In the opinion of Jerry Yu of Korean-American Coalition, the main cause of friction between Korean shopkeepers and the black community is "economic disempowerment." He notes that "south-central L.A. is a huge area, and yet it has no major employers. It doesn't even have a bank. People have no hope. And that was true even before Korean-Americans started moving into the area and opening businesses. In 1965, when the Watts riots occurred, there weren't any Korean merchants there."

Because Koreans have established businesses in the area, Yu says, "We do have an interest in trying to improve the situation. The Korean community is trying to reach out, to work with the black community." At the same time, though, he says there is "no way that one or two communities are going to solve a problem this big. It will require a concerted effort at the local, state, regional, and federal levels."

Meanwhile, many Asian-Americans are increasingly concerned about intra-community crime. Street gangs, many composed of young Vietnamese men, have been preying upon other Asian immigrants in a number of major cities. One favored

(continued on next page)

(continued from previous page)

tactic is the home invasion, in which gang members burst into a house in an Asian neighborhood, tie up family members and threaten to beat them until money and other valuables are surrendered. Before leaving, the thieves threaten the family with reprisals if the crime is reported to the police.

Oftentimes, the warning is heeded. California Rep. Matsui has observed that many Asian-Americans "came from totalitarian regimes where going to the police is simply not standard practice. Tragically, many of these immigrants also believe that the violence they face here is simply part of life in America."

Discussion Questions

1. What is your opinion of the two verdicts discussed in the reading?

2. Why do you think the autoworker and Soon Ja Du received the sentences they did?

3. What causes hate crimes and tension between ethnic groups? Stanley Mark says they are caused by pure bias, but Jerry Yu says economic disempowerment is one cause. What do you think?

People tend to think that prejudice and stereotyping occur only between different ethnic, racial, or religious groups. Although it is true that they do occur between different groups, prejudice and stereotyping can also occur within a single group. Take, for example, the experience of Mohammed Naseehu Ali, who writes about his first years in the United States in the following article.

Blacks Can Be Racist, Too

Mohammed Naseehu Ali

I spent my first three years in the United States at a **boarding high school** for the arts in northern Michigan. Being thousands of miles away from my home in Ghana, West Africa, I was fortunate when a White family opened their house and invited me to spend my vacations with them. I never encountered any **overt** racial prejudice in the three years I lived in their all-White neighborhood. Ironically enough, it was during this period that I began to gain a clearer understanding of the universality of prejudice. More specifically, I was reminded once again how prejudiced Blacks can be toward one another.

It all started when an African-American schoolmate vehemently **reproached** me for having too many White friends and accused me of "**selling out**" to "**the Man**,"

boarding high school a school where students live instead of going home every day

overt open, not secret

reproached criticized

"selling out" to "the Man" being disloyal to the black race and favoring whites

(continued on next page)

(continued from previous page)

conveniently ignoring the glaring fact that only 7 percent of the school's student body was Black! And, as if these accusations were not enough, she repeatedly **called me out** for not eating exclusively at an all-Black table in the campus dining hall.

called me out scolded me

I tried repeatedly to convince her that I chose my friends not for the **pigmentation** of their skin, but because we shared similar personalities and principles and common goals. Still, nothing I said could change the mind of my young schoolmate. She remained wholly convinced that Blacks who befriended Whites had to be "ashamed" of their skin color, something I am not nor will ever be.

pigmentation the color of living things

To this day, I'm not sure my African-American schoolmate actually *hated* Whites. However, she often defended the racially blind myth that "we [Black people] are not capable of racial prejudice." As an African, I have never held such an illusion. Growing up in an area of Ghana where my tribe was in the minority, I witnessed Black-on-Black prejudice at an early age. Instructors at my elementary school often blatantly compared the IQs of pupils from my tribe to those of animals (one of the teachers referred to children not of his tribe as "a flock of sheep!"). Most natives who have traveled along the coast of West Africa can tell you similar horror stories. When Ghanaians travel to Nigeria or Nigerians go to Ghana, they are treated like second-rate citizens. And our French-speaking neighbors from Togo, the Ivory Coast and Benin often treat English-speaking Africans—Ghanaians and Nigerians—as if they were not human beings at all.

Like every other continent, Africa has its share of problems among its peoples. Africa's turbulent tribal conflicts, often based on erroneous judgments and prejudices among different ethnic and language groups, are well documented. However, the first time that I *personally* became the victim of overt prejudice was on a bus ride from New York City to Newark, New Jersey. It was there an African-American male who overheard us speaking Hausa, our native language, said to his friend, "I hate these Africans: They're always speaking their stupid language." Not long after, a Black co-worker asked me, "Why are the African women I see here so ugly? Why are some of your people so dumb?"

I offer these examples in hopes of proving to my former schoolmate and other African-Americans who share her opinion that the claim that Blacks are incapable of racism is false. Black-on-Black prejudice, whether based on religion, nationality, skin color, sexuality, ideological preference or even one's physical appearance, is **thriving** and is just as harmful as White–Black prejudice.

thriving healthy or well developed

Perhaps no human being is completely innocent of some form of prejudice. It seems innate to human nature to use our own ethical, moral or religious standards to prejudge others. But as humans we are also blessed with an even greater natural ability to love, a quality that can guide us toward tolerating, understanding and even appreciating our differences.

It is not my intention to prescribe a romantic remedy for the prejudice that exists in this country. I am still looking for its cure myself. But I have learned that false egocentric claims can only prevent the kinship that should exist between Africans of the **diaspora**. Let us make a quest for racial harmony, rather than racism, among our diverse peoples—including **sojourners** like me—our common agenda.

diaspora a situation in which people live outside their homeland and are scattered all over the world

sojourners visitors, guests

Discussion Questions

1. Why do some African-Americans think they can't be prejudiced?

2. Why does the author think that they are?

— · — · — · — · — · — · — · — · — · — · — · — · — · — · — · — · — ·

This passage was written in 1961 by a man named Jesús Colón. Colón came to New York as a stowaway; that is, he hid on a boat without paying for a ticket. Like many other immigrants, he hoped to find greater opportunity than in his native Puerto Rico. Sometimes his hopes were met; at other times, he was disappointed.

Little Things Are Big
Jesús Colón

It was very late at night on the eve of Memorial Day. She came into the subway at the 34th Street Pennsylvania Station. I am still trying to remember how she managed to push herself in with a baby on her right arm, a **valise** in her left hand, and two children, a boy and a girl about three and five years old, trailing after her. She was a nice-looking white lady in her early twenties.

valise small suitcase

At Nevins Street, Brooklyn, we saw her preparing to get off at the next station—Atlantic Avenue—which happened to be the place where I too had to get off. Just as it was a problem for her to get on, it was going to be a problem for her to get off the subway with two small children to be taken care of, a baby on her right arm and a medium sized valise in her left hand.

And there I was, also preparing to get off at Atlantic Avenue, with no bundles to take care of—not even the customary book under my arm without which I feel that I am not completely dressed.

As the train was entering Atlantic Avenue station, some white man stood up from his seat and helped her out, placing the children on the long **deserted** platform. There were only two adult persons on the long platform some time after midnight on the eve of last Memorial Day.

deserted empty

I could perceive the steep, long concrete stairs going down to the Long Island Railroad or into the street. Should I offer my help as the American white man did at the subway door placing the two children outside the subway car? Should I take care of the girl and the boy, take them by their hands until they reached the end of the steep long concrete stairs of the Atlantic Avenue station?

Courtesy is characteristic of the Puerto Rican. And here I was—a Puerto Rican—hours past midnight, a valise, two white children and a white lady with a baby on her arm **palpably** needing somebody to help her at least until she descended the long concrete stairs.

courtesy good manners

palpably clearly

But how could I, a **Negro** and a Puerto Rican, approach this white lady who very likely might have **preconceived** prejudices against Negroes and everybody with foreign accents, in a deserted subway station very late at night?

Negro black; African-American (most people stopped using this word in the 1960s)

preconceived already formed

(continued on next page)

(continued from previous page)

What would she say? What would be the first reaction of this white American woman, perhaps coming from a small town with a valise, two children and a baby on her right arm? Would she say: Yes, of course, you may help me. Or would she think I was just getting too familiar? Or would she think worse than that perhaps? What would I do if she let out a scream as I went toward her to offer my help?

Was I misjudging her? So many **slanders** are written every day in the daily press against the Negroes and Puerto Ricans. I hesitated for a long, long minute. The ancestral manners that the most **illiterate** Puerto Rican passes on from father to son were struggling inside me. Here was I, way past midnight, face to face with a situation that could very well explode into an outburst of prejudices and **chauvinistic** conditioning of the "divide and rule" policy of present day society.

It was a long minute. I passed on by her as if I saw nothing. As if I were insensitive to her need. Like a rude animal walking on two legs, I just moved on half running by the long subway platform leaving the children and the valise and her with the baby on her arm. I took the steps of the long concrete stairs in twos until I reached the street above and the cold air slapped my warm face.

This is what racism and prejudice and chauvinism and official artificial divisions can do to people and to a nation!

Perhaps the lady was not prejudiced at all. Or not prejudiced enough to scream at the coming of a Negro toward her in a solitary subway station a few hours past midnight.

If you were not that prejudiced, I failed you, dear lady. I know that there is a chance in a million that you will read these lines. I am willing to take that millionth chance. If you were not that prejudiced, I failed you, lady, I failed you, children. I failed myself to myself.

I buried my courtesy on Memorial Day morning. But here is a promise that I make to myself here and now; if I am ever faced with an occasion like that again, I am going to offer my help regardless of how the offer is going to be received.

Then I will have my courtesy with me again.

slanders insults

illiterate unable to read; uneducated

chauvinistic showing excessive attachment to one's own group

Discussion Questions

1. What does the author mean when he says that "the ancestral manners that the most illiterate Puerto Rican passes on from father to son were struggling inside me"?

2. Why did he decide not to help the woman?

3. Do you think this could still happen today?

Thinking about the Topic

Now that you have read several articles dealing with issues of prejudice and stereotyping, discuss the following questions.

1. How do you think people form stereotypes about other groups? Are stereotypes useful in any way?

2. What might make people change their views?

3. What do you think is the source of prejudice among individuals? in society more generally?

4. Look at the following cartoon. What point is it trying to make?

2. GENERATING IDEAS AND DRAFTING

❧ ABOUT THE WRITING PROCESS

Everyone has different ways of writing; everyone has different ways of getting ideas, organizing them, and putting them down on paper. Some people get great ideas in the middle of the night, some like to use formal methods of generating and exploring their ideas, and still others simply write a bunch of notes on a scrap of paper and do the organizing later. Some people like outlines; others hate them. Some writers use note cards; some have numbering systems. Some people start writing a draft immediately and revise substantially later. Some writers already have a good idea of what they want to say, and they can start with a clear introduction to their paper, but many people write about their ideas first and work out a way to introduce them later.

There is no one right way to write. One of the things you will be trying to figure out as you go through this text is what works best for you. However, there are some steps we all probably go through in producing a piece of writing.

All writers need to start out by assembling a set of rough ideas, and they need to make a first try at putting their ideas together on paper. This is the **first draft**. You will need to go back to that first draft at least once to make sure it says what you want it to say, in a process called **revising**. You will often have to make major changes during revision. For instance, you may decide that your first paragraph doesn't have much to do with the rest of your ideas and that you need to write a new introduction. You may need to add or re-arrange material. Don't be afraid to throw out much of what you have written in the first draft if it no longer fits what you want to say. If you draft and re-vise on a computer, your job will be much easier.

Finally, you will usually have to go over your writing again to check for errors in the sentences, such as spelling, tense choice, and punctuation. This step is called **editing**.

Writing is a complex process, and it is difficult to put all the pieces together at once. This text will help you through all of these stages of writing, one step at a time.

❧ WRITING FOCUS: WRITING WITH A POINT

In this first unit, you will write from your personal experience about prejudice and stereotypes. Writing from personal experience is often the easiest because you write about a topic that is familiar to you. However, it is not enough simply to write a story. As you write, ask yourself, "Why am I telling my reader about my experience?" "What point am I trying to make?" "Will my reader finish reading about what happened to me and say, 'So what?' "

What does the story you are telling say about something beyond you and your life? Every time you write, there must be a **point** (beyond just doing your homework assignment!) to what you have written. **This is the first and most fundamental lesson of writing well.**

As you have just read, the main point is a fundamental element of a well-written essay. If the main point is missing or unclear, the reader won't know what the writer means. Now you are going to read several versions of a paragraph. As you read, try to find the main point in each one. Is it clear?

Draft

Some children are very bad. They behave especially badly at school. When I was in the second grade, there was a little boy named Leonard. Leonard never paid at-tention when the teacher was trying to talk; he even stuck his tongue out at her when her back was turned. He threw spitballs at other children and hid the chalk and erasers. He never knew the answer when the teacher called on him because he was always fooling around. The teacher tried everything to make him behave. She scolded him and sent him to the principal's office once a week. One day, she even made him stand in the wastebasket for the whole afternoon.

This is a short story about a bad little boy named Leonard. Maybe it's sad; maybe it's funny. Does it have a main point? Does it make you think about anything? Or does it make you ask, "So what?" Why would we tell you this story, anyway? Now look at a new version of the story.

First Revision

Some children are very bad. They behave especially badly at school. When I was in the second grade, there was a little boy named Leonard. Leonard never paid attention when the teacher was trying to talk; he even stuck his tongue out at her when her back was turned. He threw spitballs at other children and hid the chalk and erasers. He never knew the answer when the teacher called on him because he was always fooling around. The teacher tried everything to make him behave. She scolded him and sent him to the principal's office once a week. One day, she even made him stand in the wastebasket for the whole afternoon. The principal finally decided that she would visit Leonard's parents to discuss his behavior. When she got there, Leonard's house was a mess and there were seven other screaming children, ages two months to fourteen years, but no parents. The oldest child told the principal that her father had left ten years ago and her mother worked two jobs to earn enough money to pay the rent and buy food and clothes.

Have you changed your mind about the point of the story? Does the second version still make you say, "So what?" What do you think the writer's main point might be? It might be something about the relationship between the quality of a child's home life and his behavior at school. Yet it's not absolutely clear, so it is a good idea to write the main point into the story itself. In the next version, look at the sentences in bold. Do they answer the question "So what?"

Second Revision

Some children are very bad. They behave especially badly at school, **but this may be because they have problems at home. If there is no one to pay attention to them at home, they may try to get their teacher's attention by misbehaving. I once knew a boy in this situation.** When I was in the second grade, there was a little boy named Leonard. Leonard never paid attention when the teacher was trying to talk; he even stuck his tongue out at her when her back was turned. He threw spitballs at other children and hid the chalk and erasers. He never knew the answer when the teacher called on him because he was always fooling around. The teacher tried everything to make him behave. She scolded him and sent him to the principal's office once a week. One day, she even made him stand in the wastebasket for the whole afternoon. The principal finally decided that she would visit Leonard's parents to discuss his behavior. When she got there, Leonard's house was a mess and there were seven other screaming children, ages two months to fourteen years, but no parents. The oldest child told the principal that her father had left ten years ago and her mother worked two jobs to earn enough money to pay the rent and buy food and clothes.

In this second revision, the main point is evident to the reader. When you write the assignment for this unit, make sure that the experience you relate has a clear point, so that your readers will not be left thinking, "OK, but so what?"

CHOOSING A TOPIC

In this unit, you have discussed several readings as well as some of your personal experiences regarding prejudice and stereotypes. Now you will begin writing an essay describing an experience in which you either:

a) were the object of a stereotype or prejudice, or

b) held a stereotype yourself and perhaps later changed your mind.

Can you think of any experiences in your own life relating to prejudice or stereotypes? Perhaps there is something you already discussed with your classmates earlier in the unit, or perhaps there is some other experience you want to write about. Look at the topics again and make your decision.

GENERATING AND ORGANIZING IDEAS

Once you have decided on the topic you are going to write about and the experience you are going to describe to your reader, you will probably want to make some notes to get started. People do this in lots of different ways. For example, some people list all the ideas that come into their heads as they think about the topic and then decide which ones to keep and how to organize them. Here is what one student did for topic (a):

```
everybody thinks Chinese are smart        1
my high school math class      2 ◄─────────────────────────┐
everybody thinks Chinese all know kung fu                  │
   I tried to show people that I was like them in school  3 ◄─┐
my brother told me to ignore it                             │ │
my friend always told me how smart I was in math          ┐ │ │
nobody believed me that I learned math in China already   ┘3 ◄┘
sleeping in class                                          │
my teacher let me do whatever I wanted in class  ┐         │
I wasn't the smartest in my class in China       ┘2 ◄──────┘
```

First this writer listed all his ideas, and then he connected the ideas that related to one another with arrows and used numbers for the order he thinks he will use in the essay. He crossed one idea off his list because he decided it didn't fit his topic. Remember that the list is only a first step; the writer is merely using it to get started. He will fill in the examples and details when he writes the essay. He may also add more ideas as he begins to write his draft, or he may reorganize completely.

Some people like to use some form of an outline. Here is what another student did for topic (b):

```
  I. Introduction—Stereotypes come from when people are
     afraid or don't know each other

 II. My experience
     • I didn't know any black people I was afraid
     • I had a hard time in school at first
     • I saw a black girl everybody said was mean and
       I was afraid at first
     • the girl was nice to me
     • she was the only one who helped me with my work in
       school

III. I was wrong about her—you have to know a person not
     just their color
```

Even though this student has organized her notes more than the first writer, she still made some extra notes that she did not put in her original outline. She may change or reorganize her ideas once she starts to write.

Even more important, the first writer has made notes only about his experience, but the second writer has included some ideas for a main point in the introduction section of her outline. It is important for your essay to have a main point that tells the reader what your experience means (remember the question, "So what?"). You may not always be sure what that main point is before you start writing. You may discover the main point as you are writing your first draft. Again, there is no right or wrong way to begin as long as your essay has a main point when you are finished with it.

Activity 1.2

A. *After you have decided on a topic, make a list of all the ideas you want to include. Write them all down; don't try to decide which ones to keep or throw out. You can do that later, as the writer of the first example did. Use the space provided to make your list. Your instructor may set a time limit for you.*

_____

_____

_____

_____

_____

_____

_____

_____

_____

B. _Once you have some written notes about your topic, think about how to organize your ideas. Look at the list you made and answer the following questions. You may want to use arrows and numbers as the first writer did, or you may want to make an outline as the second writer did._

■ Which ideas belong together?

■ What is the best order for the ideas?

■ Can you think of anything more you need to add?

■ Is there anything on your list that doesn't belong in your essay?

THE • WRITING • PROCESS

DRAFTING: WRITING YOUR FIRST DRAFT

Now that you have a set of organized notes, it is time to write your first draft. As you begin, keep in mind that this is only the **first draft**. Most writers make revisions at least once, and you probably will too. Your goal here is to write an essay with a clear main point about an experience you had. It may take more than one try to accomplish this goal, which is why when you have finished a first draft, you will begin work on the next stage, evaluating an essay.

3. REVISING

 EVALUATING ESSAYS

It is often useful to look at other people's work. It can help you look at your own work with new eyes. Sometimes it is easier to see the problems in other people's writing than to see those in your own. When you go back to your own work, you may realize that your writing has some of the same problems but now you can see them more clearly. Therefore, in this text, you will generally work on samples in the book and help your classmates with suggestions for revision before you start trying to revise your own first drafts.

Responding to the work of others in ways that are helpful is challenging. The best way to judge the quality of a response is to **ask whether the writer could act on it**. It's nice to get compliments, but sometimes they are not as helpful as constructive criticism. Responses like

```
It was really interesting.
```

are not much help because the writer can't do much with them. Similarly, responses like

```
The paper was unclear.
```

don't provide much guidance. Try to give more specific information.

- Say which part was interesting and why.
- Tell the writer which section was unclear and why.
- Express what you think the writer meant to say.
- Suggest how he or she could say it better.

In each unit, you will have a sheet to guide you in providing responses to essays in the text or from your classmates. This Response Sheet will focus on different things in different units, but the format will be similar throughout. In this first unit, you will look at several first drafts written by students like you and then practice giving constructive responses. You will use the peer responses you receive in revising your writing for a **second draft**. At this point, you will look only at the ideas and organization and will postpone working on grammar points until later.

Activity 1.3

Look at a piece of writing that a student wrote for assignment (b). Write an essay describing an experience in which you held a stereotype yourself. On the next page is a sample Response Sheet, which offers suggestions for revisions. Look at the responses. Which ones do you think would be helpful to you as a writer and why?

Student Essay 1

1   In our world, there are many people who come from
2   different cultures, who speak different languages, and who
3   look different from one another. Some people stay in the
4   small world in which they live and they have family and
5   friends with similar points of view about life. Sometimes
6   when those people go outside of their groups and meet dif-
7   ferent kinds of people, they assume that they don't like
8   them because they are different or because they have heard
9   stories about them. They hate them or are afraid of them
10   even if they don't really know them. They only believe in
11   a stereotype about those people.
12   This happened to me when I first came to this coun-
13   try. Many white people have a prejudice against black peo-
14   ple. Many Asian people have stereotypes about them too.

15 Since Korean and Chinese people have come the United

16 States, they have lived with black people and sometimes

17 they have trouble. They are afraid of black people and

18 despise them. I had the same feeling about them even

19 though I never knew any black people. When I went to high

20 school, I met someone who changed my mind about blacks.

21 When I was a sophomore in high school, I came to the

22 United States by myself and studied at a U.S. high school.

23 My school was really small and had only a few black stu-

24 dents. For a year, I had a really hard time in school.

25 The language and cultural barriers were too high for me

26 to manage. I couldn't understand any of the work in my

27 classes. I couldn't even ask questions because I under-

28 stood so little. Speaking was even harder. I was afraid

29 to speak because I thought people would laugh at me.

30 During my first week, everyone looked at me with cu-

31 riosity and asked me a lot of questions. Even though ev-

32 eryone was very nice to me, I was lonely and their

33 curiosity sometimes made me uncomfortable. When I needed

34 help, they were useless. That year, there was only one

35 black student in my school. I heard she was mean and a

36 troublemaker. They said she was always fighting with some-

37 one. I was afraid of her because of the stories but also

38 because she was black. I thought she was mean and I didn't

39 even like her accent. By the end of the year, however, I

40 discovered she was not that kind of person at all.

41 During my first year, I had two classes with her. The

42 classes were very small and everyone knew everyone else

43 very well. I can't say exactly what it was that changed

44 my mind about her. I just found that whenever I needed

45 help, she was the one who was helping me. It was really

46 hard for me to do what the teacher asked and when I asked

47 my classmates for help, they did help me. Even when they

48 helped me though, I could see that they were annoyed at

49 me for asking. I could hear them talking behind my back.

50 Sometimes they ignored me when I asked for help. In these

51 situations, I found that it was the black girl who was

52   the main one helping me. She always asked me how I was
53   doing and told me things that I didn't understand. She
54   never showed the attitude that the others did. She was
55   never mean to me. I also found that she had a beautiful
56   voice.

57   I was wrong about her. She was not a person I should
58   be afraid of or despise. She had a warm heart. I had a
59   stereotype about blacks so I thought the same thing about
60   her. Now, I don't believe all black people are mean or
61   are troublemakers. It's always better when you get to know
62   each person.

Hong

RESPONSE SHEET

Writer: *Hong*   **Responder:** *Dusan*

1. Does the writer give a main point or idea? If so, what is it? That is, what is he or she trying to tell you about his or her experience? If not, what do you think the main point **should** be?

Yes, the writer has a main point. She is saying that sometimes people have the wrong idea about other people because of stories that they have heard, but then when they really meet a person, they find out it's not true.

2. Why do you say this? Write the sentence(s) that make you think that this is, or should be, the main point.

Some people stay in the small world in which they live and they have family and friends with similar points of view about life. Sometimes when those people go outside of their groups and meet different kinds of people, they assume that they don't like them because they are different or because they have heard stories about them. They hate them or are afraid of them even if they don't really know them. They only believe in a stereotype about those people.

3. Where in the paper does the main point appear (e.g., first paragraph, conclusion, etc.)?

In the first paragraph (lines 3—11)

4. What examples does the writer give to support the point? List them.

She writes about when she was in high school, she thought all black people were troublemakers, but then she met one black girl who helped her a lot and made her change her mind.

5. Are the examples strong enough to convince you of the main point?

Yes.

6. Are there any parts of the paper that are unclear or need more explanation? Explain.

The last paragraph is not clear.

7. What other suggestions can you give for the writer's next draft? Be specific.

Put in more examples.

Write more about how we can avoid believing stereotypes.

The writer has written a strong paper with a clear main point, as Dusan indicates. She has told a story from her own life, but she does so to illustrate the negative effect of prejudice and how personal experience can change a person's views.

The writing is not perfect, though, and Dusan does give some suggestions. He feels that the last paragraph is not clear. This may be true, but he doesn't really say what is unclear about it. A more helpful response might be:

```
What do you mean when you write, "it's always better to get
to know each person" (lines 61-62)? How is that related to
your story and your main point?
```

Dusan offers two suggestions for the next draft:

```
Put in more examples.

Write more about how we can avoid believing stereotypes.
```

Which suggestion do you think is better?

The first suggestion is rather vague. Where and why does she need to put in more examples? Does Dusan think this one long example is not convincing enough? He needs to say why he thinks she should include more examples. The second one is more helpful because the writer would be able to make some changes based on this suggestion. Perhaps she might expand her last paragraph to say something about the importance of knowing people as individuals and how this can help us avoid the stereotypes that can lead to prejudice.

Later in this unit, you will see some examples of how writers use the suggestions made by peers to revise and improve their drafts.

WRITING FOCUS: EXPRESSING A MAIN POINT

Remember, it is not enough to simply describe an experience of stereotyping or prejudice. If a writer gives an example of a stereotype or prejudice, that's a good beginning, but he or she isn't finished yet. The experience should be used to make a point about stereotypes, as the writer did in the paper you just read. The writer chose to tell that particular story. Why? What is she trying to say about stereotypes? In this case, you know that the writer's experience with her friend changed her views about blacks.

A **main point** is central to writing **any** essay, not just one about personal experience. From now on, make sure all your essays have a clear main point. The main point is usually stated in the beginning of the essay, and the rest of the essay is used to explain the point more fully with examples and details.

Now you are going to look at another piece of writing, this time an essay for assignment (a)—Write an essay describing an experience in which you were the object of a stereotype or prejudice.

Activity 1.4

As you read the essay, think about both the example the writer gives of stereotyping and the main point. After you read, complete the Response Sheet. Remember to make your responses as specific as possible. Ask yourself, "If someone wrote these comments about my paper, would I be able to use them to make changes in my writing?"

Student Essay 2

1 In my high school I experienced a lot of stereotyp-
2 ing. In my first year algebra class, my teacher did not
3 care what I did in class. I was allowed to sleep, to draw,
4 or to do anything, as long as I did not bother the other
5 students. I just had to turn in my homework on time and
6 do well on tests. So, everyone in class thought that Chi-
7 nese people were smart, and especially, good in math. They
8 all wondered why the most difficult class for them was
9 the easiest for me.

10 One day, my friend who sat next to me asked for
11 help on a homework problem. After we finished, he said,
12 "Thanks. Chinese people are so smart. It takes me forever
13 to solve these problems and it only took you a minute."
14 "You're kidding," I answered. "No, I'm serious," he said.
15 "You were sleeping in class, but every time, you are the
16 first to turn in the test and you rank first in the class.
17 I don't understand why you do better than me, since I was
18 paying attention in class. If you're not smart, then why?"
19 "I am not smarter than anyone else in the class. You know
20 that I do poorly in my other classes," I explained to
21 him. "I finish my homework quickly and do well on tests
22 because I already learned this math in China. In China,
23 we have to do these problems over and over again. You
24 also think all Chinese people do kung fu too, right?"
25 "Yes," he replied. I said, "Actually most Chinese people
26 don't know any kung fu. You just watch too many movies."
27 I told him if he already knew it, he would be better than
28 me.

Tran

Writer: _Tran_   **Responder:** _____

1. Does the writer give a main point or idea? If so, what is it? That is, what is he or she trying to tell you about his or her experience? If not, what do you think the main point **should** be?

_____

_____

_____

_____

_____

_____

_____

2. Why do you say this? Write the sentence(s) that make you think that this is, or should be, the main point.

_____

_____

_____

_____

_____

_____

_____

_____

_____

3. Where in the paper does the main point appear (e.g., first paragraph, conclusion, etc.)?

_____

_____

4. What examples does the writer give to support the point? List them.

_____

_____

_____

_____

_____

_____

5. Are the examples strong enough to convince you of the main point? _____

_____

_____

_____

6. Are there any parts of the paper that are unclear or need more explanation? Explain.

_____

_____

_____

_____

_____

_____

_____

7. What other suggestions can you give for the writer's next draft? Be specific.

_____

_____

_____

_____

_____

_____

_____

_____

🔥 RESPONDING TO A PEER'S WRITING

Now that you have looked at a couple of essays in the book and given some suggestions, you are going to read a classmate's essay and make suggestions. Looking at others' writing and examining the strengths and weaknesses can help when you sit down to reevaluate your own essay.

Activity 1.5

Exchange papers with your partner and read his or her draft all the way through. It's much easier to respond to something when you read the whole piece than when you have read only part of it. Use the Peer Response Sheet as a guide. You may photocopy this sheet if you are going to respond to more than one of your classmates' essays. Be as specific as you can in your answers, and **remember that your comments should be about the ideas, not the grammar.** *You will work on grammar later when you edit your paper.*

When you complete the Peer Response Sheet, be sure to put your name and the writer's name at the top of the page. Give the sheet to the writer when you have finished so he or she can refer to it later on. Discuss your answers with the writer and ask any questions you have about the paper. You may also want to ask questions about the comments your classmates made about your own paper.

Writer: _____   **Responder:** _____

1. Does the writer give a main point or idea? If so, what is it? That is, what is he or she trying to tell you about his or her experience? If not, what do you think the main point **should** be?

_____

_____

_____

_____

_____

_____

_____

2. Why do you say this? Write the sentence(s) that make you think that this is, or should be, the main point.

_____

_____

_____

_____

_____

_____

_____

3. Where in the paper does the main point appear (e.g., first paragraph, conclusion, etc.)?

_____

_____

4. What examples does the writer give to support the point? List them.

_____

_____

_____

_____

_____

_____

_____

5. Are the examples strong enough to convince you of the main point?

_____

_____

_____

_____

6. Are there any parts of the paper that are unclear or need more explanation? Explain.

_____

_____

_____

_____

_____

_____

_____

_____

_____

7. What other suggestions can you give for the writer's next draft? Be specific.

_____

_____

_____

_____

_____

_____

_____

PREPARING FOR A SECOND DRAFT

By this point, you have both given and received feedback on a first draft. What is the next step?

Look at what one student did when his first draft came back. You have already seen this particular paper and even offered some suggestions of your own. Now look at the suggestions that one of his classmates gave him and see how he responded to those suggestions. Then look at how those suggestions helped this writer to shape his second draft.

Notice that he did not accept all of the suggestions that were given to him. He evaluated what he saw as the most important ones and then either used them or explained why he decided not to. The first draft is reprinted here so that you can refer to it more easily.

Student Essay 1
First Draft

1   In my high school I experienced a lot of stereotyp-
2   ing. In my first year algebra class, my teacher did not
3   care what I did in class. I was allowed to sleep, to draw,
4   or to do anything, as long as I did not bother the other
5   students. I just had to turn in my homework on time and
6   do well on tests. So, everyone in class thought that Chi-
7   nese people were smart, and especially, good in math. They
8   all wondered why the most difficult class for them was
9   the easiest for me.
10   One day, my friend who sat next to me asked for help
11   on a homework problem. After we finished, he said, "Thanks.
12   Chinese people are so smart. It takes me forever to solve
13   these problems and it only took you a minute." "You're
14   kidding," I answered. "No, I'm serious," he said. "You
15   were sleeping in class, but every time, you are the first
16   to turn in the test and you rank first in the class. I
17   don't understand why you do better than me, since I was
18   paying attention in class. If you're not smart, then why?"
19   "I am not smarter than anyone else in the class. You know
20   that I do poorly in my other classes," I explained to
21   him. "I finish my homework quickly and do well on tests
22   because I already learned this math in China. In China,

23 we have to do these problems over and over again. You

24 also think all Chinese people do kung fu too, right?"

25 "Yes," he replied. I said, "Actually most Chinese people

26 don't know any kung fu. You just watch too many movies."

27 I told him if he already knew it, he would be better than

28 me.

Writer: *Tran*   **Responder:** *Constantina*

1. Does the writer give a main point or idea? If so, what is it? That is, what is he or she trying to tell you about his or her experience? If not, what do you think the main point **should** be?

This paper doesn't really have a main point. It mostly just tells a story about what happened to the writer when he was in school. I think what he is trying to say is that people have a lot of stereotypes about Chinese people, like they are all smart and good at math and can do kung fu. It seems like, even though the stuff about math is a nice stereotype, Tran didn't like it very much.

2. Why do you say this? Write the sentence(s) that make you think that this is, or should be, the main point.

There isn't really one sentence but I got the idea from this part: "You also think all Chinese people do kung fu too, right?" "Yes," he replied. I said, "Actually most Chinese people don't know any kung fu. You just watch too many movies." (lines 22–26)

3. Where in the paper does the main point appear (e.g., first paragraph, conclusion, etc.)?

The last paragraph.

4. What examples does the writer give to support the point? List them.

His friend thinks he is good at math just because he is Chinese and he also thinks they all can do kung fu.

5. Are the examples strong enough to convince you of the main point?

They are OK.

6. Are there any parts of the paper that are unclear or need more explanation? Explain.

I did not understand the last sentence. If he already knew what?

The first paragraph was not very clear.

7. What other suggestions can you give for the writer's next draft? Be specific.

Write what your main point is in the first paragraph. Say why you are telling this story.

Give some more examples.

Now that Tran has Constantina's comments, how can he use them to revise and write his second draft? He must sort through them and decide how to respond to each one. Some comments may be clearer than others. Some may be more important than others, and some he simply may not agree with. He needs to respond and organize his thoughts. Look at the worksheet **What to Do When the Draft Comes Back** to see how he did this.

WHAT TO DO WHEN THE DRAFT COMES BACK

Name: *Tran*

1. Read through your instructor's comments and the Peer Response Sheet.

2. Find some of the suggestions they have made.

3. Write the most important ones here. Then write what you think of each suggestion. How will you respond to it? If you do not plan to follow it, why not?

A. *She said I need to make it more clear why I have told the story.*

   i. I plan to ignore the suggestion because

   ii. I plan to change my draft in the following way:
I am going to put in a new first paragraph explaining why I think even stereotypes that say good things about you can be hard to deal with.

B. *She said the last sentence was hard to understand.*

   i. I plan to ignore the suggestion because

   ii. I plan to change my draft in the following way:
I need to connect the last sentence to the rest of the story about math. I am going to rewrite it and put it earlier.

C. *She said the first paragraph is not clear.*

   i. I plan to ignore the suggestion because
I think when I rewrite my first paragraph that this part will be clearer.

   ii. I plan to change my draft in the following way:

4. Perhaps you have thought of some other changes you would like to make. List them here:
I am going to write a little bit more about the kung fu example.

5. Are there any comments or suggestions on your paper that you did not understand? You may want to discuss them with your peer response partner or arrange a conference with your instructor. List them here, and bring this sheet with you to help guide your conference.

She said that I need more examples. I don't understand why she said that. I think I have enough to make my point.

Activity 1.6

Discuss the following questions with your classmates.

- Which of the responder's comments do you think were the most helpful? Why?
- Why do you think the writer took some of the suggestions and rejected others?

Based on the suggestions on the Peer Response Sheet, the writer revised his paper. This is his second draft. The changes are in bold.

Revision

People have a lot of stereotypes about the Chinese. Most stereotypes say negative things about people, but I found that most Americans have positive stereotypes about Chinese people. At first I took this as a compliment, but soon, I realized that even positive stereotypes can cause trouble. The stereotype that bothers me the most is that everyone thinks that Chinese people are good at math. Some Chinese people are not good at math and they feel bad when people expect them to be smart and they can't do the math problems.

In my high school I experienced a lot of stereotyping **about math**. In my first year algebra class, my teacher did not care what I did in class. I was allowed to sleep, to draw, or to do anything, as long as I did not bother the other students. I just had to turn in my homework on time and do well on tests. So, everyone in class thought that Chinese people were smart, and especially, good in math. They all wondered why the most difficult class for them was the easiest for me.

One day, my friend who sat next to me asked for help on a homework problem. After we finished, he said, "Thanks. Chinese people are so smart. It takes me forever to solve these problems and it only took you a minute." "You're kidding," I answered. "No, I'm serious," he said. "You were sleeping in class, but every time, you are the first to turn in the test and you rank first in the class. I don't understand why you do better than me, since I was paying attention in class. If you're not smart, then why?" "I am not smarter than anyone else in the class. You know that I do poorly in my other classes **like English and history**," I explained to him. "I finish my homework quickly and do well on tests because I already learned this math in China. In China, we have to do these problems over and over again. I **am not smarter, I just have done it all before." I told him if he already did this math the year before, he would be better in math class than me.**

Math is not the only stereotype that is common about Chinese people. A lot of people also think everyone does karate and kung fu. I asked my friend, "You also think all Chinese people do kung fu, right?" "Yes," he replied. I said, "Actually most Chinese people don't know any kung fu. You just watch too many movies." **Even though I explained to everyone in my class that I had learned algebra in China and I never did kung fu, they still believe that Chinese students are intelligent and the best at math and kung fu. I don't know what else I can do to change their minds.**

| Activity 1.7 | *Look at the revisions that this writer has made. Can you see where they came from? Most of the changes came from suggestions on the Peer Response Sheet. Others the writer thought of himself. He listed some of them on the* **What to Do When the Draft Comes Back** *sheet. He may have thought of others while he was rewriting his second draft. Look at each revision he has made and try to trace it back to see where it came from, such as the Peer Response Sheet or the* **What to Do When the Draft Comes Back** *sheet.* |

🌿 EVALUATING YOUR OWN WORK

Up until now, you have been looking at the work of others. Now it is time to return to your own **first draft**. Perhaps now you can look at it again and see new ways to improve it when you write your **second draft**. Your instructor will return your draft with comments, and you will also get comments and suggestions from at least one of your classmates.

Sometimes it's hard to know which suggestions to follow. Only you know what you are trying to say; others can just make suggestions. Not every suggestion from your classmates will be appropriate, perhaps because they don't understand what you mean. Sometimes even your instructor will have trouble understanding what you are trying to express. If your instructor is confused by any parts of your essay, this probably does mean that you need to revise. After you have carefully considered all of the advice you have received, the final decision about how to revise is up to you.

Activity 1.8	*Reread your first draft, the Peer Response Sheet(s), and your instructor's comments. Use the* **What to Do When the Draft Comes Back** *sheet on the next page to guide you in revising your writing. You do not need to respond to every suggestion. Try to figure out which ones are the most important and decide how you will respond to those. Use the plans you have developed on this sheet to help you revise your paper and write a second draft. Concentrate on the comments and suggestions about your ideas and organization. Feel free to correct grammar errors that you find, but try not to focus on those right now. You will look at those issues after you have completed your second draft.*

Name: _____

1. Read through your instructor's comments and the Peer Response Sheet.

2. Find some of the suggestions they have made.

3. Write the most important ones here. Then write what you think of each suggestion. How will you respond to it? If you do not plan to follow it, why not?

A. _____

_____

    i. I plan to ignore the suggestion because

_____

_____

_____

_____

    ii. I plan to change my draft in the following way:

_____

_____

_____

_____

B. _____

_____

    i. I plan to ignore the suggestion because

_____

_____

_____

_____

    ii. I plan to change my draft in the following way:

_____

_____

_____

_____

C. _____

_____

    i. I plan to ignore the suggestion because

_____

_____

_____

_____

    ii. I plan to change my draft in the following way:

_____

_____

_____

_____

4. Perhaps you have thought of some other changes you would like to make. List them here:

_____

_____

_____

_____

_____

5. Are there any comments or suggestions on your paper that you did not understand? You may want to discuss them with your peer response partner or arrange a conference with your instructor. List them here, and bring this sheet with you to help guide your conference.

_____

_____

_____

_____

_____

PREPARING FOR A CONFERENCE

When you schedule a conference with your instructor to discuss your paper, it is important to be well prepared. If you have prepared, you will learn much more from the experience. You should bring to the conference your essay with your instructor's comments, the Peer Response Sheets that your classmates filled out for your essay, and the **What to Do When the Draft Comes Back** sheet.

Activity 1.9	*Review all this material beforehand and mark the sections of your essay that you want to discuss with your instructor (using a highlighter is helpful). Use the following lines to write down any questions or thoughts you have about your essay.*

1. _____

_____

2. _____

_____

3. _____

_____

_____

4. _____

_____

_____

Make sure you address these issues with your instructor. Remember that this is your conference and that it's up to you to use the time productively.

WRITING YOUR SECOND DRAFT

You should have a clear plan now for how you will revise your essay. Look over your **What to Do When the Draft Comes Back** sheet and any notes you took during your conference with your instructor. Write your second draft. Concentrate on expressing your ideas clearly and on making sure that your reader will be able to understand your main point.

4. EDITING

ABOUT THE EDITING PROCESS

Your instructor will read your second draft. This time when you get it back, he or she may have made suggestions that are very different from the ones on the first draft. This time, your instructor may have commented on grammatical errors you have made. Throughout this unit, we have stressed the importance of expressing your ideas clearly. However, writing accurately is also important. If your essay has lots of mistakes, your reader may not be able to concentrate on what you are trying to say. Now that you have finished the second draft in which you made changes in ideas and organization, it is time to begin the editing process. During this phase of the writing process, you will identify and correct grammatical errors.

You may have done a lot of grammar exercises in other courses. Maybe you do them very well. However, you may also continue to make mistakes when you are writing. At the end of every unit of this text, there is an Editing Practice section, which is designed to help you with some of the grammar problems you may have **when you write**. Each Editing Practice section has a set of guidelines with a brief explanation of the grammar point. Most also include a writing sample containing some errors on this grammar point. You will practice by editing the writing sample before you edit your own essay and turn in your final draft.

There are additional Editing Practice selections at the end of the text. As you go through this text, you may want to consult earlier Editing Practice sections when you write papers in later units. You may even continue using them after this course is over when you write papers for other courses. Get to know which grammar points are a problem in your writing and focus on those specific editing guidelines to help you find and correct errors in your drafts.

At the end of each Editing Practice, there is an abbreviation for a specific type of error. Your instructor may use this abbreviation to indicate that you have made a grammatical error. Later on in the course, he or she may stop pointing out your errors and ask you to find them yourself.

Editing Practice

#1 Finding and correcting fragments

Note: If the concepts in this Editing Practice section are new or difficult for you, look at Editing Practice #6, Working with Sentence Boundaries, at the back of the text. It provides background information that will make this Editing Practice easier for you to understand. If the material there is already familiar to you, you can begin working on Editing Practice #1 right away.

A **fragment** is not a complete sentence. It might be just a phrase, or a dependent clause without an independent clause with a period at the end. With that period at the end, it might *look* like a complete sentence. However, it is not, and it needs to be changed.

Read through the writing sample and then look at the guidelines. The guidelines contain examples of correct and incorrect usage from the writing sample and show you how to correct **fragments**.

Sample

1   I have had problems with my parents about many things.

2   For example, studying, my social life and behavior. My

3   biggest conflict has been about studying. They have al-

4 ways thought the best plan was to study pharmacy, medicine,

5 or law. I have tried to change their minds. But they do

6 not want to listen to me.

7 The problem came up again a few days ago. They say

8 I should study pharmacy, but I say I want to study inte-

9 rior design. Because I think it is best to live my life

10 doing what I want without pressure. However, my parents

11 do not accept this. They say I have to study something

12 useful. At least until I get married. They say pharmacy

13 is a better choice than interior design because I will

14 make more money. I told them I am not smart enough to

15 study pharmacy. But they just say to try harder. They have

16 also told everyone that I was going to study pharmacy.

17 Including my relatives. Now I don't like to talk about it

18 with them because they are so stubborn.

19 A few days ago I had a chance to understand my par-

20 ents' point of view a little bit better. When I interviewed

21 some people about the conflicts that children and their par-

22 ents have about education. I found out that most parents

23 want their children to study so they can get a good job.

24 That's why they put a lot of pressure on their children.

25 In addition, many parents said that they had not studied

26 hard when they were in school. So they don't want their

27 children to be like them. After I had interviewed these

28 people. I decided that I should talk with my parents again.

29 I told them that I understood their feelings. But I also

30 said that I wanted to study interior design very much. Fi-

31 nally they said they would give me a chance to study. The

32 field that I really love. Although they also said if I get

33 a low grade, I will have to change my major to pharmacy.

34 I think many children may have similar conflicts with

35 their parents. If they can all discuss their problems hon-

36 estly though, they may understand each other better. Dur-

37 ing my interviews. I started to understand the significance

38 of discussing these important things. I think that even

39 if the two generations think differently, they are still

40 a family.

Activity 1.10

With a partner, follow these steps to check for fragments in the sample. The examples that follow can help you find and correct them.

A. *Underline any instances of* **but** *that are at the beginning of a sentence. Remember that* **but-type connectors**[1] *cannot begin a sentence. These are fragments, and you need to repair them.* **Either:**

1. change the **but** to **however**

Example:

INCORRECT: I told them I am not smart enough to study pharmacy. **But** they just say to try harder.

CORRECT: I told them I am not smart enough to study pharmacy. **However,** they just say to try harder.

or:

2. attach the sentence to the one before it.

Example:

INCORRECT: I told them I am not smart enough to study pharmacy. **But** they just say to try harder.

CORRECT: I told them I am not smart enough to study pharmacy, **but** they just say to try harder.

B. *Underline any instances in the sample of* **while-type connectors,**[2] *such as* **because, if, when,** *and* **since,** *that are at the beginning of a sentence. (Check Table EP.1 on p. 225 for others.) These connectors usually mark dependent clauses.*

1. Is there an independent clause in the same sentence? If not, this is a fragment and you have to repair it. You must attach it to an independent clause, as in the following example.

Example:

INCORRECT: They say I should study pharmacy, but I say I want to study interior design. **Because** I think it is best to live my life doing what I want without pressure.

CORRECT: They say I should study pharmacy, but I say I want to study interior design **because** I think it is best to live my life doing what I want without pressure.

2. A fragment usually appears **between** two independent clauses, so you must decide which one to attach it to. Usually only one choice makes sense, as in the following example.

---

[1]See Editing Practice #6 at the back of the text for an explanation of these terms.

[2]See Editing Practice #6 at the back of the text for an explanation of these terms.

Example:

INCORRECT: So they don't want their children to be like them. After I had in-terviewed these people. I decided that I should talk with my par-ents again.

Attaching the following sentence makes sense.

CORRECT: After I had interviewed these people, **I decided that I should talk with my parents again.**

In contrast, when you attach it to the preceding sentence, the result makes no sense.

INCORRECT: So they don't want their children to be like them after I had in-terviewed these people.

Notice the **comma** in the correct version. Remember that if the dependent clause comes before the independent clause, the two clauses must be separated by a comma.

> In future drafts, you may see the abbreviation **frag-d.c.** This means fragment-dependent clause, and you need to repair it.

C. *You also need to watch for other types of fragments: "sentences" with no main verb. Check over each sentence in the sample. Find any that are missing a main verb. Look at the examples that follow to guide you.*

Examples:

INCORRECT: Including my relatives.
INCORRECT: During my interviews.
INCORRECT: The field that I really love.

These phrases are not complete sentences. What about your relatives? What happened to them? There is no verb in this phrase.
What happened during your interview? Again, this phrase contains no verb.
What about The subject that you really love? Although the last one does con-tain a verb, it goes with the subject I. The main subject, **field,** *also needs a verb.*
In fact, all three of these fragments need a verb and must be repaired. You might find the verb you need in a nearby sentence, or you might be able to attach the frag-ment to a sentence that comes before or after it.

CORRECT: *They also told everyone*, including my relatives, *that I was go-ing to study pharmacy.*
CORRECT: *During my interviews, I started to understand the significance of discussing these important things*.
CORRECT: *Finally they said they would give me a chance to study* the field that I really love.

In future drafts, you may see the abbreviation **frag-noV**. This means fragment-no verb, and you need to repair it.

🔥 EDITING YOUR OWN WORK: THE FINAL DRAFT

Now reread your own paper and see if it contains any errors like the ones in the sample.

Activity 1.11

Follow the steps in the guidelines and correct any errors that you find. You may also find other errors that you need to correct. Once you have finished editing, you are ready to turn in your final draft. Be sure to keep your final draft so that you can refer to it when you write other papers.

COMPUTERS AND CHANGE

Task
• Gathering and analyzing data from questionnaires

Writing Focus
• Making claims and providing support

Editing Focus
• Comma splices and run-on sentences

In the last unit, you used a personal experience to make a point about preju-dice or stereotyping. The information you needed to write was readily avail-able because it was in your memory. In this unit, you will gather new information from other people. You will be asking them about their use of computers and using this information to document a trend and to say what you think this trend could mean.

In Unit One, you learned about writing a clear main point at the beginning of your essay. This will continue to be a crucial element of every essay you write. In this unit, you will learn more about making **claims** and providing strong **supporting evidence** in the body of your essay.

Computers seem to be everywhere these days, from classrooms to super-markets, from the Internet to the post office. Some people call it a revolution, but not everyone is comfortable with the widespread use of computers. Some people are even a little bit afraid of them, whereas others can't seem to get enough of them. In this unit, you will be finding out if and how some people use computers as well as how they feel about them. You will try to figure out if there is any pattern to this use and to these attitudes.

I. EXPLORING IDEAS

READINGS

The widespread use of computers has made many aspects of our lives easier. There is a darker side of the information age, however: You can get the information you need quickly and easily, but someone else can

• 53 •

*also get information **about you** quickly and easily. People who are computer experts can use this ability in order to hurt others as well as help them. This article explores the issue of easy access to information on the World Wide Web.*

No Privacy on the Web
Joshua Quittner

Want to see how much the world knows about you? Try this: log on to the World Wide Web, fire up a search engine (one of those Websites with names like HotBot or AltaVista that scour the Internet for key words), and type in your name. You're probably listed somewhere, especially if you've been mentioned in a newspaper or magazine article during the past few years.

Big deal. Now type in your Social Security number. If you're an official in the military, if you've filed papers with the Securities and Exchange Commission, or if you're a student or a faculty member at a university that uses Social Security numbers for IDs, you may well be among the people whose numbers have made their way into the all too public record.

Want to get really creeped out? Click over to InfoSpace, "the Ultimate Directory," whose People Search Directory has the home address of everybody with a listed phone number, all 112 million of them. Type in your name, and out pops a map of your neighborhood, with a little *X* marking your residence. Click on the icon to get written directions to your house.

And that's just the free stuff. If you're willing to pay for **dirt**, dozens of info brokers are waiting on the Web to supply you with just about anyone's Social Security number, listed (and unlisted) phone numbers, voter registrations, driving records, court records, real estate holdings, liens and, well, you name it. Even such **esoterica** as companies registered in Switzerland, corporate profiles of Japanese businessmen, and Nevada divorce petitions are all stored neatly online and available for a price.

Databases filled with gobs of juicy, personal information have been around since computers were invented, of course. But what was once the exclusive domain of skip tracers, private eyes and investigative reporters is now available to anyone with access to the Net. Today you too can be a **gumshoe**. Or a **stalker**. Or, if you're willing to work with borrowed credit cards, a thief.

Civil libertarians are understandably alarmed. "More needs to be done to protect privacy in the online world," says Marc Rotenberg, director of the Washington-based Electronic Privacy Information Center. "As technology has raced ahead, safeguards have failed to keep up."

Case in point: recently, after a public outcry, the Social Security Administration shut down a portion of its Website that showed taxpayers' earnings and ben-

dirt slang term for often unflattering information about someone

esoterica facts that only specialists can use or understand

gumshoe detective

stalker someone who is obsessed with another person and tries to find out everything about him or her; the stalker may follow the person home or to work, harass him, and, in some cases, may hurt him or her

civil libertarian someone who is interested in protecting individuals' rights

(continued on next page)

(continued from previous page)

efits. All an ex-spouse or divorce attorney needed to do was punch in five items: name, Social Security number, mother's maiden name, birth date and birthplace. After *USA Today* publicized the site last month, it was besieged with up to 80 requests a second. Two days later it was shut down.

"Anytime you have a large database, you're going to have a few people who misuse it," says Glen Roberts, a computer consultant who has made a hobby of exploring the opportunities for database misuse. His ironically named Stalker's Home Page has become the definitive source for information about how your privacy can be violated online. His theory is that by exposing the most **egregious** Websites to public scrutiny, he will force them to shut down.

egregious worst; most outrageous

Recently, for instance, he learned that Indiana University had a database open to the Net that listed names, Social Security numbers, phone numbers, research qualifications and job titles of 2,760 faculty members. Roberts grabbed it and publicized portions on his own site, along with a press release. University officials were not amused. They took the database off line, of course, and **sicced** the authorities on Roberts, who agreed to take his off line as well. Curiously, though, no one ever asked him to erase the data, which still reside on his home computer. "The only time people care about this is when they can see it. As soon as they can't see it, they think there's no issue. But the problem is still there."

sicced (*slang*) make someone (or something) else attack; for example, *He sicced the dog on the burglar.*

Information brokers point out that databases are the **lubricants** that keep modern business running. Personal data, after all, help establish you as an upstanding citizen and a worthy credit risk—and help creditors track you down in case you're not. "It's not really useful to say that the records could be misused by a few people, so let's remove access for everyone," says Jeff Alperin of Information America, one of the world's largest providers of public records and investigative services. "How in the world could you transfer property if you didn't know who owned it?"

lubricant grease; a substance that makes a process work more smoothly

True enough, but where do you draw the line? Last month U.S. Senators Dianne Feinstein and Charles Grassley introduced the Personal Information Privacy Act of 1997, which would make it tougher for businesses to sell Social Security numbers, unlisted phone numbers and other kinds of personal data. The legislation was prompted when Feinstein's staff members claimed to have found her Social Security number on the Net in less than three minutes. "People are losing control of their identities," Feinstein says. "Our private lives are becoming commodities with tremendous value in the marketplace."

That's the bad news. The good news is that at least someone is making money on the Web.

Discussion Questions

1. Do you think this easy access to information is a real threat? How might the fact that information about you is available on the Internet affect you?

2. Do you think the advantages of easy access outweigh the disadvantages? Why or why not?

3. If you have access to the Internet, see if you can find yourself on the World Wide Web. Try to find your parents; try a friend. If you find any information, what sort of information is it? How does it make you feel?

———·———·———·———·———·———·———·———·———·———·———·———·———·———

People use computers for many purposes: for work and play, to get information, and to communicate. This article describes a new game that is popular in Japan. Instead of simulating fighting a battle or flying a plane, this program simulates the game of love. Some men are finding virtual women easier to communicate with than real women.

Japan's Newest Young Heartthrobs Are Sexy, Talented and Virtual

Andrew Pollack

heartthrob object of romantic love and devotion

Shiori Fujisaki is a 17-year-old high school junior with long reddish hair and dreamy eyes who is about to release her first record. Shingo Hagiwara is a 21-year-old college sophomore who **idolizes** her. He goes to nearly every event at which she appears and has bought calendars, posters, watches and mugs with her picture on them. "Shiori does everything perfectly," he sighed. Perfect she might be, but Shiori is not real. She is a character in a video game called Tokimeki Memorial, the goal of which is to get Shiori or one of her friends to date you and fall in love.

idolize adore

Shingo Hagiwara, on the other hand, is quite real. He is one of the growing legion of young Japanese men who have given their hearts to a virtual girl. So-called "love simulation" games, normally sold on CD-ROMs, have become one of the hottest categories in Japan's home video game industry. The girls in such games are animated characters that have only limited ability to converse. Players cannot type in whatever they want to say; rather, they use the video game controller to pick a topic of conversation or a multiple-choice reply. In most games, the text of the conversation is also printed on the bottom of the screen.

In the Ascii Corporation's game called True Love Story, a player walking home from school with a girl can pick a topic of conversation, like the weather or fashion. Or, he can choose an action, like staring at her, praising her, giving her a present, taking her hand, asking for a date or parting ways. A beating heart and other meters in the upper left corner of the screen indicate the girl's emotional state. Pick a conversation topic that interests her and the heart beats faster. When it is beating fast enough, the player can try to hold her hand. But if he is too forward, the girl will blush and say, "Sorry, I'm going home."

Some players become so absorbed in their pursuit that the girls become real to them. Some young men send love letters and birthday cards to their favorite characters. "Everybody has one character for whom he could sacrifice his life," said Mr. Hagiwara, the college student.

(continued on next page)

(continued from previous page)

So a strange phenomenon is occurring: the video characters are becoming celebrities. Shiori has an official fan club with 10,000 members and a newsletter. There are Tokimeki gatherings and merchandise. At a recent news conference, dozens of reporters scribbled with straight faces as the Konami Company, which makes Tokimeki Memorial, announced Shiori's first compact disk and previewed the two songs, "Teach Me, Mr. Sky," and "Let's Go With the Wind."

The action is not limited to dating games. Cute girls with fan followings are also appearing in fighting games, car racing games and adventure games. Horipro, a talent agency, has used computer graphics to develop a virtual teen-age idol singer named Kyoko Date. There is even a magazine, *Virtual Idol*, devoted to these girls of the CRT screen. Unlike most video game magazines, *Virtual Idol,* which says it has a circulation of 150,000, deals not with game-playing strategy but with the hobbies, life experience and physical measurements of people who do not exist. It also profiles the real women whose voices are used in the video games and on the records. *Virtual Idol* "is just the right kind of magazine for a person like me who's not interested in real girls," one reader, T.Y., from Shiga Prefecture, wrote in a letter printed in the October issue.

There have been some slightly similar games in the United States. Sierra Online's Leisure Suit Larry games for personal computers involve trying to **pick up** women. But in America, where computer communication is more common than in Japan, people tend to do their hunting in on-line chat rooms, where the person on the other end of the line is real, albeit not always what he or she pretends to be.

> **pick up** try to get dates, usually with strangers

Another reason for the difference is that role-playing games in general are more popular in Japan, whereas Americans prefer sports and action games. Also, comic books and animations are popular in Japan among adults, not just children. Most of the girls in the love simulation games look exactly like Lolitas in Japanese comics and cartoons—with shapely figures but innocent faces and big doe eyes.

The players of the love simulation games are often male computer nerds ranging in age from their teens to their 30's. Such people are called "otaku" in Japan, a word that literally means "home" and may refer to the observation that these guys do not leave their rooms very much.

Fans of the games say they can relive their high school days, but with more success than they had back then. Also, rejection is easier to take from a machine. "I can do things I couldn't do," said Yukio Watanabe, a 25-year-old game developer. Asked what he meant, he said, "I wanted to tell a girl that I liked her but I couldn't." The game characters also tend to be sweeter than real high school students and will not tell their awkward **suitors** to **get a life**. "That kind of tender girl no longer exists," said Yasunobu Goto, a 19-year-old vocational school student.

> **suitor** man who wants to date a particular woman
>
> **get a life** (*slang*) Go find something better to do

Some say there is a danger that players will never find real relationships satisfying. "There's something called a two-dimensional complex, which means you fall in love with the animated character and you can't fall in love with a real woman," said Satoshi Suzuki, a 22-year-old post office worker.

(continued on next page)

(continued from previous page)

Some games have some nudity or suggestions of sex. There are X-rated games as well, mainly for personal computers. But the games like Tokimeki Memorial and True Love Story that are sold for Nintendo, Sega and Sony game machines are generally tame.

The **progenitor** of the love simulation games was not a dating game at all, but Princess Maker, a child-rearing game that appeared in 1991 and is sold by Gainax. There are now many dating games like Graduation, Classmates, M and Noel. But the standard-setter has been Konami's Tokimeki Memorial, which came out in 1994 and has sold 1.1 million copies. Tokimeki is a Japanese word for palpitating or throbbing, as in a heart.

Tokimeki was developed by male programmers based on their fantasies, with no input from women. "The person who created the game wanted to have experiences like this back in his high school days," said Akiko Nagata, a Konami director. The object of the game is to win the heart of Shiori, the most popular girl at school, or one of 11 other students with their own personalities. But Shiori will only say "I love you" on graduation day, three years from the start of the game. You must first live through your anxiety-prone high school years, week by week, so the game can take several hours.

Whether Shiori will say the magic words depends on how you get along with her and on characteristics like your **grooming**, athletic ability, social skills, stress level and knowledge of arts and science. Choose to concentrate on sports one week, for instance, and your athletic rating goes up, but your knowledge level goes down. Study too little and you will flunk your exams, lowering your appeal. You must also **play the field** wisely. If you focus too much on one girl, the others will have a low opinion of you. Then, even the girl of your choice will reject you, because no one wants a boyfriend who their friends think is a **dweeb**.

Periodically, you should call your male friend, Yoshio, who provides advice on date spots and tells you how each girl is rating you. You can call a girl and propose a time and place for a date. This time, you're in luck. Even though she barely knows you from a hole in the wall, Shiori has agreed to go to the amusement park with you next Sunday. First, you choose a ride. How about the Ferris wheel? "That was a nice view," she says when the ride is over. You reply:

1. "Yes."
2. "I was sleeping."
3. "I was looking only at your face."

Even an otaku can figure out which reply is appropriate here. Choose No. 3 and Shiori looks at you with her doe eyes and says: "I'm embarrassed but I'm happy. It was fun. Please invite me again."

Tokimeki, tokimeki, tokimeki.

progenitor the one that came before; what something came from

grooming physical appearance

play the field pay attention to many different women (or men)

dweeb (*slang*) nerd

More champagne, darling?

Discussion Questions

1. Why do you think the men in this article prefer virtual women to real ones?

2. Tokimeki was developed by men. Do you think Shiori would be different if women had been involved in her development?

3. What do you think of these "love simulation" games?

As more people regularly use the Internet, helping people search the Net has become big business. There are several different ideas about the best way for people to find the information they need. This article explores one company's approach. The company discussed here is called MiningCo.com. It has now been renamed About.com.

Minefields: MiningCo.com Is Digging for Online Gems So That You Don't Have To

David Batstone

In the beginning, there was a nice, uncluttered Internet populated by only a handful of researchers. Then along came the World Wide Web, and a lot of regular folks started sharing information from both work and home. Quickly, the Net became a tangled mess. Lots of good things were out there, but they were very hard to find. The Net didn't have a way to make sense of it all. Then, just when it seemed like chaos would reign, The Mining Company was born, and gave control over the Net back to the people again. And that, sisters and brothers, is the gospel of Scott Kurnit, founder and CEO of The Mining Company. Kurnit took a simple concept—employing Net surfers to provide contents and links for hundreds of subjects ranging from cooking to mutual funds to gay erotica—and built an entire company around it. Adding the **prerequisite** ".com" to its name for its February IPO **juggernaut**, MiningCo.com promised to make the Net work for users. Although **navigation sites** are among the most popular and financially profitable on the Internet, a CommerceNet/Nielsen Media Research study suggests that only Yahoo! has firmly established its brand. When asked to name the navigation site they use most frequently, 40 percent of Web surfers responded, "I don't know."

Maybe they realize that the search results they receive are a small sample of what is available on the Web. Not all navigation sites work the same, however. Directories such as Yahoo! manually classify Websites into categories by subject. Search engines such as AltaVista **trawl** the Web for documents that match word requests. But how effectively do they do their job? A September 1998 study conducted by the NEC Research Institute—a follow-up to an NEC study published five months earlier in *Science* magazine—found that no one search engine covered more than half of the total pages on the Web. The most **prolific**, AltaVista, boasted a 44 percent coverage, while Lycos limped behind at 9 percent coverage. Given the phenomenal growth of the Web and new methods of posting information on its pages, the search engines seem to be falling further and further behind.

"We mine the Net so you don't have to," announces the banner that hangs over the entrance of The MiningCo.'s Manhattan headquarters. Why do we need another navigation portal, you might ask? Because Web users need guidance finding their way through the online jungle. "The Net's not full of content; it's full of garbage," says the ever-provocative Kurnit. "Our guides use search engines but throw away 95 percent of their stuff, mining the gems for our customers." In other words, Kurnit is turning the numbers game on its head: We're better because we offer less.

The Mining Company was launched in February 1997 with the financial backing of several private investors led by Doll Capital Management and Crystal Internet Ventures. Its special-interest Websites, now a network about 645 strong, are

(continued on next page)

prerequisite something that is necessary before something else can be done; requirement

juggernaut a great, unstoppable force; in this case, the launching of MiningCo.com, that would destroy the competition

navigation site Web site that offers a variety of services, such as search engines and directories to guide users to topics of interest

trawl conduct exhaustive or extensive search

prolific producing a large amount

(continued from previous page)

individually created by guides who scour the Net for what they deem to be worth-while information. Beyond a selected list of links, guides generate their own unique content and initiate discussions and chats with members of their community.

In many respects, the site could be considered a **community portal** as much as a navigation site. But unlike community portal and chat sites such as GeoCities or Talk City where, Kurnit points out, all content providers are equally welcome, MiningCo.com tightly controls what gets listed. Each guide reports to a company editor who wields ultimate authority for quality control and ensures that site material is updated regularly. To dramatize the point, Kurnit relates that he put up a site on GeoCities more than three years ago, and recently went back to find out that it was still there, untouched, practically a time capsule.

Delivering timely content ranks high on MiningCo.com's priority list. David Schwalbe, for example, a librarian and amateur historian who runs the "American History" site, orders nearly all his content around current events. During the Senate impeachment trial of President Bill Clinton, he ran a feature on Andrew Johnson's 1868 trial, juxtaposed news of Elizabeth Dole's possible candidacy with a two-part column on Victoria Woodhull, the first woman to run for president, and produced a series of short biographies of noteworthy African-Americans for Black History Month. Schwalbe also publishes an evolving list of best links (visitors are encouraged to "Suggest a Site"), hosts a discussion bulletin board, and updates an events calendar related to American history.

Users searching for information at MiningCo.com are not limited to the 645 or so **vertical portals** of the company's **flagship**. They can also search by word to find topics that cross subject areas. Type in the words "venture capital," for example, and you'll see a list of more than 80 topic areas that direct you to sites dedicated to entrepreneurs, investing, and small business, among others. MiningCo.com claims that its **aggregated** content translates into close to 12,000 subject areas and more than 400,000 prescreened links to other Websites. All roads lead back to the guided communities, however, where relationships grow around passion and interest. After all, the company's **breakthrough** concept is people, not another piece of Internet hardware.

community portal Web site or service that guides and directs users through the Web based on a specific group's interests

vertical portal Web site or service organized by topic (for example, movies or farming) that guides and directs users through the Web

flagship a company's major, most important product or service

aggregated collected

breakthrough major advance

Activity 2.1

If you have access to the World Wide Web, check out About.com's Web site, www.about.com, and answer the following questions.

1. Click on the Internet/online channel and find the webopaedia. What's the term of the day?

2. Look in About Today. What's the top story?

3. Choose another channel that's of interest to you. Explore it and report to your class about what you found.

Discussion Questions

Based on the article (and your exploration of the Web site if you have access to it), answer the following questions.

1. What makes About.com (the new name for MiningCo.com) different from other navigation sites? Do you like it more or less?

2. What do you think Kurnit means when he says that About.com is better because it offers less? Do you think he is right?

Thinking about the Topic

After you have read the articles about computers, discuss the following questions.

1. Do you think increased use of computers is more likely to isolate us from one another or bring us together in a new kind of "community"?

2. In what ways do you see your own use of computers changing?

Activity 2.2

A. *Most of you probably already use computers and related equipment for some tasks. Not everybody uses computers for the same purposes, though. What are some of the ways that computer use might vary?*

For instance, some people have just a basic personal computer, whereas others may have all sorts of peripherals, or extra pieces of equipment, such as modems or CD-ROMs. They also may use computers for different purposes. If you use them just for writing papers for homework, chances are you are simply doing word processing. However, there are many other, quite basic functions that a computer performs. Give some examples here.

_____

_____

_____

_____

_____

_____

_____

_____

_____

B. *Do you and your classmates use computers for the same purposes?*

1. Discuss these questions to help you find out.

   - What sorts of equipment do you use, and for what purposes?

   - What about the rest of your classmates?

   - Have you noticed changes in your use of computers as you have grown—for instance, when you first used a computer, in high school, and now, in college?

• **Table 2.1** •

CHANGES IN THE CLASS'S COMPUTER USE

NAME	FIRST USE		H.S.		COLLEGE	
	equipment	use	equipment	use	equipment	use
Kyu			p.c.	mostly games	p.c. + CD-ROM	net surfing, writing papers
Hugo			none		p.c. + modem	e-mail, programming, homework
Lupe	used friend's p.c.	games	p.c.	homework, games	p.c., modem, DVD	homework, chat rooms, shopping

2. Now make a table on the blackboard like the one that has been started for you above. If high school was the first time you used a computer, leave the first two columns blank.

C. *What patterns in computer use can you find among your classmates? Discuss the questions that follow.*

1. What has changed since you started using a computer?

■ Are you using different equipment? Are you using different software?

■ Has your use of the Internet changed? How?

2. Who is using what technology and for what purposes?

■ What kinds of students use e-mail?

■ Who is playing computer games?

■ Who is using data base and spreadsheet software?

■ Who spends time in chat rooms?

■ Does anyone shop online?

3. Write in a few sentences the most important patterns you have found in your classmates' computer use. For instance, has your classmates' use of computers changed over the years? Do women have a different pattern of use from men?

_____

_____

_____

_____

4. Do you think you would find these same patterns among people outside of a college or university?

Short Write

Most of your assignments will require that you write more than one draft. Sometimes, however, writing a quick one-draft piece is helpful in generating ideas about a topic. Most of the Short Writes in this book are about personal experiences. Choose one of the following topics for a one-draft paper:

1. How has computerization helped you personally? How has it caused you difficulties?
2. Describe the first time you used a computer.
3. Discuss the things you love and hate about using computers.

2. GATHERING INFORMATION AND DRAFTING

You have been discussing and analyzing how your classmates use computers. Now you will develop a written questionnaire to hand out to fifteen to twenty people between the ages of twelve and thirty-five. Your assignment will be to collect data on their computer use. This could include information about people's attitudes toward computers, their habits (where they use computers and what they use them for), the kinds of hardware and software they have, or any other aspect you want to explore. You may decide to focus on one or several areas.

The data you collect in your survey of the fifteen to twenty people will be the basis for your essay in this unit. You will analyze the information in your questionnaire responses to identify patterns or trends. As in Unit One, you will write an essay with a clear main point, but in this unit, you will also work on three important elements of body paragraphs:

(1) telling the reader what the paragraph will be about,

(2) making a claim, and

(3) providing supporting evidence for your claim.

🔥 GENERATING IDEAS

In the last unit, you used lists and outlines to put some ideas down on paper before you started writing. Another useful way to get started is to use questions with WH words—*who, what, where, when, why*, and *how*.

Think about how people use computers. For instance, a question about habits might be: *Where do people use computers most?*

Activity 2.3

A. *Use the lines provided to write some questions with WH words about people's computer use. Make your questions cover areas you think you might want to find out about. Write as many as you can.*

_____

_____

_____

_____

_____

_____

_____

B. *Look back over the questions you have just written. Pick one or two that are the most interesting to you; these will give you a good idea of the areas you should probably explore further in your questionnaire. What area or areas do you think you are going to focus on? Write your answer here.*

_____

_____

_____

PREPARING A QUESTIONNAIRE

Once you have decided on an area or areas to focus on, you need to think about some specific questions. What are you going to ask? This is very important because the information you gather will be the basis for your essay. With these ideas in mind, think about what makes a good question. For example, if you want to find out how much time people spend on the computer, there are several ways to ask. You could ask:

```
Do you use the computer a lot?
```

Your respondents will answer "yes" or "no." This gives you some information, but it is limited. How much is a lot? One person may think twenty hours per week is a lot, whereas another thinks five hours per week is a lot. You won't be able to tell what the person had in mind when he or she answered the question. A multiple choice question will give you more information than a *yes/no* question, but you still must think about the kinds of choices you give. What if you ask:

```
How much do you use the computer?

a) never

b) sometimes

c) often

d) very often
```

This time, your respondents will tell you more than "yes" or "no," but the same problem presents itself as with the first question. How much is "sometimes"? Look at one more option.

```
How much do you use the computer?

a) more than five hours per day

b) between one and five hours per day

c) less than one hour per day

d) less than one hour per week
```

With this question, you have given specific choices and you will receive much more specific information on the questionnaire. Here, the question asks about hours per day or week. In this case, rather than finding out only that a certain number of people use the computer "often" (which could mean a variety of things), you will have a clear idea of how many hours people spend using it. This will make it easier to compare one response with another later on when you report these results as part of your paper.

In a question about people's attitudes toward computers, the choices offered would be a bit different. In this case, answers that were too vague for the time question could work. For example:

```
Are you afraid of computers?

a) very

b) some

c) a little

d) not at all
```

Because attitudes are harder to define, these kinds of choices may give you enough information to find patterns among computer users. When you ask a question with a sliding scale in which the respondents choose only one answer, give no more than four choices.

Another way to find out about people's attitudes is to ask about a specific issue, as in this question about the drawbacks of the Internet:

```
What bothers you most about the Internet? Choose one an-
swer.

a) Pornography is too easy to find.

b) It's too hard to figure out what the Web site is from
   the URL.

c) It wastes too much time.

d) Web sites change too fast.
```

You may also ask questions in which the respondents could choose more than one answer, such as:

```
What activities do you do on the Internet?

a) e-mail
```

b) chat room conversations

c) Web browsing

d) research

e) shopping

f) other _____

When answering this question, your respondents can mark as many choices as apply to them. In these cases, give no more than six options. The questionnaire should be easy to fill out; providing a limited number of answers for each question makes the respondents' job simpler.

Activity 2.4

A. *Now it's time for you to write your questionnaire. You already know which area or areas you want to ask about, and you have some guidelines on how to structure your questions. Write as many questions as you can, but write at least twelve so that you will have enough data for your essay.*

B. *After you have finished a draft of your questionnaire, exchange it with a partner. As you read your partner's questionnaire, answer these questions and discuss them.*

1. Do you understand all the questions? If not, what is unclear?

_____

_____

_____

2. Are the choices given for each question specific enough? If not, what suggestions can you make?

_____

_____

_____

3. Are there any other questions you think he or she should ask?

_____

_____

_____

_____

C. *Based on your partner's and your instructor's responses to your questionnaire, what changes are you going to make? Write them here.*

_____

_____

_____

_____

Have you thought of other changes you want to make or questions you want to add? Write them here.

_____

_____

_____

_____

D. *Before you prepare the final copy with your revisions, there is one more component to include: What do you need to know about the participants? Although you don't really need their names, you do need to know something about them. At the top of your questionnaire, you should include a section to collect this information. What will you ask? Remember that respondents will range in age from to twelve to thirty-five. Is this information specific enough?*

Another thing you probably need to know is their occupation. Why do you think this would be useful information to have? What questions could you ask about occupation? Some examples are:

■ What kind of work do you do?

■ Are you a student? In junior high? high school? college?

On your questionnaire, you will need to make a space for this information, as in the following example.

■ Occupation:

    Student: yes ____ no ____

        College ____

        High school ____

        Junior high ____

    Working: yes ____ no ____

        Type of job _____

    ■

    ■

You will notice that there are extra bullets in the box. Discuss with your classmates what other information you think you will need to include. Fill in the rest of the box together, using the bullets provided. Put this information in a box at the top right-hand corner of your questionnaire when you type up the final draft.

Your questionnaire is ready now. Be sure to make enough copies to conduct your survey. **Now hand out your questionnaires to your respondents. Bring the completed questionnaires to your next class.**

IDENTIFYING TRENDS

When you did an informal survey of your classmates' use of computers at the beginning of this unit, you tried to find some patterns. Perhaps you found that male students used computers more than female students, or more specifically, that male and female students used them for different purposes. Maybe you found that the men played more computer games and the women used e-mail more often.

Now you have a lot more data from a more diverse group of people. How can you turn this information into something interesting to say in a paper? Look at one attempt in the following excerpt:

```
I gave my survey to 12 people. This is what they said. Re-
spondents 1, 3 and 11 said they used their computers less
than 5 hours a week. Respondents 4 and 6 said they used them
between 5 and 10 hours per week. Respondents 1 and 5 said
they used their computers mostly for writing papers. Respon-
dents 2, 10, 11 and 12 used them for communicating with their
friends on e-mail. . . .
```

What's wrong with this way of writing up the data? Do you think anyone would want to read it?

For one thing, it's really boring to read! It is very repetitive and, most important, it makes the reader do all the work. You need to analyze some of the data for the reader and presents it in a way that will make sense and be interesting. To do this, you need to go through your results and find some general *trends* in your data in the same way that you did when you surveyed the class.

A **trend** means a pattern or general tendency. In general, who is using computers? What are they doing with them? How do they feel about them? Where do they use them most often? How much do they use them? You will notice the repeated use of the words "they" and "them." Who are "they"? What can you tell your reader about "them"? Look at the next excerpt:

```
Half of the respondents in my survey are scared of comput-
ers; the other half love them.
```

It won't tell the readers much if you write this, unless you also tell them who the first half is and who the second half is. Do the respondents who are afraid have anything in common? Do they fall into any particular age group? Do they have similar kinds of jobs? They don't all have to be exactly the same for you to claim that you have found a trend. If seven of them are over thirty, but one is twenty-one, you can still make a statement about the relationship between age and being afraid of computers, such as:

```
In my survey, most people who said they were scared of com-
puters were over 30.
```

Similarly, in the earlier excerpt, the reader can't draw any conclusions about "Respondent 11," unless you write something about who Respondent 11 is.

The important thing about trends is that they relate two separate pieces of information. For example, List 1 contains one kind of information and List 2 contains another kind of information.

List 1: Category of Users

Some examples might be:

■ women

■ high school students

■ engineers

■ mothers working in the home

■ people between fifteen and twenty-one

■ engineering students

(You may remember that this kind of information is already on your questionnaires, in the box on the front page.)

List 2: Statement about Attitudes or Use

Some examples might be:

■ never use computers

■ use computers only at work

■ use computers for word processing

■ get information on-line for school work

■ use computers between four and six hours per week

■ love computers

■ check electronic bulletin boards

Now you can put the two parts together by using some sample data.

```
Respondents between the ages of 15 and 21 generally used
their computers 3-5 hours per week; most respondents between
the ages of 22 and 27 used their computers 5-7 hours per
week; respondents between the ages of 28 and 35 used their
computers 0-3 hours per week.
```

This is important information that points to a significant trend in the data; however, the reader has to work too hard to find the trend. Look again at the category of user in the excerpt you just read. What is a more general way of referring to all of those people?

Age, of course. The writer is referring to people in various age groups.

What does the writer want to **claim** about the people in these various age groups? Look at the second half of each of the statements in the excerpt: . . . generally used their computers 3–5 hours per week; . . . used their computers 5–7 hours per week; . . . used their computers 0–3 hours per week. Clearly, these statements address how much or how often these people use their computers. Can you think of one general sentence that states the trend in the data presented in the excerpt, one that summarizes all of the bits of information? Write it here.

Your sentence should be something like this:

`Age` seems to be an important factor in **how much people**

use their computers.

You have now linked the general category, *age*, with a general statement about *amount of use*. This kind of statement is a good way to begin a paragraph because it tells readers what it will be about. Every paragraph should contain a sentence that gives this kind of information. It is always important to let readers know where you are going with your ideas. First you will practice writing general statements like this one based on data in Lists 1 and 2. Later you will write them using your own data.

Look back at Lists 1 and 2. The items in these lists are a good place to start, but you need to use more general terms. In the example sentence you just read, the general term was *age*. Look at List 1 and think of general terms for each of these types of computer users. For example, "women" can be included in the more general category of *gender*. A good way to determine a more general category is to try to list some other, similar items and then think of a broad term that will cover all of the items in the list.

Activity 2.5

A. *Look at Table 2.2. Some lists have been started for you in column A. Now, look at the more general terms in column B. Two of them have been filled in for you. You fill in the last blank.*

• **T a b l e 2 . 2** •

COMPUTER USERS

A. EXAMPLES	B. GENERAL TERM
women, men	gender
engineers, doctors, teachers. . . .	_____
engineering students, liberal arts students, architecture students. . . .	type of student

How about items in List 2? These provide specific information about attitudes toward computers or about use of computers. You will need to come up with something more general in your statement. One item from the list is:

■ use computers only **at work**

The important part of this statement seems to be **at work**. If you were making a list as you did with the items in List 1, it might look like this:

```
use computers only at work,

at school,

at the library,

at home,

at home and at work . . .
```

What is a general way of referring to all of these items? Write it here.

_____

If you combine what you have just written with one of the general terms from Table 2, you have the two elements for another trend statement like this one:

```
Gender makes a difference in where people use computers.
```

B. *Look at List 2 again. Table 2.3 has been started for you with a list of examples and a general term:* getting information on-line, shopping on the Web, *and using* e-mail *are all* **on-line uses of the computer***. Fill in the blanks in the rest of the table. First think of some other examples and write them in column A of Table 2.3. Then try to think of some more general ways of talking about attitudes and use and write them in column B of Table 2.3.*

• **Table 2.3** •

ATTITUDES AND USE

A. EXAMPLES	B. GENERAL TERM
■ get on-line info for assignments ■ shop on the World Wide Web ■ send e-mail ■ use computers for word processing ■ _____ ■ _____ ■ love computers ■ _____ ■ _____	on-line uses _____

Activity 2.6

A. *You have been analyzing data that have been provided for you. Now it's time to think about your own data. What kind of trends do you expect to find?*

_____

_____

_____

B. *Look through your survey data again and try to find three trends. Use the general terms from Tables 2.2 and 2.3 to help you focus on general categories. You may find* *more than three trends. If so, choose ones that seem the most important or the most interesting, or ones for which you have the strongest evidence. For instance, if all the women answered in a certain way, that would be a good trend to choose because you can support it by reporting the responses from your survey.*

In the space provided here, write a statement about each trend. Make sure that each statement addresses general categories for users and for attitudes or use.

1. _____

_____

2. _____

_____

3. _____

_____

By now you have written several statements about the trends you found in your data. You will use these trend statements to begin paragraphs in the **body** of your paper. The body is the main part of your paper. It will follow an introduction, but for now, you should not be concerned with the introduction. Look again at this general statement.

```
Age seems to be an important factor in how much peo-
ple use their computers.
```

This is a good way to begin a body paragraph because it gives your readers some idea of where you are going. *Orienting your reader* is the first of three crucial elements of most body paragraphs. In your next step, you need to be more specific.

- What *about* age?
- *How* is it an important factor in how much people use their computers?

You need to explain this to your readers. It is done for you in the next example.

```
Age seems to be an important factor in how much peo-
ple use their computers. Computer use rises with age and
then falls again.
```

This second sentence makes a **claim**. A claim is a statement that the writer would like the reader to accept as a fact, although it may or may not be true. Some examples of claims are:

- Men are better at parking cars than women.
- The search for the missing child went on for days.
- Scientists are discovering the causes of aging.

*Making a **claim*** is the second crucial element of most body paragraphs. When you write body paragraphs, make sure you make a claim about your topic.

What's next? When readers see a claim, the next thing they expect is proof. *Supporting a claim with specific evidence* is the third essential element of most body paragraphs. In the example that follows, **support** is provided for the claim that is made. The claim, which is made in the second sentence, is followed by evidence in the form of specific data.

```
Age seems to be an important factor in how much peo-
ple use their computers. Computer use rises with age and
then falls again. Respondents between the ages of 15 and
21 generally used their computers 3-5 hours per week; most
respondents between the ages of 22 and 27 used their com-
puters 5-7 hours per week; respondents between the ages
of 28 and 35 used their computers 0-3 hours per week.
```

When you write your own paper, you will need to make claims and provide support for them. Your evidence will come from your survey data.

Summary of Essential Elements of a Body Paragraph

1. A general statement that tells readers what the paragraph will be about:

```
Age seems to be an important factor in how much people use
their computers.
```

2. A sentence that makes a claim:

```
Computer use rises with age and then falls again.
```

3. Specific supporting evidence for the claim:

```
Respondents between the ages of 15 and 21 generally used their
computers 3-5 hours per week; most respondents between the
```

ages of 22 and 27 used their computers 5-7 hours per week; respondents between the ages of 28 and 35 used their computers 0-3 hours per week.

Drafting Tip

Making sure your evidence is specific

It is important to be as specific as possible when you report your data. Don't just say,

"Some people said . . ."

"A lot of women are . . ."

This information is too vague to be useful. In the example you just read, there were words like "most respondents" and "generally." This is fairly specific because it suggests that probably 75 percent or more of the people in that category responded in this way. You can also use actual numbers or percentages:

"Half of the men claimed . . ."

"Thirty percent of the high school students use . . ."

"Eight out of ten working people said . . ."

Activity 2.7

Now look back at the general statements you wrote on page 71. Remember that a general statement is the first important element of a body paragraph because it tells readers what it will be about. Next you need to make a claim and provide support for it based on your survey results. Use the lines that follow. Begin with your general statement.

Body paragraph #1

General statement: _____

_____

Claim:

_____

Supporting evidence:

_____

_____

_____

_____

_____

_____

Body paragraph #2

General statement: _____

_____

Claim:

_____

Supporting evidence:

_____

_____

_____

_____

_____

Body paragraph #3

General statement: _____

_____

Claim:

_____

Supporting evidence:

_____

_____

_____

_____

_____

_____

WRITING FOCUS: LINKING BODY PARAGRAPHS TO THE MAIN POINT

You have now written most of the body of your paper. It's time to think about other parts of the paper. Reread the example.

> Age seems to be an important factor in how much people use their computers. Computer use rises with age and then falls again. Respondents between the ages of 15 and 21 generally used their computers 3–5 hours per week; most

```
respondents between the ages of 22 and 27 used their com-
puters 5-7 hours per week; respondents between the ages
of 28 and 35 used their computers 0-3 hours per week.
```

Could you begin the paper with this paragraph? Maybe. However, that would make readers think that the whole paper is going to be about age and the number of hours that people use their computers. That may not be true; there may be other paragraphs about topics unrelated to age. Also, readers would want to know: Respondents to what? Who are you talking about?

Some sort of **introduction** is needed. It will have to do two things. First, in the introductory paragraph, readers usually expect to get an idea about the **main point** the writer is trying to make. Second, the introduction should also tell the reader where you got your information.

Activity 2.8

A. *Remember that every piece of writing must have a main point. What will be the main point of your paper? It should bring together the ideas that are in all of the paragraphs that you just wrote. Write it here.*

_____

_____

_____

_____

B. *You need to include information about where your evidence comes from. How did you collect your information? In your survey, of course. Who completed your questionnaires? How many people? These details will help readers to evaluate the evidence you give to support your claims. Write the information you need to include.*

_____

_____

_____

_____

_____

_____

_____

 DRAFTING: WRITING YOUR FIRST DRAFT

Now, go back over what you have written so far and try to put the pieces together for the first draft of your paper on trends in computer use and/or attitudes. Remember:

(1) Include your **main point** in your introduction.

(2) In your body paragraphs, (a) make **claims** and (b) provide **support** for your claims.

3. REVISING

EVALUATING ESSAYS

Once again, you will look at what another student wrote about this topic, as well as how one of his classmates and his instructor suggested that he revise his first draft. As you review this material, think about how the writer might benefit from the suggestions. Also, try to notice which responses you would find most helpful if you received them. Later, you will offer suggestions for improving another paper on the same topic.

***

Student Essay 1

1   In this world, almost everyone uses computers. Com-
2   puters improve people's way of life. I surveyed some peo-
3   ple to find out exactly what people do with computers. I
4   asked people from 12 to 35 years old who were students
5   and working people. I found out that there are some dif-
6   ferences between age groups. There are people who use com-
7   puters a lot and there are people who don't like to use
8   computers at all. There is a lot of cool stuff like hard-
9   ware, software programs and Internet services that makes
10   computers useful for different groups.

11   There were a lot of people who use computers and some
12   who were scared to use the computer. About 20% of the
13   people don't like to use the computer. These people were
14   a little bit older than the others. They were 32 to 35
15   years old. People from ages 12 to 26 use their computer
16   in school or at home and people from 27 to 35 use it at
17   work. Most people aged 12 to 18 use computers for enter-
18   tainment and to do homework. People from 18 to 27 use it
19   for research, entertainment and to send e-mail. These peo-
20   ple spend lots of time doing all these things. People from
21   27 to 35 years old usually use the computer for work.
22   They do word processing and spread sheets and send e-mail.
23   Most people use the computer to make their lives easier.

24   Most people have a computer at home. These people
25   have lots of hardware for the computer. New computer users

26 usually have great hardware. About 40% of the people have
27 the IBM 486 DX2 66. Another 50% have a Pentium (70, 90,
28 and 133) and the other 10% don't have computers. All these
29 computers have a CD-ROM, a sound card and a modem/fax. As
30 technology grows these things have become basics that all
31 computers carry.

32   Older people use the Internet more than younger peo-
33 ple. In my survey, almost everyone over 18 years old uses
34 the Internet, but no one in junior high or high school
35 does. There are a lot of cool services on the Internet.
36 People send mail, buy things, do research, and even talk
37 to each other on the chat lines. About 70% of the people
38 in my survey use the Internet and about 90% of them use
39 it to send mail to their friends and people at work.

Bu

RESPONSE SHEET

Writer: _Bu_   Responder: _Phataboot_

1. Look at the first paragraph. Does it tell you what the main point of the essay will be? Explain.

I am not sure. It is hard to tell what the main point is because he writes about many different things, such as age and hardware and software.

2. Does it tell you where the information in the essay comes from? Explain.

Yes. He says he did a survey and asked people from 12 to 35 years old about what they do with computers.

3. What trends are discussed in the body?

In the first body paragraph, he writes about how people of different ages use their computers for different things. He also writes about whether people like computers. In the second body paragraph, he writes about different kinds of equipment, but I don't know what the trend is. In the final body paragraph, he says that older people use the Internet more than younger people.

4. Is each trend discussed in a separate paragraph? If not, explain.

No. It seems like the first body paragraph is about two things and the last paragraph talks about age again, just like in the first paragraph.

5. Are there specific claims in each body paragraph? If so, write them.

I only found one in the last body paragraph. "Older people use the Internet more than younger people." (lines 32–33)

6. Does the writer give specific supporting evidence for each claim? If so, write the evidence here.

He gives a lot of data about age differences. He also tells a lot about different kinds of equipment. He says who uses the Internet and what they use it for.

7. Are there parts of the essay you don't understand? What are they?

I don't understand all the parts about the different equipment and why it is important.

8. What other suggestions do you have for the writer's next draft?

I think he should make his first paragraph clearer. After I read it, I didn't really know what the essay was going to be about. Also, the paragraph about equipment seems kind of different from the other parts.

Here's what Bu's instructor had to say about the essay.

➤ You have a lot of interesting data here about how different age groups use computers and about the kinds of hardware people have. Body paragraphs 1 & 3 each deal with two issues: in #1, it's the attitudes of different age groups **and** the ways different age groups use the computer, and in #3, it's what age group uses the Internet and services available on the Internet. In both paragraphs, you seem to be talking mainly about the relationship between age and computer use. Is this your main point? Your peer response partner had trouble figuring out what it was. Make sure it's clear in your introduction.

Also, try dividing the body paragraphs up and discussing one trend per paragraph. In each paragraph you should clearly state the trend you found and make some claim about it. I agree with Phata-boot's answer #5 that the first two paragraphs contain no claims. You may find that after you break up the paragraphs you need more supporting evidence for some of your trends. Perhaps you can combine your two discussions of computer use in one paragraph. Phata-boot's comment about body paragraph #2 is also useful. You have a lot of data, but it's hard to tell what trend you are discussing. Because the overall theme in the rest of the paper seems to be age, can you find a connection between age and types of hardware? Look back through your data and see if you find any patterns. Please reread the Peer Response Sheet and see me if you have any questions.

Activity 2.9

Before you look at what Bu did with these comments, you will respond to another paper on the same topic. Use the Response Sheet following the essay to guide you. Remember to give comments and suggestions that are constructive, that is, ones that the writer could actually use. That means you need to be clear and specific about what you think the writer should do. Be prepared to say why you have made these suggestions. Later, when you respond to one of your classmate's papers, he or she may ask you to explain your comments.

Student Essay 2

1 People have various personalities. They also have
2 different ways of thinking about computers. I conducted
3 interviews with twenty people about using computers. Those
4 people were various ages between 13 and 35, and had

5 different occupations like clerks, secretaries, and travel

6 agents. Most of the people I interviewed were students in

7 junior high, high school and college. Sometimes those stu-

8 dents were working and they had different jobs. Also I

9 had a couple of people who had regular jobs. In my sur-

10 vey, I found that people use computers in different places

11 and they use them to do different things. Finally de-

12 pending on age, people spend different amounts of time on

13 the Internet.

14 The first trend that I found in my survey was about

15 where people use computers most. There was a big differ-

16 ence between students and working people. Almost all of

17 the high school students, that is, about 90% of them, use

18 computers only at school. The next group of people are

19 students in college. About 70% of them work on computers

20 at home rather than at school. The rest, 30%, are stu-

21 dents who are working and they use computers at home, at

22 school and at work. The other people are between the ages

23 of 26 and 35 years. They are not students, only working

24 people. About 80% of these people use computers mostly at

25 work. The rest use it at home.

26 The next trend is about what kind of things people

27 do on the computer. This time the difference I found was

28 between females and males. Most females, about 85%, work

29 on word processing. A couple of them also use it for home-

30 work and talking on-line. Males do everything on the com-

31 puter including playing games, using the Web, talking

32 on-line, programming, word processing and studying. Sev-

33 enty five percent use games the most. Ten percent use it

34 for word processing. The rest, about 15%, use the com-

35 puter to talk on-line, access the Web and do programming.

36 The last trend that I found is very interesting. It

37 is about how a particular group of people use the Inter-

38 net. In this case, it is age that divided the people I

39 interviewed. About 90% of the people between the ages of

40 13 and 22 spend about 1 to 6 hours weekly on the Inter-

41 net. People between 22 and 35 spend much more time on the

42 Internet than the other people. Eighty percent of people
43 who were 22 to 35 years old spend 7 to 15 or more hours
44 weekly on the Internet.

45   In my opinion, these trends mean that people are us-
46 ing computers more and more and that technology will grow
47 very fast. People will have to study more about comput-
48 ers because they change very fast. If people work on com-
49 puters, they will have to be up to date with information
50 about computers. Perhaps at school, children will study
51 more about computers because those skills will help them
52 in the future, so there will be more special programs for
53 them. I think the evidence I found means that computer
54 services will improve for certain groups of people. If
55 most people who are using the Internet are between the
56 ages of 22 and 35, the Internet will provide more oppor-
57 tunities for them. There will be more services that in-
58 terest that age group. Also there will be more special
59 games for men because they make up the majority of peo-
60 ple who play computer games.

Dominika

RESPONSE SHEET

Writer: *Dominika* **Responder:** _____

1. Look at the first paragraph. Does it tell you what the main point of the essay will be? Explain.

_____

_____

_____

_____

2. Does it tell you where the information in the essay comes from? Explain.

_____

_____

_____

_____

3. What trends are discussed in the body?

_____

_____

_____

_____

_____

4. Is each trend discussed in a separate paragraph? If not, explain.

_____

_____

_____

_____

_____

5. Are there specific claims in each body paragraph? If so, write them.

_____

_____

_____

_____

_____

_____

_____

_____

6. Does the writer give specific supporting evidence for each claim? If so, write the evidence here.

_____

_____

_____

_____

_____

_____

_____

7. Are there parts of the essay you don't understand? What are they?

_____

_____

_____

_____

_____

8. What other suggestions do you have for the writer's next draft?

_____

_____

_____

_____

_____

✺ WRITING FOCUS: MAKING CLAIMS AND PROVIDING SUPPORT IN BODY PARAGRAPHS

Look at the two papers you have just read. Which one do you think was better?

If you picked Dominika's, we agree with you. What was it about her paper that made you think it was better than Bu's?

If you look at the introductions, you can see that both papers make the point that computers are used differently by different kinds of people, and both state where their information comes from. So you need to look further—at the body paragraphs of the papers.

Activity 2.10

*Referring to your Response Sheet, identify the sentences in Dominika's **body** paragraphs that tell you what she will be discussing in each paragraph. (Look at the first sentence in body paragraphs #1 and #2 and the first two sentences in body paragraph #3.)*

1. _____

_____

2. _____

_____

3. _____

_____

What do these sentences tell you? As you probably wrote, each sentence clearly states what the paragraph will be about:

body para. #1—where people use computers

body para. #2—what kind of work they do on their computers

body para. #3—who uses the Internet

The reader can tell quite easily what to expect in the rest of the paragraph. If you continue, you will find that she follows each of these with some **claim** about a trend that relates to the topic.

body para. #1—there is a big difference between working people and students

body para. #2—there is a difference between the kind of work men and women do on computers

body para. #3—Internet use depends on the age of the user

What should a reader expect after a **claim**? **Support**, of course! Look at what Dominika does here.

- Does she provide support for her claim?
- Does the evidence that she offers always relate to the claim she has made?

■ Does she provide unrelated evidence, that is, information that might have to do with a different claim?

In fact, she provides relevant evidence for every claim. That is why her paper is so clear and easy to follow.

Now, look at Bu's paper and try to do the same thing. Start by looking for a sentence that tells you what each paragraph will be about.

body para. #1—It looks as if he is going to compare people who use computers and people who are afraid to use them.

body para. #2—Based on the first sentence, the reader might expect this one to be about where people use computers. In the second sentence, we see it may be about hardware.

body para. #3—The first sentence in the paragraph clearly indicates what the paragraph will be about. Based on that sentence, it appears that paragraph will be like one in Dominika's essay: the relationship between age and Internet use.

As you read further in each paragraph, does each paragraph turn out as you expected? In most cases, it probably doesn't.

body para. #1—This paragraph has a little bit of everything. It does give a lot of interesting information about the expected topic, that is, people who use computers and people who are afraid of them. However, it also focuses on age and various computer uses, as well as on where they are used.

body para. #2—This paragraph is indeed mostly about equipment, but it is not clear why he is writing about this issue.

body para. #3—There is a discussion of age and the Internet, as expected from the topic sentence, but the paragraph also addresses services available on the Net.

This paper is weak for a number of reasons.

First, it is confusing because sometimes the writer leads readers to believe a paragraph will be about one thing, and then it turns out to be about something else. A sentence that clearly states what the paragraph will be about would be helpful here. For instance, what really is the topic of body paragraph #1? It is certainly about age, but *what about* age? Bu seems to address two trends: (1) age and attitudes toward computers, and (2) age and computer use. Bu's instructor has suggested he break this paragraph up and write two paragraphs. Each paragraph should have a sentence indicating the topic and a sentence making a claim about that topic.

Second, some of the paragraphs contain pieces of information that are not really related to one another. For instance, body paragraph #3 is about age and the Internet, yet it also includes information about the Internet that has nothing to do with age. Unless Bu can relate this material to his topic, it has no place in the second draft.

A third problem is that in body paragraphs #1 and #2, Bu **never makes any claims** about trends. He gives lots of numbers, but you have to figure out for yourself why he is giving them. As you try to make sense of the paper, what you are really doing is trying to figure out what his claims are. In the end, you can't be sure. He needs to state his claims clearly, as he has done for body paragraph #3.

Now go back and look at Dominika's paper. The last thing to look at is her final paragraph. This one is a little bit different from the other body paragraphs. It doesn't make a claim or provide evidence. Instead, she says what she thinks is significant about the trends she has described. She helps readers to answer the question:

So what?

It may be interesting to read about trends in computer use, but it helps readers if the writer draws some conclusions from them. Dominika's conclusion is not simply a summary of what has been written in the rest of the paper; she makes a comment about the material and evaluates it. Bu's paper includes nothing like this, which is the final reason why Dominika's is the stronger paper.

Drafting Tip

Benefiting from Criticism

We have just suggested that Bu's paper has a lot of problems and that it needs considerable revision. **This does not mean that Bu should throw out his paper and start all over!** There is a lot of useful information in his paper, particularly data showing how age is related to computer attitudes and use, as well as important facts about hardware. It does mean that he should organize this information differently and frame it in a way that makes it easier for readers to understand.

Perhaps you sometimes get comments on a paper that make you feel like crumpling it up and throwing it in the garbage. Usually, that's not necessary! When you reread your draft, try to find the things that are worth including in your next draft and think of how you can put them in a better "package."

ANALYZING A REVISION

Now look again at Bu's paper. You have seen the comments that one of his classmates and his instructor made. Look at what Bu plans to do. You can get an idea from his **What to Do When the Draft Comes Back** sheet. You can also see how he has revised his paper in the second draft. The additions are in bold.

Name: *Bu*

1. Read through your instructor's comments and the Peer Response Sheet(s).

2. Find some of the suggestions they have made.

3. Write the most important ones here. Then write what you think of each suggestion. How will you respond to it? If you do not plan to follow it, why not?

A. *I need to make my main point clearer in the introduction. My main point should be about age.*

   i. I plan to ignore the suggestion because

   _____

   _____

   _____

   _____

   ii. I plan to change my draft in the following way:

   I will add some sentences to the first paragraph to show the main point and also tell what the body paragraphs will be about:

   (1) age and how people feel about computers, (2) age and how much people use computers, and (3) age and the Internet.

B. *I need to make claims in the first two body paragraphs.*

   i. I plan to ignore the suggestion because

   _____

   _____

   _____

   ii. I plan to change my draft in the following way:

   I will make one for each.

C. *It seems like Phataboot thinks I shouldn't write about equipment.*

   i. I plan to ignore the suggestion because

   I think equipment is very important, so I want to keep it but I will try to relate it to my main point about age better.

   ii. I plan to change my draft in the following way:

   _____

   _____

   _____

   _____

4. Perhaps you have thought of some other changes you would like to make. List them here:

I will divide the first body paragraph into two separate ones.

I think I will also write about why different age groups act differently.

5. Are there any comments or suggestions on your paper that you did not understand? You may want to discuss them with your peer response partner or arrange a conference with your instructor. List them here, and bring this sheet with you to help guide your conference.

_____

_____

_____

_____

Based on the suggestions from his instructor and on the Peer Response Sheet, Bu revised his paper. Here are his first and second drafts.

First Draft

1   In this world, almost everyone uses computers. Com-

2 puters improve people's way of life. I surveyed some peo-

3 ple to find out exactly what people do with computers. I

4 asked people from 12 to 35 years old who were students

5 and working people. I found out that ~~there are some dif-~~

6 ~~ferences between~~ age groups. There are people who use com-

7 puters a lot and there are people who don't like to use

8 computers at all. There is a lot of cool stuff like hard-

9 ware, software programs and Internet services that makes

10 computers useful for different groups.

11   There were a lot of [people who use computers] and   → *1*

12 [some who were scared] to use the computer. [About 20% of

13 the people don't like to use the computer. These people

14 were a little bit older than the others. They were 32 to   → *2*

15 35 years old.] People from ages 12 to 26 use their com-

16 puter in school or at home and people from 27 to 35 use

17 it at work. Most people aged 12 to 18 use computers for

18 entertainment and to do homework. People from 18 to 27 use

19 it for research, entertainment and to send e-mail. These

20 people spend lots of time doing all these things. People

21 from 27 to 35 years old usually use the computer for work.

22 They do word processing and spread sheets and send e-mail.

23 ~~Most people use the computer to make their lives easier.~~

24   [Most people have a computer at home.] These people   *3*

25 have lots of hardware for the computer. ~~New computer users~~

26 ~~usually have great hardware.~~ About 40% of the people have

27 the IBM 486 DX2 66. Another 50% have a Pentium (70, 90,

28 and 133) and the other 10% don't have computers. All these

29 computers have a CD-ROM, a sound card and a modem/fax. As

30 technology grows these things have become basics that all

31 computers carry.

32 Older people use the Internet more than younger peo-

33 ple. In my survey, almost everyone over 18 years old uses

34 the Internet, but no one in junior high or high school

35 does. ~~There are a lot of cool services on the Internet.~~

36 ~~People send mail, buy things, do research, and even talk~~

37 ~~to each other on the chat lines. About 70% of the people~~

38 ~~in my survey use the Internet and about 90% of them use~~

39 ~~it to send mail to their friends and people at work.~~

Second Draft

1 In this world, almost everyone uses computers. I sur-

2 veyed some people to find out exactly what people do with

3 computers. I asked people from 12 to 35 years old who

4 were students and working people. I found out that **dif-**

5 **ferent** age groups **use computers differently and have dif-**

6 **ferent attitudes about them too.** There are people who use

7 computers a lot and there are people who don't like to

8 use computers at all. **Some people really like computers**

9 **and some people are kind of afraid of them.** There is a

10 lot of cool stuff like hardware, software programs and

11 Internet services that makes computers useful for differ-

12 ent groups.

13 **Age makes a difference in how people feel about com-**

14 **puters. Most people I surveyed use computers but some**   *1*

15 **still feel scared to use them. In my survey about 80% of**

16 **the people use computers and feel comfortable with them.**

17 **These people were between the ages of 12 and 30. All of**

18 **these people learned to use the computer in school.** About

19 20% of the people **in my survey** don't like to use the com-   *2*

20 puter. These people were a little bit older than the oth-

21 ers. They were 31 to 35 years old. **This group didn't learn**

22 **to use the computer in school and has trouble under-**

23 **standing how to use it.**

24 **Different age groups use the computer to do differ-**

25 **ent things. People aged 18 to 27 do much more on the com-**

26 **puter than the younger and older groups. Everyone I sur-**
27 **veyed from 18 to 27 uses the computer. They use it for**
28 **research, shopping, chat lines, to play games and to send**
29 **e-mail. They also spend the most time surfing the Inter-**
30 **net.** These people spend lots of time doing all these
31 things. **Seventy-five percent of the people** aged 12 to 18
32 use computers **only to play games** and to do homework. Peo-
33 ple from 27 to 35 years old usually use the computer for
34 work. **Ninety-five percent said they** do word processing and
35 spread sheets and send e-mail **for work.**

36 **Ninety percent of the** people have a computer at home. *3*
37 These people have lots of hardware for the computer **but**
38 **they don't use all the hardware they have. Younger peo-**
39 **ple use more of their hardware than older people. About**
40 **40% of the people in *my survey*** have the IBM 486 DX2 66.
41 Another 50% have a Pentium (70, 90, and 133) and the other
42 10% don't have computers. All these computers have a CD-
43 ROM, a sound card and a modem/fax. As technology grows
44 these things have become basics that all computers carry.
45 **Eighty-five percent of the oldest group, ages 27 to 34,**
46 **use their computers just for typing and mailing. They**
47 **don't usually use their CD-ROM or sound card. The younger**
48 **people, from 12 to 26, use all the hardware they have.**
49 **They use their CD-ROM and sound card and send messages**
50 **with their modem/fax.**

As you can see, Bu has made several substantial changes. The second draft is **not** too late to try out new ideas; in fact, it's exactly the right time. Also, if you look back at the first draft, you will notice that some parts have been crossed out. The arrows show how Bu used a lot of material from his first draft but improved it by moving it around and adding new material to support it. Each paragraph is discussed next.

Introductory paragraph

As you saw in his **What to Do When the Draft Comes Back** sheet, Bu decided to make age the focus of his whole paper. The fourth sentence in his second draft provides the main point of his paper. Then he gives some indication of what he will talk about in the rest of his paper, one sentence for each of the body paragraphs that follow.

Match each of the sentences in the introduction to the corresponding body paragraph. Write each one here:

1. _____

_____

2. _____

_____

3. _____

_____

Body paragraph #1

This is where Bu added the most new material. He divided his old paragraph into two new ones, as he said he would on his **What to Do When the Draft Comes Back** sheet. Now body paragraph #1 focuses on age and attitudes toward computers. His first draft didn't contain enough information on this topic to support his claim, so he went back to his survey data to find more evidence. He also added a very interesting and important point: that younger people are less afraid of computers because, unlike the older users, they learned all about computers in school.

Body paragraph #2

This paragraph contains some of the material from body paragraph #1 of Bu's first draft, but now there is a new focus and a clearer claim: that age seems to influence what people use computers for. Again, he had to go back to his survey results to find more supporting information. It is also interesting to note that he has included information about Internet use in this paragraph. That information used to be in the last body paragraph of the first draft.

What happened to all the material about services available on the Internet that was also in the last body paragraph of the first draft? If you can't find it in the second draft, it's not surprising: Bu threw it out. After you have worked hard to write your first draft, it feels as if you have wasted your time if you throw anything out. Sometimes, however, it is necessary to delete material in order to make the paper clearer. In this case, because Bu decided to focus on age, describing the range of services available on the Internet was no longer relevant to his main point.

Body paragraph #3

If you look back at the first draft, you will find that about half of this material came from body paragraph #2 in the first draft. Bu's instructor and peer response partner couldn't quite figure out why he was talking about all of this equipment. His instructor suggested that he try to relate the issue of equipment to his main point, age. Has Bu managed to clearly tie age and equipment together? If so, how has he accomplished this?

RESPONDING TO A PEER'S WRITING

Activity 2.11

Now you are going to read and respond to at least one of your classmates' essays using the Peer Response Sheet provided. You may photocopy this sheet if you are working with more than one partner. As always, be as specific as you can, and think about whether or not you could make changes to an essay based on the answers you have given. Also, keep in mind that the focus here is still on the ideas in the essay, not the grammar. You will work on that in the editing section.

PEER RESPONSE SHEET

Writer: _____   **Responder:** _____

1. Look at the first paragraph. Does it tell you what the main point of the essay will be? Explain.

_____

_____

_____

_____

2. Does it tell you where the information in the essay comes from? Explain.

_____

_____

_____

_____

3. What trends are discussed in the body?

_____

_____

_____

_____

_____

4. Is each trend discussed in a separate paragraph? If not, explain.

_____

_____

_____

_____

_____

5. Are there specific claims in each body paragraph? If so, write them.

_____

_____

_____

_____

_____

_____

6. Does the writer give specific supporting evidence for each claim? If so, write the evidence here.

_____

_____

_____

_____

_____

_____

_____

7. Are there parts of the essay you don't understand? What are they?

_____

_____

_____

_____

_____

8. What other suggestions do you have for the writer's next draft?

_____

_____

_____

_____

WHAT TO DO When the draft comes back

✿ EVALUATING YOUR OWN WORK

Activity 2.12   *Now look at your own first draft, Peer Response Sheet(s), and your instructor's comments. Use the **What to Do When the Draft Comes Back** sheet to guide you in revising for your second draft.*

WHAT TO DO WHEN THE DRAFT COMES BACK

Name: _____

1. Read through your instructor's comments and the Peer Response Sheet(s).

2. Find some of the suggestions they have made.

3. Write the most important ones here. Then write what you think of each suggestion. How will you respond to it? If you do not plan to follow it, why not?

A. _____

    i. I plan to ignore the suggestion because

    _____

    _____

    _____

    _____

    ii. I plan to change my draft in the following way:

    _____

    _____

    _____

    _____

B. _____

    i. I plan to ignore the suggestion because

    _____

    _____

    _____

    _____

    ii. I plan to change my draft in the following way:

    _____

    _____

    _____

    _____

4. Perhaps you have thought of some other changes you would like to make. List them here:

_____

_____

_____

_____

5. Are there any comments or suggestions on your paper that you did not understand? Which are the ones you need to discuss with your peer response partner? List them here.

_____

_____

_____

_____

6. Are there other parts of your draft you are unsure about that you would like to discuss with your instructor? List them here.

_____

_____

_____

_____

WRITING YOUR SECOND DRAFT

Now you are ready to revise your essay. Look over your **What to Do When the Draft Comes Back** sheet. As you write your second draft, make sure your claims are clear and that you have provided adequate support for them.

4. EDITING

Editing Practice

#2 Comma splices and run-on sentences

Comma Splices

When two independent clauses are connected by a comma, this is an error called a **comma splice**.

Run-on Sentences

Run-on sentences occur when there are more than two independent clauses in one sentence.

Read through the writing sample and then look at the guidelines. The guidelines contain examples of correct and incorrect usage from the writing sample and show you how to correct **comma splices and run-on sentences**.

Sample

1   For most people, their dream is to immigrate to the
2 United States for a better opportunity to make money. The
3 reason I immigrated to the United States was to learn En-
4 glish and have a better opportunity to enter college be-
5 cause of the lack of opportunity to enter college in Peru.
6 Yet there were many unexpected difficulties, and the most
7 difficult thing to face was not knowing the language. That
8 happened to me when I first entered the United States, I
9 didn't know how to communicate with the people.
10   When I was still in Peru, many people told me that
11 I didn't have to put in much effort to learn English, I
12 would know it automatically when I came to the United
13 States. At that time, I was silly enough to believe that
14 this was true. The first moment I stepped on the land
15 of the United States, I figured out that was not true
16 at all. When we arrived at the airport, we had to make

17 fingerprints in order to get a green card, but we didn't
18 know which way to go. We were trying to ask other peo-
19 ple, but we didn't understand what the people told us,
20 and they didn't know what we were talking about, and we
21 were so worried at that moment. Finally, my father found
22 a Cuban girl to help us settle things. After that, I told
23 myself that I had to put effort into studying English, I
24 had to know English in order to get good grades to help
25 me enter college.

26   When I first went to school, I was already an eighth
27 grader. There were not many courses to study, only sci-
28 ence, history, U.S. constitution, math, and English. They
29 were all in English, I felt so scared when I opened up
30 the book. Yet I told myself that I could do it because
31 I hadn't reached my goal yet. I told myself not to ever
32 give up. Therefore, every day after school, I went home
33 and finished with my homework, and prepared the food for
34 my mom to cook dinner, then I began my homework. Although
35 there was a lot of vocabulary I didn't know, I found a
36 way to take care of that. First I read the section over,
37 then I wrote down the words and translated them to Span-
38 ish, then I would convert the meaning back to English. Of
39 course that took a lot of time, but I thought that was
40 the way to make things work out when I couldn't ask any-
41 one for help. Therefore, I finished my homework at almost
42 midnight every day although sometimes there was not much
43 homework. After I had finished with my homework, I would
44 review everything I had learned for the day to make sure
45 I understood it before I went to bed. By the end of the
46 semester, my work paid off, I earned mostly A's or B's
47 in all my classes. I was so happy, but I told myself never
48 to be arrogant because I had a long way to go.

49   The summer when I was waiting to go to high school,
50 at a family dinner, my uncle said something that was like
51 a bomb exploding in my heart. He said that my brother was
52 the only one who could go to college to gain more educa-

53   tion because he was smart. It hurt me so much, how could

54   he say that. From that time on, I told myself to study

55   harder and to get good grades to go to college, I wanted

56   to prove to him that I could do that without his support.

57   In the four years of high school, I studied very hard. I

58   studied until midnight every night, and I studied ahead

59   before the teacher taught us. I was trying to communicate

60   with the teachers and the students with my broken English.

61   Because the school that I attended had no Spanish-speaking

62   teachers, I had to speak up, otherwise I would never know

63   how to speak English. After the first year in high school,

64   people began to understand what I meant when I talked to

65   them. My English was improving by speaking to them. By

66   the time I graduated from high school, I was an A honor

67   student. That surprised my uncle, he never realized that

68   I could put all my effort into studying, and he couldn't

69   believe that I could make it to college.

70   After the six years of school, my English has improved

71   a lot, that doesn't mean there won't be any problems in

72   the future. No matter what kind of problems come, if I

73   can try my best to face them, then I'll overcome them.

Comma Splices

Activity 2.13

*With a partner, follow these steps to find and correct **comma splices** in the sample. Follow the steps and study the examples that follow to help you decide how to correct the errors.*

A. *Find all the commas and underline them.*

B. *Decide if any of the commas separate two independent clauses.*

If they do, these sentences contain comma splices and are unacceptable. You have three choices in repairing a comma splice.

1. If the sentence is short, add **and**.

Example:

INCORRECT: That happened to me when I first entered the United States, I didn't know how to communicate with the people.

CORRECT: That happened to me when I first entered the United States **and** I didn't know how to communicate with the people.

2. Use a period and start a new sentence.

Example:

INCORRECT: That happened to me when I first entered the United States, I didn't know how to communicate with the people.

CORRECT: That happened to me when I first entered the United States. I didn't know how to communicate with the people.

3. Make one of the independent clauses into a dependent clause by using a **while-type connector**[1] such as **because, when, although, before, after,** or **while.** Be sure to choose one that makes sense in the sentence.

Example:

INCORRECT: That happened to me when I first entered the United States, I didn't know how to communicate with the people.

CORRECT: That happened to me when I first entered the United States because I didn't know how to communicate with the people.

Now read over your sentence to be sure it makes sense. Sometimes something is grammatical but doesn't make sense. Look at the next example.

Example:

INCORRECT: It hurt me so much, how could he say that.

INCORRECT: It hurt me so much, and how could he say that.

Even though the two independent clauses are short, inserting **and** doesn't make sense. A period and a new sentence are a better choice.

Example:

CORRECT: It hurt me so much. How could he say that?

In future drafts, you may see the abbreviation **cs.** This means the sentence contains a comma splice, and you need to repair it.

Run-on Sentences

Activity 2.14

With a partner, follow these steps to find and correct run-on sentences in the sample. Follow the steps and study the examples that follow to help you decide how to correct the errors.

A. *Find all the **ands** and **buts** in your paper and underline them.*

B. *Check each sentence. Find the sentences that have more than one **and** or **but**. How many independent clauses are in those sentences?*

---

[1]See Editing Practice #6 at the back of the text for an explanation of this term.

If there are more than two independent clauses, this is a run-on sentence. You have two choices in repairing it. You can:

1. Choose one of the independent clauses and use it to make a new sentence. If your new sentence begins with **but**, change it to **however**.

Example:

INCORRECT: We were trying to ask other people, but we didn't understand what the people were talking about, and they didn't know what we were talking about either.

CORRECT: We were trying to ask other people. However, we didn't understand what the people were talking about, and they didn't know what we were talking about either.

2. Make one or more of the independent clauses into dependent clauses.

Example:

INCORRECT: We were trying to ask other people, but we didn't understand what the people were talking about, and they didn't know what we were talking about either.

CORRECT: Although we were trying to ask other people, we didn't understand what the people were talking about, and they didn't know what we were talking about either.

In future drafts, you may see the abbreviation **ro**. This means you have written a run-on sentence, and you need to repair it.

If you would like more practice with fragments, comma splices, and run-ons, turn to the Practice Exercise on Sentence Boundaries in the back of your text.

EDITING YOUR OWN WORK: THE FINAL DRAFT

Activity 2.15

Follow the steps in the guidelines and correct any run-on sentences and comma splices that you find. You may also find other errors that you need to correct. In particular, you should also check for fragments as you did in the last unit. Once you have finished editing, you are ready to turn in your final draft. Be sure to keep your final draft after your instructor has returned it to you so that you can refer to it when you write other papers.

STRATEGIES IN ADVERTISING

Task
- Analyzing advertising strategies

Writing Focus
- Introductions and conclusions

Editing Focus
- Using a learner dictionary

In the last unit, you gathered information from friends and colleagues about their use of computers. You analyzed that information and used it to make a claim about computer use among certain populations. In this unit, you will be gathering and analyzing a different kind of information—this time, from television commercials. Once again, you will use the data to make claims and provide support for those claims. You will also learn more about writing introductions and conclusions. It is important that these elements of your essay work together with the body paragraphs so that your main point is clear to your readers.

Advertising is a powerful force in today's world. You will explore the different strategies that advertisers use to persuade people to buy their products. In particular, we will look at how they target different populations in an effort to sell these products. You will gather information about television commercials and try to organize it so that your readers can clearly see the strategies that advertisers use.

I. EXPLORING IDEAS

READINGS

*In order to understand more about **how** advertising works, it is important that you understand **what** advertising is. This article outlines the basic principles of advertising.*

Advertising

An advertisement is a message carried in one of the various forms of "media" such as newspapers and magazines, radio and television, and the posters and neon signs we see in the street. The purpose of most advertisements is to *persuade* a particular audience to buy a product or service offered by the advertiser.

There are, of course, many advertisements with a different purpose. Some advertisements are simply *informative*. The "want ads" columns in the local newspapers, for example, may contain notices of items for sale. They include a simple description of the item, but do not normally try to use the techniques of persuasive advertising. Other advertisements may try to promote a cause or an idea. You have probably seen posters carrying messages such as "Stop the whaling" or "Say no to strangers." Sometimes the advertiser is the customer rather than the seller: in the "help wanted" columns of national and local newspapers, employers advertise for the services of employees. But most advertising is concerned with persuading people to buy.

How Advertising Works

Advertising is only one of the tools used in marketing or selling goods. The other tools—product, price, packaging, distribution to the stores, store display—also have to work to make the product sell. Manufacturers have to compete with others for a share of the market, so before any product is **launched**, market research is undertaken to find out which people will buy it and what will make them buy it instead of the competing products. These points are highlighted in the campaign.

launched put on the market for the first time

Planning the Campaign

If an advertisement is to be effective, it must reach an audience of **potential** customers: there is not much point in advertising cosmetics during a football program nor automobiles in a children's magazine. In order to choose the right combination of media the people planning the advertising campaign must study a great deal of information. Publishers of newspapers or magazines provide them with circulation figures (the number of copies sold), details of approximately how much their readers earn, their age and much else. Television companies provide audience viewing figures and information about the income and professions of the audience. The prices charged for advertising in the different media range from the small amount it may cost to advertise your old bike in the local newspaper to the tens of thousands of dollars a manufacturer might pay for a 60-second spot on peak-time TV.

potential possible

Advertising costs are built into the purchase price of any product that we buy. For some products the advertising budget will be small and may only represent

(continued on next page)

(continued from previous page)

about five percent of the purchase price. Other products need heavy advertising, so half of what you pay for a soft drink might really be the cost of advertising.

The advertiser must choose the right media to target the market. It is not always the media with the largest audiences that are chosen. It all depends on the product. If, for example, you are a manufacturer of expensive designer jeans, your market research (and common sense) will tell you that the product will only be bought by a limited number of customers. So you will most likely confine your choice of media to more "up-market" magazines—that is, the magazines bought by higher income groups. If, on the other hand, you are advertising a can of soft drink that you hope will be bought in millions by adults and children alike, then you will need to spend a great deal of money on a television campaign. It is only the larger manufacturers who can afford to use such an expensive medium as television.

Once a new product has been successfully launched, that is not the end of the role played by advertising. The manufacturer cannot sit back and expect his product to continue to sell. It must be kept constantly in the mind of potential customers. The "brand image"—that is, the idea customers have of a particular product—must be maintained and kept up-to-date through improvements in the product itself, by more attractive packaging and exciting advertisements.

Advertising Agencies

Advertising agencies are multi-million dollar businesses employing thousands of people in jobs throughout the industrialized world. On behalf of the firms who employ them (whom they call their "accounts") they conduct market research, prepare the advertisements and choose the media.

In an advertising agency it is the creative director who decides on the brand image he or she wants to create for the product. Copywriters write the "copy," or text, and art directors arrange for film or photographs to be prepared. The campaign is agreed upon with the client or account, and then space is bought in whatever media have been decided upon.

Every advertisement tells a story. Some tell a "before and after" story—that is, the advertisement suggests that before you bought a particular product you were not entirely pleased with life, but now that you have it, your problems are solved. Others forget the "before" part and simply show you the "after"—how things might be if you were the product's owner. Some advertisements tell a joke, some have a catchy **jingle**. In other advertisements it is the visual image that carries the message and that people remember.

jingle song used to advertise a product

Discussion Questions

1. What is the main purpose of advertising?

2. How do advertisers choose where to advertise?

3. What does "Every advertisement tells a story" mean?

In this article, you will read about a company that is going to all corners of the world to sell its products—in this case, to the heart of the jungle along the Amazon River. The company, Avon, sells cosmetics and beauty products, such as lipstick, perfume, soap, hand lotion, and fancy underwear. When the company first started, most of the salespeople were housewives in the United States, who went door to door selling the products to their friends and neighbors. Now, with so many American women in full-time jobs, there are few women to sell the products and there are few women at home to buy them. As a result, the company has changed its strategy and has become more international. Today, Avon is growing quickly in places far from its home in the United States. Sales are increasing rapidly in China, Russia, and, as you will read, in the rain forests of Brazil.

Lotion Voyage
Michael Neill & John Maier Jr.

The 68 Tembé Indians who live in Tenetehará, in northeastern Brazil, have no love of western civilization. Last year they expelled a Catholic missionary and shut down the village's only nightclub. Tribal leaders wear feather bonnets and carry spears, and both men and women go naked above the waist. A traditional existence in the Amazonian rainforest does not, though, in Sonia Pinheiro's opinion, **rule out** the possibility that the Tembé might be in the market for some personal grooming or skin-care products. So, Pinheiro, a zone manager for Avon, has **trekked** 140 miles from Belém, impeccably dressed and without a hair out of place, to try to interest the people of Tenetehará in her products—from lipstick and **lingerie** to moisturizer and mascara.

"This is a **reconnaissance trip**," says Pinheiro, 38. "We want to see if we can offer them something. Maybe some of the women will want to become **vendors**. Who knows?" There are 36,000 registered Avon ladies (and gentlemen) in Amazonia.

This may seem a long way to go to make a sale, but it is in such rural Third World areas that Avon, the huge New York City-based cosmetics company, is enjoying its greatest growth. Fanning out through the vastness of Amazonia, much of which is still frontier, the **Avon reps**, who accept almost anything as payment, have **boosted** the company's Brazilian sales by 50 percent this year.

In Itaituba on the Tapajos River, 90 miles from where Pinheiro is meeting the Tembé, Benedita Aguiar, 34, has just sold a pair of bikini briefs to Jose da Silva, a barefoot fisherman. In return she gets a string of day-old *mapará*, a type of catfish. She would have preferred some of da Silva's fresh-caught piranha, and he would have liked some Touch of Love deodorant and Vita Moist body lotion, but they couldn't strike a bargain.

rule out exclude

trekked traveled

lingerie women's underwear

reconnaissance trip a first trip to gather information
vendors sellers

Avon reps representatives of the Avon Company
boost increase

(continued on next page)

(continued from previous page)

In Patrocino, a gold-mining boom town in the center of the Amazon basin, the Avon reps do not have to settle for payment in fish, but they have other worries. During six years of living in the town, saleswoman Antonia Conceição, 40, a divorcée with 14 children, has been stung by a scorpion (although she has thus far **eluded** the area's many poisonous snakes) and has contracted **hepatitis, malaria and dengue fever**. Worse, Patrocino, with a population of 2,000, has 40 bars and 23 **brothels**, but no doctors. Still, Conceição thinks the profits—three times what she could make in a safer place—are worth the risks. "Dangerous?" she says, laughing, "Only if you get bitten by a snake or real sick. Then you probably die."

Half her customers are miners like Rosivaldo Silva, who weighs out 1.5 grams of gold dust to pay for two tubes of Silicon Gloves hand lotion. Then, there are the town's many prostitutes. "The miners get all the gold," Conceição says, "but they spend it on the women."

Becoming an Avon lady is one of the few respectable ways for a woman in the Amazon to become financially independent—and her profit often comes at the expense of some tender **male egos**. "I couldn't stand the idea of my wife leaving home and visiting all those houses," says Rossimar Perreira, 38, whose wife, Teresinha, 33, is the most successful vendor in Itaituba (pop. 50,000). "My neighbors asked me how I could let her go out like that." The Perreiras fought daily for weeks, but when he saw the cash Teresinha was bringing in—at least $500 a month, sometimes much more—Rossimar quit farming to become his wife's assistant. Now, he says, "I no longer care what my neighbors say. We're the ones leading the good life."

Back in Tenetehará, Pinheiro is finding out that the Tembé are just not interested. She shows some of the tribeswomen Red Temptation lipstick, but they are unimpressed. "We have that," says one. "It's *uncuru*." *Uncuru*, it turns out, is a greenish nut with a red core—and for the Tembé it fulfills the same function as Red Temptation. Finally, Marrioca, the village chief, takes a whiff of Cool Confidence deodorant and immediately decrees it: "*Nekatu!* [bad]." He politely tells Pinheiro, "This may be good for you, but not for me. I like the way I smell." Undaunted, Pinheiro shares a lunch of chicken and rice with the villagers, then one of the tribesmen rows her back upriver. There, her air-conditioned car awaits her. Somewhere out there, she knows, are jungle dwellers who need a **makeover** and are willing to pay for it.

---

eluded avoided

hepatitis, malaria and dengue fever dangerous, mostly tropical diseases that can be fatal

brothels houses of prostitution

male ego a man's feeling of his own importance

makeover a new appearance as a result of new makeup and hairstyle

---

Discussion Questions

1. Does it surprise you that Avon would try to sell its products to residents of the Amazon basin? Why or why not?

2. Why do you think the fisherman wanted the bikini underpants and body lotion?

3. Why does Ms. Pinheiro still think there are "jungle dwellers who need a makeover and are willing to pay for it" even after the Tembé people rejected the Avon products?

All advertising is designed to sell something. The ads you are about to look at are a little different from what people typically see. They are made by advertising companies who want to sell their services to other businesses.

Discussion Questions

1. What is the message in each of these ads, that is, why would businesses want to hire these advertising companies?

2. One of these ads reads, "We don't translate ads into Spanish. We translate Spanish into sales." What do you think this means?

3. Think about the people in your own ethnic or language group. What do you think an advertisement aimed at them should emphasize in order to be effective?

How do you take your advertising?

Well, if you want it to be successful,
you take it rich and full-bodied.
And if you want it to be strong, you
take it Black. Because for the
African-American market,
whose annual buying power is
$438.4 billion and growing, your
advertising must be energetic
and daring enough to get their attention.
Look to Don Coleman Advertising, Inc.,
for strong, impactful advertising
that promises to wake them up.

We taught
a bar of soap
how to speak
Spanish.

JMCT PUBLICIDAD

Ever wonder how
Latinos eat
such
spicy food?

JMCT PUBLICIDAD

How do you say
"I quit"
en español?

JMCT PUBLICIDAD

We don't
translate ads
into Spanish.

We translate Spanish
into sales.

JMCT PUBLICIDAD
Hispanic division of Jordan, McGrath, Case & Taylor Inc.

A Chinese symbol of luck.
More related to courage in Japan.
In India, he's one of Vishnu's most important incarnations.
Just a reminder from Mosaica:
Your Asian American advertising can't swim
if you don't know what a fish is.

EXPERT MARKETERS WITH ASIAN EXPERTISE
CHINESE FILIPINO INDIAN JAPANESE KOREAN VIETNAMESE

MOSAICA
A Young & Rubicam Agency

Thinking about the Topic

After you have read all of the articles on advertising, discuss the following questions.

1. Would society be better off if there were no advertising? Why or why not?

2. Some people claim that the job of advertising is to sell happiness. Others say it is the opposite—to sell discontent and unhappiness. Explain why you think people might say both these things. What do you think?

Activity 3.1

You will do this activity in groups. Imagine you are a team at an advertising agency. A company has approached you about its new product. You need to come up with a plan for advertising this new product.

Each group will discuss one new product. Here are some possibilities. You may think of others on your own.

- new, faster modem
- oil-free potato chips

- remote-controlled lawnmower
- new weight-loss program
- dinosaur action toy

A. *Discuss the following questions with your classmates as you formulate your plan for advertising the product.*

1. What will you call the product?

2. Who do you think is most likely to buy it?

3. How can you reach those people with your advertisements?

4. What kind of advertisements would work best?

5. Where should you advertise?

Are there any other things you will need to consider? List them here.

- _____
- _____
- _____
- _____
- _____

B. *After you have finished discussing your product, jot down the most important points. You can refer to these when you present your ideas to the rest of the class.*

_____

_____

_____

_____

_____

2. GATHERING INFORMATION AND DRAFTING

Now that you have done some reading, discussed the purpose and methods of advertising, and made a marketing plan for a new product, you are going to begin collecting information about how actual advertising strategies work.

IDENTIFYING ADVERTISING STRATEGIES

Businesses use advertising to convince consumers to buy their products. You will be exploring how they do this specifically on television commercials. What are the methods that advertisers use to convince the public that one product is the best?

Activity 3.2

Watch at least five television commercials, and make some notes about how advertisers try to convince you to buy their products. Think about the following questions as you watch.

■ What good things does the ad say will happen if you buy a product?

■ What bad things does the ad say will happen if you don't buy a product?

You will use the information in these notes for class discussion.

Activity 3.3

After you have watched the commercials, make a list of advertising strategies you found. By "strategy" we mean, what does the ad tell you that you will gain by buying the product? How will your life be better because you have bought a particular product? For example, one student watched a commercial for a pain reliever in which a woman talked about how much better she felt after she took the pills. This student summed up the ad this way:

```
If you buy this medicine, you will feel much better very
quickly.
```

Another student watched an ad for a new computer game in which a young boy who had the game became popular and a boy who didn't have it was left out of the group. This student summed up the ad this way:

```
If you buy this game, you will be popular with your
friends.
```

A. *Look at the Strategy List that follows. Fill in the sentences based on the ads you watched. Some of the sentences will fit the ads you watched and some won't. Use the ones that work for the ads you watched.*

Strategy List

If you buy _____, you will be _____.

If you buy _____, you will/will not _____.

If you buy _____, you/your children will _____.

If you _____, you/your friends _____.

If you buy _____, you/your family _____.

If you buy _____, _____.

If you buy _____, _____.

B. *Compare the different strategies you found with those of your classmates. Add any new strategies from your classmates' lists to your own. Keep this list; you will use it later when you gather information for your essay.*

GATHERING INFORMATION

Now you are going to watch a number of television commercials and again collect information about how specific products are advertised. You should choose three products that you want to investigate. As you watch, you should also note the brand. Products are things like cars or soap, as opposed to brands, such as Toyota or Dove.

This time you will look not only for the product and strategy used to sell it but also for **when the advertisement appears** and during **what type of program**. In order to collect this information efficiently, a chart like the one on page 124 is a useful tool.

Here you can see that a student has filled in the product, brand, strategy used to sell the product, type of program (movie, comedy, talk show, news, etc.), and time of day (morning, afternoon, prime time [7–10 P.M.], or late night) on the chart.

Activity 3.4

*Once you have chosen the three products you want to examine, watch at least five commercials for each product. Use the blank chart on page 125 and fill in the blanks for each product. Try to watch at different times of day. You may find a product advertised during different types of programs or at more than one time of day. If you do, list all the types of programs and times on your chart. Not all the spaces were filled in on the sample chart, but you will fill in all the spaces on your chart (except for a blank column on the right; you will fill it in later). Use the **Strategy List** you made with your classmates to help you as you watch commercials and fill in the chart. Write in all of the strategies you identify. You may find some of the strategies you have already discussed, and you may find new ones as well.*

• **Table 3.1** •

SAMPLE CHART

Product: Brand	Advertising Strategy	Type of Program	Time of Day
Cars: Volvo	You will be safer.	Movie	Late night Prime time
Cars: Cadillac	_____	News Comedy show	Evening
Soap: Dove	You will look younger.	_____	Daytime
Beer:	_____	_____	_____

Short Write

Write a one-draft response to the questions that follow. Your paper should be one or two pages.

What kind of strategies are successful in convincing you to buy a product? Write a short description of an advertisement or commercial that persuaded you to buy something. Why was the ad so effective?

ANALYZING DATA

Review the information you have gathered for your chart. Does it seem to you that certain products are associated with specific strategies? For some products, there may be only one obvious strategy to use. For example, if you were advertising vacuum cleaners, what sort of strategy would you use? It doesn't make much sense to say that one brand is safer than another, or more attractive. There is really one major thing that is important about a vacuum cleaner: the effectiveness of the product. Therefore, you would expect a commercial to boast about how well it cleans. Maybe this is because it is more powerful or because it has more attachments to clean different things, but the message is: *This machine cleans better than other machines.* Other products might use a variety of strategies.

• T a b l e 3 . 2 •

Product: Brand	Advertising Strategy	Type of Program	Time of Day

Discussion Questions

- How might a company try to persuade you to buy its beer?
- How about cars?

Once you have established the relationship between a product and a specific advertising strategy, think about **why** the company uses that strategy.

Whom does the company hope to reach with this strategy? What category of buyers is the company targeting with the advertising?

- Which buyers would care if a toothpaste gets teeth white and bright or if it gives fresh breath?

- Which buyers would care if the same toothpaste helps to prevent cavities?

- Which buyers would care if a toothpaste tastes great?

Now you have thought about how advertisers choose their target population and what strategies they use to persuade them to buy their products. The next step for the advertisers is to figure out **how** to reach that population—in this case, through television advertising.

- If a company that manufactures diapers decides it wants to advertise specifically to young mothers, what should it do?

- How can it reach this population through television advertising?

- What kinds of decisions does the company have to make about placing the commercials?

Activity 3.5

Reread the information on your chart.

1. Is there a relationship between the products and the types of programs during which they are advertised?

2. Why did the companies choose these particular programs?

3. What is the target population for the products?

Add this information about the target population for your product. Use the blank column on your chart. The chart that follows shows some examples for diapers and for denture (false teeth) adhesive.

• Table 3.3 •

Product: Brand	Advertising Strategy	Time of Day	Type of Program	Target Population
Diapers: Pampers	effectiveness (against leaks) • gives moms more **freedom**	morning, early afternoon	talk shows, soap operas	young mothers
Denture adhesive: Poligrip	effectiveness • helps teeth stay in place • prevents embarrassment	all day	news, talk shows	old people

You will use all of this information on target populations when you begin to write your draft. The first step is to turn all of this information into a clear set of claims that you can support with the data you have collected.

Activity 3.6

*For each of the three products from your chart, write a sentence that makes a **claim** about the target population for these products. Use the following questions to guide you.*

■ Why have the advertisers chosen to use these kinds of strategies?

■ Why have they chosen to place their commercials in these particular slots, for example, during the Oprah Winfrey show or during an NBA game?

Write your claim statements here.

1. _____

_____ .

2. _____

_____ .

3. _____

_____ .

You can use these kinds of statements later when you write your draft. Remember that these are an essential element of every paragraph because they make general claims *that you will support with examples from your data.*

🔥 DRAFTING: BODY PARAGRAPHS

Now you are ready to start writing your first draft. Your assignment is to write about:

How advertisers use TV commercials to target different populations.

You will begin with body paragraphs. You have already started working on them, that is, you have written statements about three products. Use these statements as a starting point. Write a paragraph about each. You need to keep two things in mind as you write:

(1) the content of your paragraphs

■ What is the advertising strategy?

■ What is the target group of potential buyers?

■ How are these two connected?

(2) the organization of your paragraphs

■ Does each paragraph make a claim?

■ Does each paragraph provide support for that claim?

Drafting Tip

Thinking about what your readers know

Remember that your readers may not know as much about this topic as you do. They may not have seen the commercials you are discussing. They may not know exactly what you mean when you write about advertising strategies. The entries on the sample charts have consisted of short notes, using words like "success" and "happiness" to describe these strategies. That works well for taking notes, but short notes like these don't make it clear to your readers what you mean. Look at the following sentence:

```
Shipping companies, such as Federal Express and UPS, use

success as an advertising strategy.
```

You know what you mean by "success," and your teacher **might** be able to figure it out, but he or she would have to do some guessing. Don't make your readers guess; make your writing as clear as you can.

When you are writing, you should always ask yourself:

1. How much do my readers know?

2. How much do I have to tell them? Think for a moment about how you could rewrite the sentence about "success" to make it easier for your readers to understand.

```
Commercials for shipping companies, such as Federal

Express and UPS, show how you will be more successful

in your job if you use their services because your

packages will arrive more quickly and with no mis-

takes. Some commercials show how happy your boss will

be with your work.
```

These statements make it much clearer what the writer means by "success." In this case, "success" means that a **person will do better at his or her job if he or she uses the product or service.**

🔥 DRAFTING: LINKING BODY PARAGRAPHS TO THE MAIN POINT

You have drafted paragraphs about three products. Now you need to think about the paper as a whole. In the first unit, you learned that every time you write, you have to make a point. What is the **main point** you will make in this paper?

Activity 3.7

Look back over all of the examples in your body paragraphs and recall your assignment: how advertisers use TV commercials to target different populations.

Describe the relationship among products, advertising strategies, and the target populations. You may need more than one sentence. Use the lines that follow.

_____

_____

_____

_____

_____

What you have just written contains the main point of your paper. This main point should appear in your introductory paragraph. It should tell to your readers what the rest of your paper will be about. Use it as a starting point for the first paragraph of your paper. Now complete your paragraph and put it together with the body paragraphs for a first draft.

3. REVISING

 EVALUATING ESSAYS

Activity 3.8 | *Once again, you will look at what two students wrote about this topic. After each student essay, you will offer suggestions for revising it for a second draft. Try to be as specific as possible in your responses.*

Student Essay 1

1   Everybody goes into business to make money. They in-
2 vest their money to produce a product and they hope it
3 will do well and make a profit for them. Once a product
4 has been made, the last step is to advertise it so that
5 people will buy it. Advertising can have a significant
6 effect on profits. Advertisements play an important role
7 in business and advertisers must choose the right way to
8 advertise: TV, magazines, or signs, etc.

9   The methods and placement of advertisements depend on
10 the product. One example is breakfast cereal. First, ad-
11 vertisers conduct market research to see what kids like
12 to eat. After they know their target, they make an ad-
13 vertisement that will appeal to kids. They use many dif-
14 ferent methods. They may use popular characters from

15   cartoons, or show how tasty the cereal is, or even show

16   the toys that are in the cereal boxes. They may also try

17   to appeal to the parents and say that the cereal is

18   healthy or that the kids will love it. Once they have

19   prepared the advertisement, companies must choose the

20   right time and place for it. Most kids watch TV in the

21   early morning and afternoon and on weekends. That is why

22   most kids' cereal advertisements appear during those

23   times.

24   Advertisers go through a similar process for cars.

25   Only adults can buy cars, so most of the car commercials

26   are during prime time. Advertisers use strategies that

27   stress safety, popular models and power. For instance,

28   they show that if customers buy this car, their families

29   will be safe. Safety is most important for women, so car

30   companies show commercials about safety when women are

31   watching. Volvo commercials show that the cars are safe.

32   Men like to drive big, fast cars, so they show commer-

33   cials that make men believe that all their friends will

34   think they are very important because they have a big,

35   new car, like a Cadillac. They show these commercials dur-

36   ing sports or action shows. They show that if customers

37   buy this car, their families will be safe and all their

38   friends will think they are very important because they

39   have a new, fast car.

40   Businesses spend millions of dollars to advertise

41   their products so that more and more people can know about

42   them. They use different methods and media to introduce

43   different products to help the right consumers to find

44   out about the products they can buy. Television adver-

45   tising is very effective because advertisers can target

46   an audience by choosing certain programs at certain times

47   of the day.

Ahmed

RESPONSE SHEET

Writer: _Ahmed_ _____   **Responder:** _____

Look at the first paragraph.

1. What does it say the essay will be about?

_____

_____

_____

_____

2. What is the writer's main point?

_____

_____

_____

_____

Now look at the rest of the paper.

3. What claims does the writer make about advertising strategies?

_____

_____

_____

_____

_____

_____

4. What evidence does the writer give to support each of these claims?

_____

_____

_____

_____

_____

_____

_____

_____

_____

5. Read the first paragraph again. Do the claims and evidence in the body paragraphs support the main point in the introduction? Explain.

_____

_____

_____

_____

_____

_____

_____

6. Are there parts of the essay you don't understand? What are they?

_____

_____

_____

_____

_____

7. What other suggestions do you have for the writer's next draft?

_____

_____

_____

_____

Student Essay 2

1   As an industry grows, advertising starts to have an
2   important role. We can see advertisements all over the
3   place: on TV, in the newspaper, in magazines, even on the
4   bus. Companies use this advertising for consumers who
5   might be interested in buying their products. If the pur-
6   pose of advertising is to persuade people to buy prod-
7   ucts, then it is important that the ads are shown to the
8   right customers. Advertisers spend a lot of time and money
9   making sure that this happens. We can see the relation-
10 ship between the kind and time of advertisements on tele-
11 vision and the kind of people that advertisers hope will
12 buy their products. Companies target different kinds of
13 people for different kinds of products, so they must be
14 careful about which programs and which time of day they
15 choose for their advertisements.

16 Every adult wants a car, so we see car commercials
17 at all times of the day: morning, afternoon and evening.
18 Of course, children cannot buy cars, so it would be silly
19 to advertise cars during cartoons or other children's pro-
20 grams. Companies use different strategies for different
21 kinds of products, such as safety, happiness and success.
22 Some car commercials appear in the morning and early af-
23 ternoon when there are a lot of soap operas on televi-
24 sion. These commercials show that the cars are safe and
25 a good value. Companies use these strategies during these
26 programs because most of the people watching are women.
27 Safety and value are important to women. During sports
28 shows or the news, the strategies are usually different.
29 They stress success and a good appearance. They show beau-
30 tiful cars that go very fast and have strong engines.
31 These are things that men care more about.

32 Fast food commercials also appear throughout the day
33 because everyone likes fast food. Advertisers use strate-
34 gies such as happiness, intelligence and success. During

35 the later afternoon, when children are watching, the com-
36 mercials show happy children eating fast food. This makes
37 the children who are watching want to be like the chil-
38 dren on TV. Later in the evening, during comedies and
39 sports shows, they show the large size, good value and
40 great taste of the food. They try to tell adults if they
41 eat this food, they will be happy and smart shoppers. Some
42 fast food companies like McDonald's try to convince adults
43 that some of the food is especially for them.

44 Advertisers use different words and strategies to in-
45 terest their customers. They are very careful about where,
46 when and how they use their advertisements so that they
47 can reach the right people. As a result, they get the
48 most people to buy their products and they don't waste
49 their money to make commercials for people who will not
50 buy their products. Television advertising is very power-
51 ful because it can affect how people act and the choices
52 they make.

Graciela

Writer: *Graciela* _____   **Responder:** _____

Look at the first paragraph.

1. What does it say the essay will be about?

_____

_____

_____

_____

2. What is the writer's main point?

_____

_____

_____

_____

Now look at the rest of the paper.

3. What claims does the writer make about advertising strategies?

_____

_____

_____

_____

_____

4. What evidence does the writer give to support each of these claims?

_____

_____

_____

_____

_____

_____

_____

5. Read the first paragraph again. Do the claims and evidence in the body paragraphs support the main point in the introduction? Explain.

_____

_____

_____

_____

_____

_____

_____

6. Are there parts of the essay you don't understand? What are they?

_____

_____

_____

_____

7. What other suggestions do you have for the writer's next draft?

_____

_____

_____

_____

✒ WRITING FOCUS: INTRODUCTIONS AND CONCLUSIONS

Think again about the essays Ahmed and Graciela wrote. Is one better than the other?

If you think Graciela's is a better essay, we agree with you. What's the difference between Graciela's paper and Ahmed's?

Start by looking at the body paragraphs. You know from Unit Two that body paragraphs should have a sentence that makes a claim and that they should also provide specific evidence to support the claim. Both essays have body paragraphs with clear, well-supported claims, so there is little difference there. You also know that the body paragraphs should support the main point of the essay, which can usually be found in the introduction. Is this true for both essays?

Look again at Ahmed's introduction. When you read it, what do you think the paper will be about? You probably think it will be about how advertising affects profits. This is a perfectly good topic and the main idea is clear. But what about the connection between the body and the introduction? Do the body paragraphs support Ahmed's main point? Not really. The body is about how advertisers target different populations with television commercials. The fact that the introduction and body are about different things is a serious problem. These two parts should work together.

So what should Ahmed do, rewrite the introduction or rewrite the body? The introduction is about advertising, but it is not about the assigned topic—how advertisers use television commercials to target different populations. In contrast, the body does address the assignment. This means he should change the introduction to make it fit with the body. It is very important that the parts of the essay fit together and that the whole essay be about the *assigned* topic.

Now look at Graciela's essay again. The introduction is about the subject of advertising and the specific topic of how advertisers use television commercials, and it has a main idea that addresses the assignment. The body has well-supported claims, and these support the main idea in the introduction. All the parts of the essay fit together. Look more closely at the introduction. What makes it work? She has first introduced the topic of advertising with the sentences:

> As an industry grows, advertising starts to have an important role. We can see advertisements all over the place: on TV, in the newspaper, in magazines, even on the bus.

This is followed by a more specific discussion of the purpose of advertising with the sentences:

> Companies use this advertising for consumers who might be interested in buying their products. If the purpose of advertising is to persuade people to buy products, then it is important that the ads are shown to the right customers. Advertisers spend a lot of time and money making sure this happens.

Finally the link is made between the purpose of advertising and the main idea that is stated in the last sentence.

> *We can see the relationship between the kind and time of advertisements on television and the kind of people that advertisers hope will buy their products, so they must be careful about which programs and which time of day they choose for their advertisements.*

In this essay, the introduction starts with general statements about the topic and then becomes more specific as it moves to the main idea. This is a very good way to begin..What about your introduction?

1. Have you introduced your topic to your reader?
2. Have you dealt with the assigned question?
3. Have you included your main idea?

Drafting Tip

When to write the introductory paragraph

Sometimes writers wonder when they should write the introduction to their paper. For many people, writing the introduction first is the most logical way to proceed. This way, the main idea is written before the body and can help a writer stay focused on the overall point of the paper. For others, it makes more sense to write the body and then write the introduction afterwards. This way, a writer can develop all the ideas in the body first and then tie them together in the introduction. This is the way it has been done in this unit. Both methods work. The order you use will depend on what makes the most sense to you. Which way do you prefer to do it?

Now that you've looked at introductions and how they fit together with the body of an essay, you need to think about how to end the essay. There are different ways to conclude. Two of the most common ways are either to summarize the information in the body, or to evaluate the information in the body. Sometimes summarizing is sufficient. Look again at Ahmed's conclusion. He summarized the information that he discussed in the body and restated the main point. This is good as far as it goes, but compare it to what Graciela has done. Like Ahmed, she summarized the information in the body of her paper, but she went a step further and evaluated this information as well, with the sentence:

> *Television advertising is very powerful because it can affect how people act and the choices they make.*

Graciela's conclusion, like Dominika's in Unit Two, answers the familiar question, **"So what?"**

By answering this question, she has tied all the parts of the essay together and made it more interesting for the reader, which makes a better essay over-all. What about your conclusion? Did you summarize, evaluate, or both? What will work best in your essay?

RESPONDING TO A PEER'S WRITING

Activity 3.9

Now you will respond to one of your classmates' papers. He or she will use this feed-back in revising and writing the second draft. A classmate will do the same for your paper.

PEER RESPONSE SHEET

Writer: _____   Responder: _____

Look at the first paragraph.

1. What does it say the essay will be about?

_____

_____

_____

_____

2. What is the writer's main point?

_____

_____

_____

_____

3. Does the essay answer the assigned question?

_____

_____

_____

_____

Now look at the rest of the paper.

4. What claims does the writer make about advertising strategies?

_____

_____

_____

_____

_____

_____

5. What evidence does the writer give to support each of these claims?

_____

_____

_____

_____

_____

_____

_____

_____

6. Read the first paragraph again. Do the claims and evidence in the body paragraphs support the main point in the introduction? Explain.

_____

_____

_____

_____

_____

_____

_____

7. How does the writer conclude?

_____

_____

_____

_____

_____

8. Are there parts of the essay you don't understand? What are they?

_____

_____

_____

_____

9. What other suggestions do you have for the writer's next draft?

_____

_____

_____

_____

🦋 EVALUATING YOUR OWN WORK

By now you should know what the next step is in revising your essay. You will notice that the form that follows is less structured than the ones in the previous units. Use it to plan the changes you will make in your second draft.

Activity 3.10

What to Do When the Draft Comes Back

Read through your instructor's comments and the Peer Response Sheet(s) and find some of the suggestions they have made. Consider the following questions as you plan your revision.

- Which are the most important suggestions?
- What do you think of them?
- How will you respond to them?
- If you do not plan to follow them, why not?

_____

_____

_____

_____

_____

_____

_____

_____

_____

_____

_____

_____

Perhaps you have thought of some other changes you would like to make. List them here.

_____

_____

_____

_____

_____

_____

_____

_____

_____

_____

✍ WRITING YOUR SECOND DRAFT

Now you are ready to revise your essay. Look over the plans you made in Activity 3.10. As you write your second draft, make sure your claims are clear and that you have provided adequate support for them. Check that your introduction clearly states your main point and that your main point is supported in the body paragraphs that follow.

4. EDITING

Editing Practice

#3 Using a learner dictionary

You probably have a dictionary, maybe even more than one. Maybe you have a bilingual dictionary and an English dictionary. Each has legitimate uses. However, if you don't have a learner dictionary, you need one. In this Editing Practice, we will try to convince you that this is true, above all, for writing.

A learner dictionary contains valuable information that second language writers need but native English writers do not. For instance, no native speaker of English needs to be reminded that *information* is a noncount noun and cannot take a plural *s*. All native speakers know this because English is their first language. For second language writers, in contrast, this can be very confusing. It is these kinds of details about words that can be found in learner dictionaries. However, it takes a little practice to learn how to use them well. Using the *Newbury House Dictionary of American English*, you will go through several features that are unique to learner dictionaries. Here are three useful things you can find in a learner dictionary.

1. Count/Noncount distinction

You can find out if a noun is count or noncount. This dictionary uses the symbol [U] for *uncountable* and [C] for *countable*. Look at the entry for **advice**.

> **ad·vice** *n.* [U] **1** opinion(s) given to someone about what to do. (*syn*) guidance. *She took my advice and did not drop out of school.* **2** direction, warning: *On the advice of her doctor, she no longer smokes cigarettes.*

Activity 3.11

Try looking up some other nouns. Are they count or noncount?

excitement _____

music _____

land _____

2. Verbs and prepositions that go together

Second language writers often have trouble choosing the right preposition to go with the verb they are using. Many verbs can occur with several different prepositions. Sometimes you will find information about prepositions in the definition. Sometimes you will have to look at the examples that follow the definition. Look at the entry for **insist**.

> **in-sist** *v* **1** to demand, show strong opinion. *I insist that you go to the hospital immediately; you are very ill.* **2** *phrasal v.* **insist on** to accept only certain things, to require. *The cook insists on the finest meat and fish.*

Activity 3.12

Try looking up some other verbs. What prepositions do they appear with?

believe _____

stand _____

thank _____

3. Choosing the best word

As you know, there are often cases where two or more words mean almost the same thing. For instance, when should you use the word **bathroom** and when should you use **restroom**? A learner dictionary can help you distinguish from among the choices. Look at the entry for **bathroom** in the dictionary. There is a section called USAGE NOTE[1] that gives you some help in deciding.

> USAGE NOTE: In the USA, *bathroom* usually means a room with a toilet and bathtub or shower in a house, but *restroom* refers to a toilet facility in a public building. *See* ladies' room, men's room, powder room.

Activity 3.13

Try looking up some other words. What special things did you learn from the usage notes?

happy _____

_____

street _____

_____

These are just a few examples of the extra resources that a learner dictionary provides. It is important for all second language writers to use one whenever they write.

ABOUT LEARNING LOGS

Now you have done at least three Editing Practice exercises. Your instructor may have also made comments and suggestions regarding areas of grammar

---

[1]Features may be different in other dictionaries.

that you need to work on. However, once you are no longer in an ESL class, your instructors may not give you this kind of assistance. Therefore, it is very important that you take responsibility for making sure that the grammar is as good as the content and organization of your paper.

There are two kinds of grammar problems. The first kind (1) occurs when you don't really understand the rule you are using; perhaps you are trying to use a more complicated structure than you have used before. It's important to try out new ways of saying things, and you should continue to do so. You will probably need an instructor's or native speaker's help with this kind of problem.

The second kind (2) is easier to fix. These occur with rules that you already know fairly well. You really can correct these yourself if you take a little extra time when you edit. It is these aspects of grammar, such as third person singular -s and sentence fragments, that you should work on in your Learning Logs. A Learning Log is a personal record that will help you focus on the little errors that you can and should be responsible for correcting.

Activity 3.14

Look back over your final drafts from the last two units. Make a list of the errors that you think are important. Which ones do you think are type (1) errors? For these, you will probably need to ask your instructor for help. Which ones are type (2) errors, the ones you can correct yourself? Your instructor may have pointed out some of these to you. Look at the type (2) errors. You need to develop a strategy to make sure that you improve in these areas. For instance, if your instructor has suggested you need to work on third person singular -s, you should include this in your Learning Log. Look at the following sample Learning Log.

I. Grammar point that I plan to work on:

> 3rd person singular -s (agreement)

II. Strategy for improving my performance:

1. Go through Editing Practice #7 before turning in my final draft.

2. Put in a ✓ mark next to each 3rd person singular subject as I go through my draft to check for agreement.

3. Write my signature at the end of each final draft, stating that I have checked for agreement errors. That makes it more like a promise.

III. Questions I need to ask my instructor:

I keep getting mixed up about "nobody" and "no one." Do both of them need an -s on the verb?

For each error, check to see if there is a relevant Editing Practice and follow the guidelines given there. You may be able to come up with some additional steps of your own, as in numbers (2) and (3) on the sample Learning Log. On the next page, there is a blank sheet where you can begin your own Learning Log. You may photocopy this sheet. In your Learning Log, write down what strategy you are going to use to correct the error you have selected. If there is no Editing Practice, consult with your instructor on a step-by-step strategy for improving your performance and write it down in your Learning Log.

Before you turn in each final draft, review your Learning Logs to remind yourself what you need to check for. It is easiest to concentrate on one thing at a time. However, soon you will have to check for everything, so it is best to establish a system now that can work for you later.

LEARNING LOG

I. Grammar point that I plan to work on:

_____

_____

_____

II. Strategy for improving my performance:

_____

_____

_____

III. Questions I need to ask my instructor: _____

_____

_____

EDITING YOUR OWN WORK: THE FINAL DRAFT

Activity 3.15

It is time once again to edit your own draft. Your instructor may have suggested that you consult your learner dictionary regarding some of the words you used in your second draft. Look these up and make any changes that you think will improve your essay. This is also the time to identify and correct any grammatical errors you can find. In particular, check for comma splices, run-on sentences, and fragments, as you did in the last two units.

Once you have finished editing, you are ready to turn in your final draft. Be sure to keep your final draft after your instructor has returned it to you so that you can refer to it when you write other papers.

NAVIGATING THE UNIVERSITY

Task
- Giving advice to incoming freshmen

Writing Focus
- Writing for different purposes

Editing Focus
- Verbal adjectives

In the last two units, you organized, analyzed, and presented information that you gathered from surveys and television commercials. The purpose of the writing tasks was to provide information for your readers. In this unit, you will analyze and critique written information in order to give your readers advice. You will also reflect on the experiences you had when you first came to college in order to try to help others who may now be in the same position.

You have been writing essays with body paragraphs that support the main point presented in your introduction. These elements are basic to almost all academic writing. However, there are a variety of ways to put these elements together. In this unit, you will work on an essay that has a somewhat different structure from those you have written up until now.

Colleges and universities can be intimidating because they are so much more complex than high schools. There are so many different offices and services that it is not always easy to get the information you need when you need it most. For your essay in this unit, you will explore one aspect of your university or college and then provide newcomers with useful information on that part of the system.

I. EXPLORING IDEAS

READINGS

Many students encounter problems when they start at a new college or university. These problems can take all forms, from simply finding the right classroom to taking notes in lectures, and everything in between.

Here is what two students had to say about their first experiences on their university campus.

Jean-Baptiste

Coming to a university, students face a totally new environment and new experiences. The habits gained in high school in many cases may be useless in this new setting and may have to be replaced with new ones. For many students, entering college is a huge first step on the way to a new, adult life. However, the adaptation to this new life is not always easy and it may even be stressful and unpleasant in the beginning. As for many others, for me, the first experience at college was a great struggle.

One of the most irritating things about starting school in a new place is the unfamiliarity of the streets and buildings. I experienced this most painfully during my first two days on campus as a part of my orientation. Trouble started as soon as I reached the campus. First, I could not decide which parking lot to use since I didn't know where I was heading. There were no directions anywhere and no one around to help those new to the university. After ten minutes of driving around campus, I finally just decided to park in any lot and walk the rest of the way. Then, it took me another half an hour to find the building where I had to be. Even though I had left for campus an hour early, I still was late for my orientation.

For the first few days of the semester, I walked around the campus with a map in my hand. I was embarrassed because I felt as if people were looking at me as if I were a "freshie." The campus seemed like a small town to me. I tried to learn the names of the buildings, but everyone used short names and abbreviations and that was hard for me to get used to. Even if I asked someone for directions, I got answers like, "Go straight past SEL and take a right at SH." This never helped me much. Now that I have been here for a while, everything is much easier. It even seems that the campus has shrunk with the passage of time.

Another aspect of college life that was new and difficult for me was the process of taking notes in large lectures. This has taken a lot of getting used to. At the beginning, I had trouble distinguishing which things were important in the professors' lectures. Even though I knew that I was supposed to take notes, most of the notes I did take were not very useful because I never seemed to write down the most important parts. I just sat there and watched other people taking notes and wondered what they were writing. Sometimes I looked at my notes a few days later and I wouldn't understand anything. This happened to me all the time during the first few months. However, as the semester progressed, I began to learn how and when to take notes during lectures. I began to understand when the professor was stressing an important point and when he was just talking about other things.

The thing that continues to be the most difficult for me is understanding the accents of some of my teachers. Most of my teaching assistants and many of my professors come from other countries and speak English with different accents. My

(continued on next page)

(continued from previous page)

chemistry T.A. is Thai and in the beginning I could hardly understand anything that he said. Eventually though, I became more used to his way of speaking. Now sometimes I even think that people with an accent are more likely to understand others with an accent because they make more of an effort. Other times though, I still get frustrated when I can't understand the chemistry.

Starting college can be very tough in the beginning. You have to learn a new way of thinking, studying and learning, as well as an entirely new place. However, as time passes, you will find that the difficulties pass with it and everything becomes routine.

Shanti

For me, the beginning of college was filled with surprises and problems. The biggest problem was choosing my classes since I didn't really know which ones to choose. I thought and I thought and I talked to other people. Then I sat down and spent four hours deciding on my schedule. I thought that everything was settled. I tried to make most of my classes in the morning so that I could work in the afternoon or else go home and do my homework. However, when I did my phone registration, the number was always busy. When I finally got through, I discovered that most of the classes I had chosen were already full. Since I did not want to have to call again and get a busy signal for one hour, I had to decide on a new schedule immediately. Everything that had taken me four hours the day before, I had to do in five minutes. I had to change most of my classes and I ended up with some classes I did not really want and also I had three or four hours between my classes. I realized that I would not be able to take a job in the afternoon and that I would have to do my homework between classes while I was still at school.

My next problem came when I arrived at the campus. I had a lot of trouble finding the right building and classrooms. I had a map and a schedule, but still, it was hard to get to the right place at the right time. I felt as if I were in a labyrinth, and in the beginning, I was always late for my classes. I felt so stupid carrying around a map with me wherever I went on campus. When I came home on the first day, I just sat down and cried because I was so frustrated. I thought I would never figure out where I should go.

I also was not used to such big classes. One of the first classes I took was biology. It was a huge class of almost four hundred students. I had never had more than 25 or 30 students in my class in high school. My problem here was taking notes in the lectures. My professor seemed nervous and jumped from one topic to another. I couldn't figure out which parts were important and which weren't, so I didn't know which things I should write down in my notes. In high school, my teachers always told us which parts we should remember and write down. Also, the way he talked made the class really boring. It was hard to stay awake in the class and a lot of people went to sleep. The professor didn't seem to care. In such a big class, it is difficult to get to know your teacher or the other students in your class. I was

(continued on next page)

(continued from previous page)

too scared to ask questions in front of the class. When I had problems understanding the lecture, I went to see the professor outside of class, but then I was so nervous because I didn't know him very well and I didn't know how I should speak to him.

In my math class I had a different problem. The class was small but it was taught by a T.A. from China. I had a lot of problems understanding him, especially in the beginning. All the students complained about him and some of them made fun of him. I felt very bad because he understood the math very well but he just couldn't explain it so that we could understand it. I also remember how frustrating it was to try to express myself when I couldn't speak English very well.

Now I am much wiser. I know where all the buildings and classes are. Now I do not regret that I have so much time between my classes because I use it to study and sometimes to relax. I think that there are many interesting things to do at college. It just takes some time to find them.

Discussion Questions

1. Jean-Baptiste and Shanti had some of the same problems. What were they?

2. What other problems did each of them face?

3. Did you have any of these kinds of problems when you started college?

Many prospective college students cannot afford to pay their whole tuition and therefore must apply for financial aid. There are many kinds of financial aid, including loans, grants, and scholarships. There are also many sources of aid: the federal and state government, as well as private foundations and individual colleges and universities. In order to qualify for financial aid, applicants are asked to provide a great deal of information and go through a complex evaluation process. The following is an outline of what applicants at one university must do in order to be considered for aid.

Application Packet
Office of Student Financial Aid

This packet contains the application needed to apply for grants, loans, and employment from various federal, state, and **institutional** sources.

Students must submit their FAFSA application to the processing agency by March 1st for **priority** consideration. Students who apply after this deadline will

institutional from a college or university

priority top

(continued on next page)

(continued from previous page)

be considered for aid but all funds may not be available and payment of funds may not occur during the first week of class.

How does a student apply for financial aid?

Step 1:

A. Fill out the FAFSA form. Read the instructions carefully before filling it out. If you received a Renewal Application for Financial Aid, you must complete it instead of a FAFSA form.

B. Mail the FAFSA or the Renewal Application for Financial Aid to the processing agency.

C. Do not complete both the FAFSA and the Renewal Application for Financial Aid. Only one form will be accepted by the processor.

Step 2:

If you have attended any other **postsecondary** institutions (except foreign schools), regardless of your enrollment or hours earned, a financial aid transcript must be completed by all previously attended schools and **forwarded** to the Office of Student Financial Aid (OSFA). This is **mandatory** even if you never received aid at the institution. Transcript forms are available at the OSFA.

postsecondary any schooling after high school

forwarded sent
mandatory required

Step 3:

You will receive a Student Aid Report (SAR) four to six weeks after you mail the FAFSA or the Renewal Application. It contains key information and an estimate of your family's contribution. If any of the information on the SAR is incorrect, make the necessary change(s) on the SAR and mail it back to the address provided on your SAR. If all the information is correct, keep the SAR for your records.

Step 4:

Eligible undergraduate students who meet residency requirements will receive notification from the Student Assistance Commission (SAC) regarding eligibility for the Monetary Award Program (MAP) within four weeks after receiving the SAR. Keep this notification for your records.

eligible qualified

Step 5:

The OSFA will receive an analysis of your application information from the processing agency. Upon receipt of this data, you may be required to submit tax returns, proof of citizenship, and/or various other documentation to the OSFA. All requested documents *must be submitted* in order to continue the processing of your file.

Step 6:

The OSFA will notify all applicants of their eligibility for federal, state, and institutional assistance. You will receive an award letter (**tentative** or official) or a **denial** letter. Carefully read the letter you have been sent. If you receive an official award letter, complete all sections and return it to our office along with any additional materials requested. If you receive a tentative award letter, you have been selected for application review and will be sent an official award letter within six to eight weeks.

tentative possible
denial rejection

Discussion Questions

1. Do you find this document confusing? Which parts? For instance:

   ■ Do you find Step 1 difficult to follow?

   ■ Is the difference between FAFSA, SAR, and MAP clear?

   ■ Is it possible to tell from this document whether you are eligible for financial aid?

2. Do you think a high school senior would understand what to do with this information?

3. Did you apply for financial aid? Did you find the process confusing? Did you experience any problems?

Students and teachers may each engage in behavior that the other finds irritating. In some cases, even though they may not realize that their behavior is annoying, their actions may adversely affect the learning process. This article provides results of a study that attempted to find out exactly which activities teachers and students find the most irritating.

Faculty and Student Perceptions of Irritating Behaviors in the College Classroom

Drew C. Appleby

The behaviors of college students that irritate their teachers and the behaviors of college teachers that irritate their students were organized into three categories: (a) teachers who are irritated by students who act bored, (b) students who are irritated by teachers who are poor communicators, and (c) both groups who are irritated by behaviors they interpret as rude or disrespectful.

Although college faculty and students are **inextricably** involved in the teaching/ learning process, they form two distinct societies. They are generally from different generations, may possess opposing value systems, and often hold **divergent** opinions about the appropriateness of behaviors. People form opinions of others by projecting their own social norms and noting the **discrepancy** between their belief about what others should do and what they actually do. The greater the discrepancy, the more negative the opinion, and the more negative the opinion, the lower the probability of meaningful interaction. When the values, opinions, and behaviors of teachers and students match, the classroom is in relative harmony. When they do not, the teaching/learning process is likely to suffer.

The purpose of this study is to identify perceptions that negatively affect the teaching/learning process. Certain student behaviors irritate faculty, and specific faculty behaviors irritate students, even though neither of these groups deliberately attempts to irritate the other. Faculty are probably unaware that some of their behaviors irritate students, and students may be equally unaware that many of their behaviors irritate teachers. The quality of the teaching/learning environment might be significantly improved if both groups become aware of the impact of these behaviors and decrease their frequency. The results of this survey are summarized by category in Tables 4.1 and 4.2.

Discussion

The results indicate considerable **consensus** among faculty about irritating student behaviors. There are several reasons why faculty are irritated with immature and inattentive student behaviors. These behaviors pose a threat to the teaching/ learning process because they are time consuming and often prevent a teacher from dealing with important materials and issues. These behaviors can also create the impression that students are not interested in the learning process or that they believe their teachers are boring. These behaviors may also play a significant role in teacher burn-out by emphasizing generational **disparity** and creating negative attitudes towards students and the learning **milieu**.

(continued on next page)

inextricably inseparably

divergent different

discrepancy difference; mismatch

consensus agreement

disparity difference; inequality
milieu environment

(continued from previous page)

• **Table 4.1** •

CATEGORIES OF IRRITATING BEHAVIORS OF STUDENTS
GIVEN BY FACULTY

Immature Behaviors
- talking during lectures (35)
- chewing gum, eating or drinking noisily (17)
- being late (16)
- creating disturbances (10)
- wearing hats (8)
- putting feet on desks or tables (2)
- being insecure or **"brown-nosing"** (1)
- complaining about work load (1)
- acting like a know-it-all (1)
- not asking for help or asking for help when it is too late (1)

"brown-nosing" flattering the teacher, doing extra work, etc., simply in an effort to get good grades

Inattentive Behaviors
- sleeping during class (18)
- cutting class (16)
- acting bored or apathetic (16)
- not paying attention (15)
- being unprepared (13)
- packing up books and materials before class is over (5)
- asking already answered questions (4)
- sitting in the back rows when there are plenty of empty seats in the front (3)
- obvious yawning (3)
- slouching in seats (2)
- asking "Did we do anything important?" after missing class (2)
- not asking questions (1)
- doing work for other classes in class (1)
- reading the school newspaper in class (1)

Miscellaneous Irritating Behaviors
- cheating (6)
- asking "Will it be on the test?" (1)
- being more interested in grades than in learning (1)
- pretending to understand (1)
- blaming teachers for poor grades (1)
- giving unbelievable excuses (1)

Note. Numbers in parentheses indicate number of responses.

• **Table 4.2** •

FREQUENCY OF IRRITATING BEHAVIORS OF TEACHERS
GIVEN BY AT LEAST FOUR STUDENTS

Communication Problems
- present poor lectures (e.g., unprepared, **monotone**, digress, too fast, ramble, repetitious, unorganized) (147)
- cannot explain concepts clearly (14)
- cannot or will not answer student questions (13)
- take lectures straight from the textbook (12)
- tell jokes that are not funny, use inappropriate humor, or laugh at own jokes (11)
- write illegibly on the blackboard (10)
- pace constantly during lectures (9)
- show no enthusiasm (for teaching, their subject matter, or their professional field) (9)

monotone a flat, boring voice

(continued on next page)

(continued from previous page)

- eat, drink or chew gum during lectures (9)
- say "ah" or "uhm" frequently during lectures (8)
- teach in a disorganized, unorganized, or unstructured manner (7)
- blow nose or clear throat excessively during lectures (6)
- appear not to understand their own subject matter (5)
- use jargon without sufficient explanation of its meaning (5)
- read straight from the textbook or notes during lecture (5)

Unresponsive to Student Needs
- keep class past end of period (52)
- arrive late for class (37)
- have obvious favorite students (i.e., teacher's pets) (18)
- have a condescending attitude toward students (i.e., treat students like children) (17)
- act as if their class were the only one that students are taking (17)
- feel that their point of view is always correct (i.e., close-minded and inflexible) (16)
- embarrass students in class (e.g., criticize, pick on, or make an example of them) (16)
- take a long time to return tests and papers (12)
- assign "busywork" that is either not collected or not graded (10)
- do not follow their own syllabi (7)
- cancel or do not show up for class frequently (5)
- ignore students' suggestions or opinions (4)
- are unavailable to help students (4)
- do not allow questions or class participation (4)

Evaluation Problems
- use subjective, too strict, unfair, inconsistent or picky grading criteria (14)
- include material on tests that has not been covered or assigned (13)
- give too few tests that cover too much material (9)
- give unannounced "pop" quizzes (9)

Miscellaneous Behaviors
- take attendance (5)
- dress in an unprofessional or shabby manner (4)

Note. Numbers in parentheses indicate number of responses.

There also appears to be consensus among college students about the behaviors of teachers that most irritate them. The two largest categories identified in the current study (i.e., communication problems and unresponsive to student needs) are similar to those identified in previous research, which found that low student evaluations of teachers **correlated** with negative personal or communication characteristics.

correlated corresponded

Conclusions and Recommendations

Students and teachers exhibit surprisingly consistent sets of behaviors that are perceived as irritating: (a) teachers are most irritated by immature and inattentive students and (b) students are irritated most by teachers who are not **empathetic** and poor communicators. A tentative conclusion that can be drawn from these results is that a circular causal relationship may exist between irritating behaviors cited by both teachers and students. A teacher faced with a lecture room filled with slouching, yawning, and sleeping students may decide that they are undeserving of the time and effort that it would take to present them with a sparkling, enthusiastic lecture.

empathetic understanding

(continued on next page)

(continued from previous page)

Students faced with an unenthusiastic lecturer may exhibit inattentive behaviors that, in turn, produce even less enthusiasm.

Faculty can help students to become more aware audience participants by discussing the perceptual consequences of student behaviors during classroom sessions. Teachers should also become more aware of their behaviors that irritate students and attempt to minimize or eliminate them. With the establishment of such mutual insight, the teaching/learning process would surely improve for both generations of participants, and student evaluation of faculty might be more positive.

Discussion Questions

1. Do you agree with the results of the study regarding the students' point of view?

2. Do you think you ever irritate your teachers with your behavior?

3. Do you think such behavior makes a difference in how much students learn?

Thinking about the Topic

Activity 4.1

A. *Think back to your first days at your university or college, and discuss these questions with your classmates.*

1. What was difficult about being new on campus? Why?

_____

_____

_____

2. Were there any university services (financial aid, registration, tutoring, etc.) that you had trouble using? What were they? Make a list.

_____

_____

_____

_____

_____

_____

3. Were there any services you didn't know about then that could have helped you? What are they? Make a list.

_____

_____

_____

_____

_____

_____

B. _Now look at the list of campus services you and your classmates have put together and choose one you would like to explore further and write about. You may choose a service you have used before, or you may choose one that you haven't used. If you decide on a service that you have used before, select one that you had difficulties with. If you decide on a new service, select something that you think could have helped you with a problem that you had. For example, if you had a hard time in a class and think tutoring would have helped but you didn't know about tutoring services on campus, you might choose this service. You might also choose it if you did try to get tutoring in the past but had some problems using the service. Write your choice here._

_____

C. _Once you have chosen a campus service to investigate, discuss the following questions with your classmates._

1. What happened when you used this service? What problems did you encounter?

2. What would have made your experience easier?

3. If you haven't used this service, what information would you need in order to use it?

2. GATHERING INFORMATION AND DRAFTING

GATHERING INFORMATION

Now you need to collect information on the service that you are going to write about later in this unit.

Activity 4.2

Make a list of the things you need to do to find out about how this service works. Write it here and compare it with your classmates' lists. The first item is done for you.

1. Collect written materials from the service.

2. _____

_____

3. _____

_____

4. _____

_____

The first item on the list suggests collecting written materials. Why should you do this? Think about the example of tutoring on campus. If you have never used any tutoring services on campus, what do you need to know? You probably want to find out who is offering tutoring and in what subject areas, the hours tutoring is available, how to schedule appointments, and how much it costs. Tutoring services often provide this information in a flyer or information packet, as do other campus services.

If you have used tutoring services on campus before and had problems, you probably want to look at copies of written materials you already have and find out if there were also materials you never received. In addition, you may want to find out if there are other tutoring services on campus you didn't know about when you initially used the service. Where do you need to go to collect written materials on the service you are going to write about?

What else is on your list? You may have included talking to someone at the service to ask questions about the written information you collected or to get help using the service. You may also want to ask about ways to avoid the problems you had when you used it in the past. Make sure you take notes as you go so you can refer to them later when you prepare to write.

Have you included talking to other students about the service? You may want to find out if other students have had similar difficulties. Again, make notes to use later.

These are just a few suggestions. Discuss these as well as any other ideas you have with your instructor and classmates and complete your list. Once you have finished your list, go out and gather all your information.

Short Write

Write a one-draft response to the following questions. Your paper should be one or two pages.

What happened when you tried to gather information about your service? Was it easy to get what you needed? Were people helpful?

ANALYZING YOUR TEXT

Now you will analyze the material you have collected. You need to do this analysis so that you can explain this information to your readers when you write your paper. In your analysis, you should focus on the more difficult parts of the text. If you can discover the source of the difficulties, perhaps you can help the next person overcome them.

Activity 4.3

Read through your text(s) and answer the following questions:

- Are there any parts of the text that you found confusing? Use a highlighter to mark these sections. Are there any parts of the text you think a new user might find confusing, even if you understand it yourself? Use a highlighter to mark these sections.

- Are there words you do not understand? Use a highlighter to mark them.

There are many reasons why a document can be difficult to understand. For instance, in the Financial Aid application that you read at the beginning of the unit, the directions in Step 1A were somewhat confusing. First they said to fill out FAFSA, but then they said not to if you had already received another form. Thus, in general, the instructions might be described as confusing, or more specifically, as *contradictory*; that is, first they say one thing and then they say the opposite.

Activity 4.4

A. *Here are some more **specific** reasons why a text might be confusing.*

A text can be confusing because it:

- is contradictory

- contains too many complicated words

- contains too many abbreviations and acronyms (like FAFSA and OSFA in the reading)

- has long and complicated sentences

■ doesn't give enough information

■ gives too much information for a first-time user

■ refers to unfamiliar places or things

■ doesn't clearly show the steps a user needs to follow

■ jumps around from topic to topic

Write some other reasons here.

■ _____

_____

■ _____

_____

■ _____

_____

B. *Of course, part of the problem may lie in what the text doesn't say! Maybe it doesn't say that if you want to sign up for help at the Writing Center, you have to be there at 7:00 A.M. on the first day of class or you'll never have a chance! Be sure to consider information like that, even though you can't actually point to the problem in the text itself. If you think there is important information missing from your text, write it here.*

_____

_____

_____

Activity 4.5

Now look over your text again carefully. Look back at the parts you highlighted in Activity 4.3 and then look at the list from Activity 4.4. For each of the parts you highlighted, can any of the reasons from the list help to explain the source of the trouble? Try to link each trouble spot to a reason. Use the lines that follow. There are five spaces here, but you may have fewer or more trouble spots that you want to address. Feel free to add more spaces or leave some blank.

1. trouble spot:

_____

_____

_____

reason:

_____

_____

_____

2. trouble spot:

_____

_____

_____

reason:

_____

_____

_____

3. trouble spot:

_____

_____

_____

reason:

_____

_____

_____

4. trouble spot:

_____

_____

_____

reason:

_____

_____

_____

5. trouble spot:

_____

_____

_____

reason:

_____

_____

_____

Typically, if you want to receive a service, you must go through a sequence of steps in order to receive it. Recall the Financial Aid application, which described the steps that an applicant must complete in order to be considered for aid. Your document may or may not make it clear what these steps are.

Activity 4.6

Read through your text(s) and try to figure out this sequence of steps. Even if you do not understand everything in each step, try to give a general idea in your own words of each step on the lines that follow.

1. _____

_____

_____

_____

2. _____

_____

_____

3. _____

_____

_____

4. _____

_____

_____

Up until now, you have been focusing on the problems presented by the text itself. However, there may be other difficulties in using the service. What might be difficult for a newcomer about using this service? *Access* may also be a problem. *Access* refers to how hard it is to get the information you need or to actually use the services. Returning to the example of tutoring services, perhaps tutoring is offered by organizations spread out all over the campus—departments, fraternities, honor societies, and clubs—so that information is not available at one central location. Maybe the service just isn't very well publicized, so that you never heard about it when you came to campus. Or, perhaps, even if you have the proper information, there is so much demand for the tutoring service that you can never get a tutor for the subject you need the most.

Activity 4.7

If access was a problem for you, describe it here. _____

_____

_____

_____

DRAFTING: WRITING YOUR FIRST DRAFT

The Body

Once you have finished analyzing the service, you are ready to begin work on your essay. The assignment is to:

Evaluate a campus service and provide advice for new students.

At this point, you have already identified some of the obstacles to using the campus service, so you already have a lot of the material for the body. The body will have three main parts: (1) your own and other students' experience with the campus service, (2) any problems you found in understanding and using the written material, and (3) your advice to new students about this service. Now look at each of these parts in more detail.

1. Your personal experience. You discussed some of your personal experience with your classmates in the beginning of this unit. Since then, you have collected information, discussed the service with other students, talked to someone at the service, and made notes about your experience. You may have also completed the Short Write assignment. All of these resources should give you plenty of material for this part of the body. Remember that you are writing for someone who is new to campus and does not know much about the available services, so your personal experience has value.

2. Problems with the written material. Much of the work for this portion of the body is already finished. Refer to the analysis of trouble spots in Activity 4.5 in order to write this section. Remember to attach a copy of your text and to use a highlighter to mark the trouble spots you address. This will allow you to discuss specific problem areas and allow your reader to refer directly to them.

3. Giving advice. Now that you have given your experience and evaluated the problems, what advice can you give to students new to campus? What do they need to know in order to use this service more effectively? Think about what you wish someone had told you earlier. Use these questions to guide you as you prepare to write this body paragraph.

- What exactly should new students do to prepare themselves to use this service? For example, do they need to collect documents, make phone calls, or visit another service or professor before they go?

- What alternatives have you found to deal with the problems you discussed earlier in the essay? That is, is there any way for new students to avoid these problems?

- If these problems can't be avoided, what other advice can you offer?

Now write your body paragraphs.

Drafting Tip-Speaking versus Writing

As you write the body paragraphs, it may be tempting to use the word *you* to refer to the students you are addressing, as in:

> *You should call ahead for an appointment at the tutoring center.*

Using second person (*you*) is generally acceptable when speaking, but is usually not used in academic writing. Start using third person (*he, she, it, they*) alternatives now to make your writing more formal.[1] Look at some alternatives for the previous sentence. Any one of the following is acceptable.

> *Students should call ahead for an appointment at the tutoring center.*
>
> *Everyone should call ahead for an appointment at the tutoring center.*
>
> *One should call ahead for an appointment at the tutoring center.*
>
> *A student who wants to use the tutoring center should call ahead for an appointment.*
>
> *Any students who want to use the tutoring center should call ahead for an appointment.*

There are a number of alternatives open to you; these are just a few possibilities. Remember that if you choose to use the singular (*everyone, one, a student*), continue to use the singular throughout. If you choose the plural (*students, any students*), use it throughout. Whatever your choice, be consistent. See Editing Practice # 7 for more information on agreement.

The Introduction

After you have finished working on the body paragraphs, it's time to think about your introduction. You may have already written it, or you may be starting it now. In either case, as in previous essays, you need to

- introduce your topic to your reader
- directly address the assignment
- include your main idea

Check for these things when you write your introduction.

---

[1] You may wonder why we have used "you" throughout this text. We have done so precisely because we want it to be more like a conversation and less formal. Unfortunately, you don't have that option!

The Conclusion

After you have written your introduction and body paragraphs, how will you conclude? In Unit Three, you learned that the most effective conclusions provide an evaluation of the information in the essay. Try to include some evaluation or commentary in your own conclusion.

Now put all of these elements together for your first draft.

3. REVISING

 EVALUATING ESSAYS

This time, you will look at what just one student wrote about this topic. After reading the essay, you will offer suggestions for revising it for a second draft. Try to be as specific as possible in your responses.

Student Essay

1   The biggest challenge for most students at a new col-
2   lege for the first time is that they must face problems
3   they do not expect. The university is a new and unfamil-
4   iar place for most of the incoming freshmen. It can be
5   very stressful if students do not know where to go for
6   help. One of the problems I faced during my first semester
7   at college was finding a job on campus. In order to get
8   a job, I had to fill out a lot of forms as part of the
9   job application. The document I had the most trouble with
10   was the W-4 form. After reading this paper, hopefully
11   other students will learn from my experience, take my ad-
12   vice and avoid trouble.

13   The process I went through to find a job took a lot
14   of time and was very stressful. First, I consulted the
15   university home page to find out about student employ-
16   ment. The Student Employment Office's web page had a long
17   list of job opportunities. I printed all of them out and
18   studied them to find a job that looked right for me. Af-
19   ter I picked the job I wanted, I called the Student Em-
20   ployment Office and they told me I had to fill out an
21   application. This is when my trouble started. They didn't
22   tell me that the office only opened at 12:00, which meant

23 I got there too early. I just had to sit and wait until

24 the office opened so I could pick up the application. They

25 gave me a thick document, about ten pages long. I started

26 to fill it out, but after a half an hour, I still wasn't

27 finished. Then I got to the tax forms, including the

28 W-4 form. I got completely confused, so I decided to take

29 it home and ask for help from a friend who had already

30 used the Student Employment Office to find a job. After

31 my friend helped me fill it out, I returned to the Stu-

32 dent Employment Office with my application, but then they

33 said they could not accept my application until I showed

34 them my alien registration card. I had to return the next

35 day. Once my application was on file, I had to go to one

36 more office to interview for the job. It took more about

37 a week to complete the application process, much longer

38 than I expected.

39   Of all of the parts of the application, the part

40 about taxes was the most difficult for me to understand.

41 There were many different parts, including the Employee

42 Information Form, U.S. Department of Justice Form, Child

43 Support Information Act Form, Educational Loan Default

44 Statement, the W-4 form and several others. I couldn't

45 understand which of the forms applied to me. The woman in

46 the Student Employment Office said the most important one

47 was the W-4 form. I found the directions very confusing.

48 They asked me to decide how I wanted the university to

49 pay my taxes, and I had to give information about my fam-

50 ily. I had to state how many deductions and allowances I

51 wanted. They give worksheets to help calculate how much

52 this should be, but I just couldn't understand what num-

53 bers I should put down on the worksheet. My friend ex-

54 plained to me that most students only need to fill out

55 the first worksheet on the first page. Since I am not

56 married, I just entered one allowance for myself. Then I

57 had to decide if I was exempt from federal income tax.

58 Since I only earn a little bit and didn't pay any taxes

59 last year, I am exempt. When I finally understood it, the

60 form was not so difficult, but for someone who has never

61 seen it before, it can be very confusing.

62   New students can find a job on campus if they know

63 how. The first thing to do is to get a list of job open-

64 ings. It is important to find out the hours of the Stu-

65 dent Employment Office before going in. The best thing to

66 do is to call ahead for an interview appointment. Immi-

67 grants must bring their alien registration card with them

68 when they go in for the application. Filling out the ap-

69 plication takes a long time because there are many dif-

70 ferent forms. It helps to have a friend come along who

71 has gone through the application process before. That will

72 make everything go more quickly because the W-4 form can

73 be especially hard to figure out.

74   It is very tough for new students just beginning

75 their college life because there is so much they do not

76 know. However, there are many services that can help them

77 to solve their problems. In the beginning, though, it is

78 hard to understand how these services work. Asking ques-

79 tions and asking friends for help can make things easier.

80 As time passes and things are not so new and different,

81 everything becomes easier to understand. Soon the new stu-

82 dents will not be new anymore and they will be explain-

83 ing everything to the next group of students.

Kalala

WRITING FOCUS: BODY PARAGRAPHS WITH DIFFERENT PURPOSES

In the essays you have written for the two previous units, the purpose has been to inform your readers of a pattern you found in the information you collected: in Unit Two, you wrote about trends you found among different groups of computer users, and in Unit Three, it was strategies used to sell products to particular groups. In both cases, you sorted through the information, identified two or three patterns, and wrote about each one in a separate body paragraph. These body paragraphs were essentially parallel; that is, each one contained **the same kind of information**. They each had a sentence making a claim about a trend or strategy and they had supporting evidence explaining the trend or strategy. This structure works very well for many essays when the purpose is to **inform**.

In this unit, however, the purpose is somewhat different. The assignment is both to **inform** and to **advise**. The body paragraphs for this assignment are not parallel; each one has a different structure. Look back at Kalala's essay. Whereas the first body paragraph is a summary of his personal experience, the second provides an analysis of the written documents he gathered, and the third contains his advice to the new student. Varying the structure works well for this assignment. It is important to note, however, that these body paragraphs have some basic elements in common with the ones you wrote in earlier units. They still need to tell the reader what the paragraph will be about, make a claim, and provide supporting details.

Activity 4.8

Reread Kalala's essay and answer the following questions.
For each body paragraph:

■ Is there a sentence that says what the paragraph will be about?

■ Does it make a claim?

■ Are there supporting details for each of the body paragraphs?

_____

_____

_____

_____

What about the introduction? As we saw earlier in this unit, you still must introduce your topic, address the assignment, and include the main idea.

■ Has Kalala done all of these things in his introduction?

_____

_____

_____

_____

As you can see, Kalala's introduction differs somewhat from those you wrote in previous units. In those units, you might have written an introduction that included a list of the specific trends or strategies you found. That technique is fine for those essays, but it doesn't really fit for this assignment because the body paragraphs are different from one another. Here Kalala provides general information about his difficulties getting a job, but saves the specifics for the body.

The point is that not all essays have the same purpose; therefore, they are put together differently. There is no single formula for all essays. You must think about not just the information that you are providing, but also what you are trying to tell your readers about that information. The purpose will play a large part in determining how you write the different parts of your essay.

EVALUATING YOUR OWN WORK

In the past three units, you have offered suggestions for improving student drafts in the textbook, as well as comments and advice for helping classmates to revise for a second draft. Similarly, you have used the suggestions of your classmates and your instructor to improve your own papers. This is good practice, and you almost certainly have benefited from the advice of other writers. In future courses, however, it is likely that you will be solely responsible for the revision of your own drafts. Therefore, it is important that you start taking responsibility for this process now. Starting in this unit, you will respond in the same way that you have in the past, but now you will respond only to your own writing. This can be more difficult than responding to someone else's writing because it is harder to be objective. Everything is already clear to you because you know what you are trying to say. When you read over your paper, try to read it with someone else's eyes and consider whether what you have written would be clear to another reader.

Activity 4.9

Use the following questions to guide your response.

1. Look at your introduction.

- Have you told your readers where your information comes from?
- Have you included a clearly stated main point?
- Are there any ways in which you think you can improve your introduction?

_____

_____

_____

_____

_____

2. Look at the body paragraphs.

- Have you discussed an experience you had using the service?
- Have you presented a clear analysis of your text? Have you offered the reader some advice?
- Do all of the paragraphs relate to the main point?
- Does each body paragraph contain a sentence that tells what the paragraph will be about?
- Does each body paragraph contain a claim?
- Are there any ways in which you think you can improve the body of your paper?

_____

_____

_____

_____

_____

_____

_____

3. Look at the conclusion.

■ Have you provided a conclusion that offers some sort of comment on the information in the paper, rather than just summarizing it?

■ Are there any ways in which you think you can improve it?

_____

_____

_____

_____

_____

4. Now read over your whole paper again.

■ How do you think your readers will respond when they read your paper? Is there anything you would like to change or add to make sure your readers find it interesting? Explain.

_____

_____

_____

_____

_____

■ Do you think any of the material in your paper is irrelevant and should be omitted? Which material? _____

_____

_____

■ Do you need to change the order of any of the material in your paper? Which material?

_____

_____

_____

_____

Now put your paper aside and do something else for a while before you come back and read it again. Sometimes you see problems in your paper more clearly if you get away from your writing and then come back to it later.

In previous units, you have filled out a **What to Do When the Draft Comes Back** sheet, basing your plan, in part, on what your classmates suggested. This time, however, you have only your own suggestions and perhaps those of your instructor. Because of this, you will also have to structure your own revision plan.

Activity 4.10   *Look over your own suggestions and your instructor's comments, if you have them. How do you plan to revise for your second draft?*

- What do you plan to change?
- What do you plan to add?
- What do you plan to delete?
- Which parts are you happy with?
- Which parts are you still unsatisfied with?
- Are there some parts you need to ask your instructor about?

Write your plan here.

_____

_____

_____

_____

_____

_____

_____

_____

_____

_____

_____

_____

WRITING YOUR SECOND DRAFT

Now you are ready to revise your essay. Look over your first draft and your plan for revision. As you write your second draft, make sure your essay contains all of the important elements, including supporting details and examples.

4. EDITING

#4 Verbal adjectives

You may have noticed that there are many adjectives, like *interesting* and *bored*, that look a little bit like verbs. In fact, they are called **verbal adjectives** because they come from verbs, but this similarity can sometimes cause confusion. One type of verbal adjective comes from the present participle (the *-ing* form) and the other one comes from the past participle (the *-ed* form).

There are several things you need to know about verbal adjectives.

1. The adjectives that take the *-ing* ending, such as *boring*, describe something that **causes** a reaction or a feeling. You can really see how closely this is related to the verb *bore*. The first sentence in the example contains a verb; the second contains a verbal adjective.

Examples:

Physics really **bores** me.
Physics is so **boring**. (It causes a feeling or reaction of boredom.)

2. The adjectives that take the *-ed* ending, such as *bored*, describe the person or thing that **experiences** this reaction or feeling.

Example:

My physics class is so long. I get very **bored**. (I experience a feeling of boredom.)

It is easy to mix up the two adjective forms, but they mean very different things. If you mix them up, you may end up saying something that you do not mean.

Example:

INCORRECT: I get so **boring** that I think I will scream.
CORRECT: I get so **bored** that I think I will scream.

Bored is the correct choice because you are **experiencing** boredom.

Example:

INCORRECT: Some people think computers are really **excited**.
CORRECT: Some people think computers are really **exciting**.

Exciting is the correct choice because the computers **cause** excitement.

3. The bare form (*bore*) is a verb, not an adjective. It cannot be used as an adjective. This is probably the most common mistake writers make.

Example:

INCORRECT: I think he is **embarrass** that they don't understand about computers.

CORRECT: I think he is **embarrassed** that they don't understand about computers.

Activity 4.11

Now read and check the following sample. Are the verbal adjectives in the correct form? If there are errors, correct them.

1   Some people think computers are really excited. I
2   don't understand why. To me, they seem so boring. When-
3   ever a group of people get together and start discussing
4   and comparing computers, I get so boring that I think I
5   will scream. My brother spends all of his time playing
6   games on the computer and surfing the internet. Since we
7   have only one phone that means the phone is always busy.
8   My parents get really annoy with him when they find out
9   their friends are trying to call and they can't get
10   through. He says they just don't understand new things
11   and that they are scare of new technology. I think he is
12   embarrass that they don't understand about computers.

13   Computers are OK; they are really useful. However, I
14   am not interesting in knowing all about what is inside
15   them and how they work the way my brother and his friends
16   are. I use a computer to write my papers for homework and
17   we have to use them for our science labs too. Usually,
18   it works out pretty well, but once in a while something
19   goes wrong with the software and it gets so frustrate that
20   sometimes I just give up and use a pen and paper. Some-
21   times I call my brother to help me figure out what the
22   problem is, even though it is a little embarrassing to
23   admit that I can't figure it out by myself. He is usu-
24   ally pretty nice about it, though.

> In future drafts, you may see the abbreviation **v-adj**. This means there is an error in the verbal adjective form, and you need to repair it.

Here is a list of some common verbs that can be used in both the *-ing* and *-ed* adjective forms.

amaze	confuse	embarrass
amuse	convince	excite
annoy	depress	fascinate
astonish	disappoint	frighten
bore	disgust	interest

puzzle	surprise	upset (note that the
relax	thrill	-*ed* form is also
satisfy	tire	*upset*)

EDITING YOUR OWN WORK: THE FINAL DRAFT

Activity 4.12

A. *Check your draft to see if you have used any of these words in your writing. Have you used the appropriate form? If not, correct it for your final draft. You should also identify and correct any grammatical errors you can find. In particular, check for comma splices, run-on sentences, and fragments. If you are unsure of the meaning or form of any of the words you have used, look them up in a learner dictionary.*

B. *This is also the right time to review the strategies you wrote in your Learning Log. Use these strategies in preparing your final draft. Once you have finished editing, you are ready to turn in your final draft.*

LEARNING FROM YOUR FINAL DRAFT

Activity 4.13

Look over your final draft from this unit. You may also want to review your other final drafts. Are there some new grammar problems that you think you should start working on?

■ Choose at least one new entry for your Learning Log.

■ Decide on the strategy you are going to use to try to improve.

■ Include an Editing Practice if there is one. If there is no Editing Practice, consult with your instructor on a step-by-step strategy for improving your performance and write it down in your Learning Log.

Be sure to save your final draft after your instructor has read it so that you can refer to it when you write other papers.

Keep your Learning Log so that you can consult it when you are writing papers for other classes. It will help you to turn in papers with fewer grammatical errors. When your paper has fewer errors, your professor can concentrate on the content of your paper.

ATTITUDES ACROSS GENERATIONS

Task:
- Analyzing information from oral interviews

Writing Focus
- Taking risks

Editing Focus
- Present and past tense shifting

In the last unit, you analyzed some written material and offered some personal experience and advice to your readers. In this unit, you will gather information about the beliefs and practices of people in your community. In Unit Two, you used a written survey. This time, you will gather your information by conducting oral interviews. Oral interview data are sometimes more difficult to analyze than written survey data because there are often no clear numbers to use. The generalizations don't just jump out at you the way they sometimes do with numerical information. You will have to search through your data and make these generalizations yourself.

The topic of your interview will be to some degree up to you, but it will have something to do with people's views about how much immigrant communities should maintain their own culture and how much they need to adapt to a new one. The terms that are sometimes used to describe these two situations are *cultural maintenance*, that is, keeping up the culture that immigrants bring with them, and *cultural assimilation*, that is, moving toward the culture of the country in which they now live. People of different ages sometimes have vastly different views on which alternative is preferable. Often, too, younger and older people have different ideas about how they should live and behave, and how they should relate to other people. You will explore these issues in your interviews.

I. EXPLORING IDEAS

READINGS

Parents raise their children differently in different cultures and may have contrasting ideas about what their responsibilities are to their family. This article is from a book about teenagers in America. In this excerpt, the author interviews Steven Truong, whose family emigrated from Vietnam when he was a young boy. Truong talks about the very different ways teenagers are expected to behave in American and Vietnamese culture.

A Totally Alien Life Form: Teenagers

Sydney Lewis

Steven Truong: Chicago

We meet at a public library in Uptown, an inland port for immigrants from **Appalachia** to Southeast Asia. The library serves as the headquarters of What's Uptown?, a monthly newsletter put out by local high school kids, for which Steven is a columnist. He's wiry and edgy—twisting, swiveling and sprawling on the carpeted floor as we talk. "I don't know about being a **hyper** person, I just like to move," he says. "I can't sit still for long. The only time I'm still is when I'm sleeping. Sitting still is, like, boring and a waste of time." He notes that in May he'll be 16, able to get his driver's permit. His **alias** in the book is Michael Huang.

[What follows is in Steven's own words.]

In Vietnamese culture being a teen really has no meaning, because you have like maybe an ounce more freedom than when you were 2. The culture is very family oriented. You reach 18 and start working—you still live with your parents. And then you start raising them, you know what I mean? They raise you, you raise them, and then your children raise you. You are not really an individual, so rebelling and being a teen has no meaning—there's no point in it. Actually, if you do rebel, you're looked down upon, and every other teen thinks you're crazy.

In Asian culture disappointing your elders is a big **taboo**. If I do something bad, it's like my whole family has been cursed. I do something bad, my grandma thinks when she walks out in the street people are going to look at her. You are not an individual: Your actions affect everyone else. Which is not like the American way. I am myself, so you can kiss my . . . , for all I care! [laughs] And sometimes I bring that attitude home to my parents, which is terribly wrong. You know, going outside and coming back home are two different worlds—totally different. When I'm at school, the American way, I'll talk back to anyone I feel like. Of course, I know better. When I am at home I do not talk back to my parents. But sometimes I forget that I'm at home, [laughs] and I *will* talk back to my mother.

As a teenager, you're in an in-between stage. Your parents are like, "You're grown up," but then, "You're still a kid." You get two contrasting things going. I like to think I know everything but I really don't. Teenagers think they know everything because they know much more than they did when they were like 9 or

(continued on next page)

Appalachia a mountainous region of Kentucky and West Virginia

hyper (*slang*) short for *hyperactive*; unable to remain still

alias a false name

taboo something that is forbidden

(continued from previous page)

10 years old, and that's a really big leap. Since it's such a big leap, you think, "Oh, I've reached the **pinnacle** of knowledge—I can't be any smarter."

pinnacle the highest point

Some kids just rebel, because their parents are really strict and don't know how their life is. And there's no way, I mean, *no way*, your parents will know what you're going through. You gotta really make the effort to let it be known what's going on with you. But some of these kids, they're frustrated and they don't know what to do. They go home and it's all strict, then they go outside and they see how everyone else has freedom, how everyone else has the right to express themselves, and they don't—so they rebel. And that's where the gang thing comes in.

If you walk the other way down Broadway, you'll see by the video rental store so many of them standing there—in the summer outside, and in the winter inside—'cause there's an arcade in there. After school, they'll spend like maybe from 3 to 8 there. They don't know where they're going, no direction or anything. They're frustrated and they feel a sense of hopelessness because they think they're not gonna make it through their teenage years. All those kids, they wear their low, big, baggy clothes and stuff, just to be like everyone else. A lot of parents object to that, but what can they do?

Discussion Questions

According to Truong,

1. Why doesn't teen rebellion occur in Asian families?

2. Why does it occur in American families?

3. What happens when the two systems meet?

Sometimes after immigrants come to a new country as children and live there for some time, they find that some of their views are different from those of their parents or older generations, whereas some of their views remain the same.

Hardship and Dreams

My Mother and I
Vang Vang

Vang Vang, twenty-three, was born in Laos. When she was three, her family fled the Communist regime and lived in a refugee camp in Thailand. Two years later, they moved to the United States. She now lives in Boston and is in the process of becoming an American citizen.

"Tell me what you were like when you were my age," I asked my mother one winter afternoon when I was home from college. My mother stopped her sewing and looked up, surprised at my question. "I was never like you," she said. "I never dreamed of being a doctor, professor, or anything other than a wife, mother and grandmother. I was the eldest of twelve children and every waking moment was filled with work and responsibilities. Back then, there was only one career for girls, and it was being a hard-working wife." My mother grew up in Laos where, like most other people from the Hmong tribe, she lived with her family in a remote mountain village. She fled her homeland during the war in Vietnam, and became one of the 125,000 Hmong people now living in the United States.

Most Hmong refugees brought little with them but their traditions—including the custom of marrying young to preserve the race under **adverse** conditions. In Hmong culture, honor, respect and family solidarity **take precedence over** individual desires—and men, the bearers of the family name, take precedence over women. "Men are important," my mother would tell me when I asked why women always ate last. "They are stronger and wiser—therefore they always eat before us."

That winter afternoon I sat in silence until she spoke again. "This story is between us," she said, "because it is shameful for me to tell it. I hated my mother. I worked so hard for her. Every night—before washing the dishes, sweeping the floor, and preparing rice for tomorrow's meal, I would go into my parents' bedroom, wash their feet with warm water, and tuck them in for the night. My mother never once said, 'Thank you' or 'Chee Lee, you're a good girl.'"

I stared out the window, remembering how I grew up, always wanting to hear a word of praise from her, and getting only rules and expectations I could never live up to. I remembered the years she made me get up at six every morning and

adverse hostile, hurtful

take precedence over are more important than; come ahead of

(continued on next page)

(continued from previous page)

cook breakfast for the family before leaving for school. I remembered the slumber parties, dances and after-school sports that I missed because she didn't approve of them.

She looked down at her sewing and continued. "Nothing was ever good enough for my mother. I was glad to leave her when I married your father. Well, it's too late to tell her now, and she wouldn't understand anyway. And I know she did love me, even if she never said so. If she didn't, she wouldn't have cared whether I did my chores correctly or not."

I was too shocked to speak. Growing up, my mother had never initiated a serious conversation with me. It was always lectures about my attitude, clothes, and hairstyle; about how I'd have to control my anger and thirst for knowledge in order to be a good wife.

Through generations of **famine**, disease, and war, Hmong women had taught their daughters what they needed to survive: how to cook, clean, haul water, and manufacture textiles; how to be productive, obedient, respectful, and patient. But as a teenager growing up in America, I found it hard to take these lessons as evidence of love.

famine widespread starvation

"I told you this shameful story for a reason," my mother said. "Yes, I have many children, and I love them all. But you are my first child, the first in everything to me. I've been very strict and hard on you, but I raised you in the only way I knew how. I am proud of you."

The Tequila Luck Club

Eduardo Jiminez

Eduardo Jiminez, twenty-one, is the son of Mexican immigrants. He was born in Oakland, California.

There is a group of old men who sit around in my backyard in Oakland, talking about world politics and economics. They're Mexican men who have worked under the hot sun all their lives, and it has not only toughened them physically but transformed them mentally: They're proud people who don't trust anything they don't do with their own hands. They don't like it here in the United States, but they have families to feed, and my backyard is an oasis for them. There, they are members of the **Tequila** Luck Club. It's like **Amy Tan's *Joy Luck Club***, but instead of old Chinese women, the members are old Mexican men.

tequila a strong alcoholic drink made in Mexico

Amy Tan's *Joy Luck Club* a book about two generations of Chinese women

The Tequila Luck Club is a place where they're free to be men, drink hard, and discuss life with friends. They're not academically schooled, but they're commonsense wise. None went higher than elementary school, but they know exactly what effects **NAFTA** will have on Mexico, how the Mexican government is failing them, and what separates a good tequila from a bad one.

NAFTA an economic agreement between Mexico, the United States, and Canada

I used to sit in my room and look out the windows, wishing I could be part of the club. I was always too ashamed to go outside and join them, because I haven't

(continued on next page)

(continued from previous page)

worked a hard day in my life. My hands are soft from sitting behind a desk all day studying, while they are out constructing buildings and homes. More important, I felt I didn't belong because I am an American, not Mexican like they are.

I dreamed of doing something that would make them accept me, that would prove to them I was a man. I wasn't making my own living yet, and to them, that made me a kid. But last May, when my friends and I decided to go on a trip to **Tijuana**, I saw my chance. I remembered hearing stories about men smuggling bottles of tequila back from Mexico, and I decided that's what I'd do. I'd smuggle back some of the best bottles I could find and use them as an initiation offering. I thought I could handle whatever Tijuana tossed my way, but I was wrong. The club members had the street smarts to handle the temptations of that seedy city, but I was naive. Within hours of arriving I was picked up by two Mexican police officers. I'd been caught with an open bottle of tequila, walking through the streets like I owned them. I'd failed to obey the first law of the club—"Respect the host's home"—and now I was heading for a Tijuana jail. I had nothing to protect me but the money my dad had given me before I left. The officers told me to empty my pockets, and they took it all.

The cops took more than my money. They made me realize I was not a Mexican but an American tourist in my parents' homeland. They sent me home empty-handed—another club rule broken—insuring I'd never be a part of the group that assembled in my own backyard.

It turned out that I underestimated the Tequila Luck Club. I'd thought membership could be bought, but of course it couldn't. When I told the members what had happened in Tijuana, they laughed and laughed, and their laughter let me know I was accepted—even without a bottle to offer. They liked me not because of what I'd brought them, but because I'd gone on a life-experience journey.

Tijuana a Mexican city at the United States border

Dreaming in Estonian

Romy Ruukel

Romy Ruukel, nineteen, came to the United States from Parnu, Estonia, when she was twelve. She became an American citizen last year.

I remember how I used to sit at the kitchen table with my grandmother, begging her for stories about her childhood. My favorites were the ones about the land that was so far away I didn't even dare to dream of going there.

In my imagination, this fairy-tale kingdom called America was the greatest place in the world. Over there, they had so many flavors of ice cream and candy that you couldn't try them all in a lifetime. They had Barbie dolls and toys I'd only seen in magazines, and happy people who never stopped smiling.

My grandmother had traveled to America, and I yearned to know every detail—what she'd eaten, what she'd seen on TV, what the children there had been

(continued on next page)

(continued from previous page)

like. Compared to my reality in Estonia—standing in line for hours for a loaf of bread, never knowing if we'd have heat or hot water in the apartment when we woke up in the morning—it all seemed miraculous.

When I was 11, my mother took a trip to the United States to visit her aunt. She called one afternoon a few weeks later. "She says she's got wonderful news," my grandmother told me. "She's met a wonderful guy and gotten married." At first, I didn't understand. It was as if the words had no meaning. When they finally registered, I burst into tears and ran into my room. My mother wasn't coming back. As time passed, I got used to the idea and hoped it meant I would get to go there myself. A year later, I did.

My stepfather tells me that when I first stepped off the plane, all he could see were my big brown eyes, wide open, looking around in awe. At first, America met all my expectations. Going to Safeway for the first time and seeing the huge variety of food took my breath away. All the people I met were happy and smiling. And I couldn't get over the 52 channels we got on cable—50 more than we'd had in Estonia.

There were so many new things that I wanted to try—but soon I realized I couldn't afford most of them. It didn't take me long to realize how naive I'd been to think that everyone in America would be rich and happy. Back in Estonia, I had never encountered gangs or drug dealers. I had never met any homeless people either, and for a long time I didn't know how to act when I saw them standing on street corners, asking for money. This wasn't what America was supposed to be like.

At night I'd lie in bed with my eyes squeezed shut and imagine I was still in my old room. Sometimes I fooled myself into thinking that I would wake up to the sounds of my grandmother making breakfast and my grandfather listening to the news on the radio. Somehow I had forgotten the troubles back home, and the country I had left replaced America as the wonderful place of my dreams.

There's so much that I miss from home: the sound snow made under my boots when I hurried to school on winter mornings, the first day of school when we all got dressed up and brought flowers to our teachers, seeing my whole family around the dinner table on my birthday.

Last winter, I went back to visit Parnu. It felt so good to find my roots. My friends had changed, but so had I. Estonia will always be the country of my childhood memories, but America is the country of my future. As for constantly wishing I'm wherever I'm not—I think that will always be my nature.

Discussion Questions

1. What do you think Vang Vang thought about her mother before she heard her mother's story? What about after she heard the story?

2. Why does Eduardo Jiminez say he had underestimated the Tequila Luck Club?

3. What is the difference in the way Romy Ruukel views life in America and the way her grandmother viewed life in America? Why do you think their views are different?

Cultural differences between immigrant groups and Americans who have been here for generations can occur in many aspects of home and work life. As the values of immigrant children begin to shift, there are sometimes clashes between the generations. This article examines differences between the ways Americans and immigrant groups choose to discipline their children.

For Many Immigrants, a Cultural Reluctance to Spare the Rod
Celia W. Dugger

The immigrant mothers sat along the edges of Brooklyn playgrounds and talked about two methods of discipline: the American way, and the way they brought with them from their homelands. American parents, they say, give a young child a timeout or ground an older one, then may even feel guilty about it. The immigrant parents believe sterner is better, they say. They would slap a fresh mouth, spank a disrespectful child or beat one who dared to lie or skip school.

But that approach requires them to walk a fine line. If they administered the kind of **lickings** they endured while growing up in the islands, they say, they might lose their own children to foster care, or even face arrest. "The first thing a child learns here, 'If you spank me, I'll call 911,'" said Emma Henderson, a mother of three who grew up in Dominica. "There's something wrong about it."

At a time city planners estimate that more than half of New York's population is made up of immigrants and their children, one of the central cultural clashes is about where spanking ends and child abuse begins. Many immigrants, from cabdrivers to baby sitters to schoolteachers, say Americans spoil their children by **sparing the rod**. The police and child protection workers are too quick to cry abuse, they say.

The child protection system, with many social workers who are themselves immigrants, has not had an easy time resolving some cultural differences. Critics say that too often, caseworkers judge **excessive** punishment as acceptable, and have called for better training for agency workers.

These issues have come to the fore in two recent child welfare cases, with the arrest of a Nigerian immigrant charged with assaulting his son, whose wrist was found to be broken, and of a Cambodian immigrant couple that the authorities said beat their disobedient daughter with a plastic curtain rod. The Nigerian father, Shakiru Adebayo, told the police he was following the disciplinary ways of his coun-

(continued on next page)

lickings beatings

sparing the rod deciding not to hit children as punishment

excessive too much

(continued from previous page)

try. The city caseworker who investigated an earlier abuse report on the family had decided the beatings of the boy were signs not of abuse, but of the father's cultural beliefs, school officials said. But Olikoye Ransome-Kuti, a pediatrician who was minister of health in Nigeria from 1985 to 1993, said last week that Adebayo, if guilty of the charges, had crossed the line into brutality even in the context of his own culture. Breaking a child's wrist is "clearly **beyond the pale**," said Ransome-Kuti, now a consultant to the World Bank in Washington.

beyond the pale over the line of appropriateness; too much

In New York City, city officials concede, the city has done a poor job in recent years of training the new workers to make complex judgment calls about when a child is being abused. In a confidential November 1995 memo, Gene D. Skarin, associate general counsel of the city's Human Resources Administration, voiced alarm about caseworkers who have lived in the United States only a few years and see "excessive **corporal punishment** being an acceptable form of discipline."

corporal punishment physical punishment

Immigrants who think that hitting is the best way to teach children to be respectful and studious are running into a contrary view, held by many doctors, psychiatrists and social workers, that physical discipline can deaden a child's spirit and lead to violence later in life. That view, along with a growing awareness of child abuse, has contributed to an **evolving** definition in the United States of what constitutes excessive corporal punishment, which is against the law. In many parts of the country, and in New York in previous decades, for example, principals routinely paddled the mischievous. But for more than 30 years, corporal punishment has been forbidden in New York City schools.

evolving changing

Immigration experts say the issue is a highly **charged** one for many people locating in the New York metropolitan area from all over the globe: Nigerians, West Indians, Dominicans, Mexicans, Eastern Europeans and Russians, among others. Often, the parents have come to America for the sake of their children, only to feel they are losing them to the rebellious ways of American youth. Separated from the extended family members and neighbors who had helped keep children **in line** back home, and separated from their children by the long hours they put in at work, panicky immigrant parents may rely more on harsh discipline, experts say. Mary C. Waters, a Harvard University sociologist who interviewed West Indian immigrants and their children in New York City from 1991 to 1993, said corporal punishment was the central issue for them. "When I asked what's different about the United States," she said, "they said: 'The state comes between you and your children. Americans don't discipline their children well, and when you do it the right way, there's the danger your kids can call social services on you.' They **were at a loss** as to how to discipline your child if you couldn't hit them. It cut across class lines."

charged emotional

in line in order; behaving properly

were at a loss did not know

Una Clarke, a Jamaican-born City Council member from Queens, said that immigrants must learn new ways to discipline their children as part of their adaptation to American culture. When she worked for the city supervising day care centers, Ms. Clarke said, she tried to teach parents, for example, that they can tell children they will not get a new pair of sneakers until they behave. "Many families saw that

(continued on next page)

(continued from previous page)

as bribery," she said. "You have to tell them it's a reward for appropriate behavior. Clearly, there is a clash of values. But the law of this country has to be one law."

The conflict between West Indian parents and children is intensified by the particular pattern of their migration, in which the mother typically arrives first, with her children following years later, often as teen-agers. Parents then discipline children who are resentful at having been left behind, and who in some cases may not know their parents well.

"The kids all knew they could call **D.S.S.** on their parents," Professor Waters said. "When new kids arrived from the West Indies, that was one of the first things they'd tell each other. They saw it as a lever to use against their parents. They could threaten this and maybe reduce the beating they were going to get."

D.S.S. Department of Social Services—the department in charge of child welfare in New York City

George Mathelier, a Haitian immigrant, said he sees the power struggle between immigrant parents and children taking place at Prospect Heights High School in Brooklyn, where he is a social worker. The Caribbean children who were used to beatings in their schools in the islands "quickly realize the system here is lax and loose and they can get away with murder." He described the case of a 14-year-old Haitian who had been neglecting his homework and taking money from his parents. His father, a cabdriver, gave him a beating and the son called 911. The father was arrested and taken away in handcuffs. The case was resolved with a court recommendation of family counseling. The father pretended he was no longer angry, Mathelier said. Next summer, the family went to Haiti on vacation. At the airport there, the father pulled out a leather strap and whipped his son on the spot. Two days later, the family flew back to New York, leaving the teen-ager in Haiti with relatives.

The clash of cultures is especially acute for the thousands of immigrant women who work as baby sitters, often 50 or more hours a week caring for the children of upper-middle-class professionals. Daily they come face to face with two opposing attitudes toward discipline. Barbara Solomon, who was a schoolteacher in Tobago, took a job as a baby sitter when she first immigrated two years ago. One day, the 4-year-old girl in her care came in from school and dropped her coat and lunch bag on the floor. "I told her to take it up," Ms. Solomon said. "She started screaming and **throwing a tantrum**. I thought, 'If she was my 4-year-old, I would have slapped her.' Her brother picked up for her. She told me her mom did not allow her to put her things away. I believe in children learning to pick up after themselves." Ms. Solomon, who now works 12-hour shifts seven nights a week caring for an elderly person and spends another 20 hours a week in college studying tourism, said her four children have not challenged her right to discipline them. She said she tells them that if she cannot punish them here she will take them home to do it, an effective threat since they love living in the United States. "Beating or flogging a child was the parents' way of getting them to conform," she said. "It's because we love them that we use it."

throwing a tantrum having an emotional outburst, often including lying on the floor, kicking, and crying

Like many other West Indian parents, Ms. Solomon said she understood the difference between discipline and abuse. She said she was careful not to bruise her

(continued on next page)

(continued from previous page)

children or hit them so hard their skin swells. She said she always explained the reason for the spanking. "If I cannot beat them and they get out there, the police will shoot them when they do wrong," she said. "I love my children more than the system loves them."

The immigrant mothers in Brooklyn talked of their own mothers' pelting them with whatever came to hand, a bar of soap, a cup, a pot spoon; or whipping them with a broomstick, a shoe or a **switch**. Ingrid Neverson, a 24-year-old from St. Vincent, who works as a baby sitter, vividly remembered the time she told her grandmother she was going to the library to study, but instead went to the beach. Her uncle spotted her and called the grandmother.

switch stick or twig used for beating

When Ms. Neverson got home, her grandmother found her wet bathing suit, took the 15-year-old Ms. Neverson to the bedroom and gave her a beating that left welts all over her back. "It was long," she said. "It was painful." At the time, Ms. Neverson tried to move in with her father or her grandfather, but both backed up her grandmother. Now, she said, she thinks that her grandmother did the right thing.

As the 2-year-old boy she looks after tugged affectionately on her hand at a playground in Prospect Park, Ms. Neverson seemed shocked when asked if she had ever slapped him. She said the boy is well disciplined and that she would never hit him. When asked what she would do when she has children of her own, she replied: "I would spank my kids. Those are my kids. I would discipline them how I see fit."

Discussion Questions

1. How much corporal punishment, if any, do you think is appropriate from parents? at school?

2. Are American-born children spoiled?

3. Should the government have a say in how parents discipline their children?

Thinking about the Topic

For your paper, you will interview people of different ages from your community on a topic related to cultural maintenance and assimilation. First, however, you must select the topic for your interview.

Often younger and older generations have different views about traditions, behavior, education, relationships, rules, and responsibility.

Activity 5.1

Discuss some of the following questions with your classmates. This activity may help you to focus on an issue that interests you.

1. Have you or your siblings ever had a conflict with your parents, when you thought their views or their rules were old-fashioned? Have you or your friends

ever felt that your parents were acting as if they were still in their home country? Do you think their expectations of you are fair?

2. In the United States, children's views are often different from those of their parents; we call this a "generation gap." Some people say that this doesn't exist in other cultures. What do you think? Do you share most of your parents' opinions? Do you think there is a bigger or smaller "generation gap" in immigrant families than in American-born families?

Activity 5.2

A. *What are some of the areas that you think cause the greatest conflict between parents and their children as they grow up? The last reading selection mentioned discipline. Some other possibilities include:*

- rules for seeing friends, dating
- importance of education
- children's responsibility to their family

These are just a few suggestions. With a classmate, make a list of some others.

_____

_____

_____

_____

Now combine your suggestions with those of your classmates. Make a list on the blackboard.

B. *You will need to focus on some specific topics in your interviews. Look at the list the class has created as well as the topics that were suggested in part A. You may notice that many of the topics are somewhat related, for instance, children's responsibility in the family and discipline. In doing your interview, it makes sense to choose two related topics. This will help your interviews go more smoothly because questions about one topic will flow naturally into questions about the other topic. At the same time, two topics will ensure that you will always have plenty to talk about.*

Which two topics do you think you would like to explore in your interview? Write them here.

1. _____

_____

2. _____

_____

C. *Finally, you need to state the aim of your interview project. This will help you stay focused on your topic. What are you trying to find out? Write it here.*

_____

2. GATHERING INFORMATION AND DRAFTING

PREPARING FOR AN INTERVIEW

To gather information for your paper, you will need to interview six people from your community: three from your parents' generation and three from your own generation. When you choose the participants, you may include members of your family such as aunts or uncles, but not your own parents, brothers, or sisters.

The next step is to think about how to conduct an interview. What kind of questions are you going to ask? How will you get people to tell you their opinions? In Unit Two, you wrote a questionnaire that a fairly large number of people filled out and returned to you. This task will involve fewer people but they will respond in much more detail. Once again, you must ask yourself what makes a good question. Because an interview is a sort of guided conversation, the questions will be a little different from those in Unit Two. You still want to get beyond a simple "yes" or "no" answer and to find more information, but because you will be participating in the conversation, you can ask different kinds of questions.

An example may help make this clearer: One student interviewed people about discipline in the family. One of the things he wanted to find out was how the two generations thought children should act toward their parents. The first question he asked was:

```
Do you want your children to do whatever you say?
```

How do you think people would answer this question? Most people will probably either say "yes" or perhaps will find the question difficult to answer. Should they do **whatever** their parents say? That is not a simple question for everyone. In either case, the answers may not be very informative. Look at how the student rewrote this question.

```
Do you think children should do whatever their parents say?

Why or why not?
```

This is better because it asks for an opinion and an explanation about children in general, rather than about their own children. It's likely that the student will find out more in some of the interviews than if he had asked the first question, but he still may find that people give a very short answer. What else can he do to improve the question? Perhaps if he gave some context or background for the question, it would be easier to get people talking. Look at what this student finally ended up asking:

```
Some people say kids today don't respect their parents be-
cause they don't always do everything their parents tell
them to do. Do you think this is true?
```

This form of the question not only gives people something to agree or disagree with but is also much more conversational than the previous questions.

This can help people relax and talk more. This form of the question also leads naturally into follow-up questions such as:

```
What do you think parents should do if their children dis-
obey them?
```

Every question should have follow-up questions that address specific issues you want to explore. It is important to prepare follow-up questions for every question that you write so that the conversation continues and you can gather the information you need.

Drafting Questions

Think about the two issues you want to explore in your interviews; you will need to write a series of questions on these topics. There are several things to keep in mind as you work on this. First, as we just mentioned, the interview should be in the form of a conversation, so structure your questions with this in mind.

Second, every interview will be different. Some people will talk more readily than others. If someone is telling you a lot, you may not ask as many questions as you would of someone who is more hesitant. The point is that you should have plenty of questions ready, but you may not use all of them in every interview.

Finally, in some instances you may end up with slightly different questions for the different generations. Using the same example of discipline, the student might ask someone from the older generation:

```
How were you disciplined by your parents if you disobeyed
them? Is it different from the way you discipline your own
children?
```

He then might ask someone from the younger generation:

```
How have your parents disciplined you? Do you think you
would discipline your own children in the same way?
```

The questions are slightly different, but the topic is the same.

Activity 5.3

Write at least ten questions for each issue you have chosen.

_____

_____

_____

_____

_____

_____

_____

_____

_____

_____

_____

_____

_____

_____

_____

_____

_____

Revising Questions

Activity 5.4

Now that you have a draft of your interview questions, exchange it with a partner.

A. *Read your partner's draft and answer these questions.*

1. Do you understand all the questions? If not, what is unclear?

2. Is there enough context given in the questions?

3. Are there follow-up questions?

4. Are there questions that can be answered with just a "yes" or "no"?

5. What other suggestions can you make?

6. After reading the questions, are there any others you think your partner should ask?

B. *Reread your interview questions and look at your partner's responses. Revise your questions using your partner's responses and any new ideas you have.*

Practicing the Interviews

Activity 5.5

After you have made your revisions, it is a good idea to practice your interviewing techniques on a classmate before you conduct an actual interview.

A. *Using the questions you have developed for a member of the younger generation, interview a classmate. Take notes as if you were doing a real interview. When you take notes, focus on getting down the main idea or what you think is most important. Sometimes people will talk a lot; some of what they say will be relevant and some of it won't. Don't try to write down everything they say or to write out whole sentences. If you try to write out the whole conversation as you go, you will be so busy that the conversation may stop altogether!*

B. *After you have finished this practice interview, you may find that some questions worked better than others and that you need to make more revisions. What happened when you interviewed your partner?*

1. Did your partner give many one-word answers? If so, for which questions?

2. Look at those questions again. Do you need to provide more context? Do you need to ask a different question before asking this question? Do you need to change the question completely?

3. If your partner never stopped talking and you couldn't ask some of your important questions, how can you change your questions to get the answers you need?

Make any changes you think are needed and prepare the final draft of your questions.

Finally, if you think the person you are interviewing would be more comfortable talking in his or her first language, you should be prepared to ask your questions in that language. You may wish to prepare a second set of your interview questions in that language.

Conducting the Interviews

Once you have completed the final draft of your questions, you are ready to start your interviews. You should be prepared to take notes during the interviews. You should also try to use a tape recorder if possible. This will help you later on when you prepare to write your essay. **If you do decide to tape the interviews, make sure you have permission from the person you are interviewing**. It is very important that people agree to be taped. Sometimes people are a little nervous at the beginning of an interview, especially if there is a tape recorder. However, most people will relax and forget about the recorder after the first few minutes.

ANALYZING THE DATA

Now that you have completed your interviews, you need to consider how to use this information in your paper. In transforming this information into material for an essay, the first and most important thing you will need to do is look through your material and see if you can make some generalizations. Look over your notes or, if you have recorded your interviews, review your tapes. What general statements can you make about the responses to your questions? For example:

- Were the responses of all the older people similar? the younger people? In what respect?

- Were the two generations' responses similar on one topic, for example, marriage, but different on another, for example, dating?

- What were the reasons that they gave for their responses? Can you make any generalizations? For instance, older respondents may have said their children must marry only members of their own community because others would not understand their culture. Younger people may say they must do so to please their parents.

Activity 5.6

On the lines that follow, write the generalizations you have made based on your data:

_____

_____

_____

_____

_____

_____

_____

_____

_____

DRAFTING: WRITING YOUR FIRST DRAFT

You should make a plan before you actually begin writing. Remember the essential elements of body paragraphs.

■ Use the generalizations from Activity 5.6 to write claim sentences for body paragraphs.

■ Use actual interview responses to support your claims.

You may have heard many interesting or moving stories from the people you interviewed. Using these stories in your essay can make it more colorful and interesting to read. Can any of the stories you heard dramatically illustrate the claims you have made? If so, be sure to use them in your body paragraphs.

Note what you plan to include in your body paragraphs. The next step is your introduction. Don't forget the elements that you need to have in your introductory paragraph. Finally, you should think about how you would like to conclude the paper. In Unit Three, you learned that a summary of your findings is not always the most effective way to end a paper, especially because the reader has just finished reading about them. Instead, it is a good idea to think about what your information means. You should try to answer the question in the reader's mind, "So what?" Can you evaluate the significance of what you found in your interviews? For instance:

■ If you found conflicting views, how might things turn out for this family? for this community?

■ If you found no conflict, what do you think that means?

This kind of information belongs in your conclusion. Now you are ready to put together your essay.

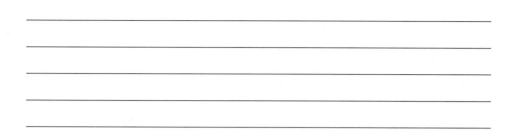

Drafting Tip—Tense Use in Reporting Interview Data

 When you write up your interview information in your paper, frequently you will have to report what other people said. It is sometimes difficult to choose which tense to use when you are doing this kind of reporting. Use the following guidelines to help you decide.

It is possible to use many different tenses when you are reporting the results of your interviews. These guidelines describe the **simplest** way.

There will be two verbs in your sentence:

(1) the reporting verb in the independent clause, such as *say, claim, report, believe*

(2) some other verb in the dependent clause

You need to be sure that the tense in each one is correct.

Example:

The older respondents claim that teenagers today do not respect their parents.
                                (1)   (2)

This is the easiest way to be sure you are doing it right:

(1) The reporting verb can be in the present or the past. This is because it is true in **both** the present and the past. They claimed it when you interviewed them, but it's likely that they still claim it today. As a result, either of the next two sentences would be fine.

(a) *The older respondents **claim** that teenagers today do not respect their parents.*

(b) *The older respondents **claimed** that teenagers today do not respect their parents.*

(2) The verb in the dependent clause should reflect when something actually happens. The preceding example sentence is about teenagers *today*, so it should be in the **present**.

*The older respondents claim that teenagers today **do** not respect their parents.*

You could also report on some action, habit, or belief from the **past**:

Example:

*Young women reported that their parents **did not let** them date when they **were** in high school.*

There are many other ways to report what people say. If you learned another way, go ahead and write it that way. These are simply guidelines to use if you are not sure about how to report the information you found in your interviews.

3. REVISING

 ### EVALUATING ESSAYS

Once again, you will look at what two other students wrote about this topic.

Student Essay 1

1 People have different ideas about how young people
2 should behave. These differences are sometimes based on
3 age and on culture. I interviewed six Korean and Korean-
4 American people, three younger and three older, about
5 dating practices. I asked what they thought about Korean-
6 American kids dating people from different backgrounds and
7 whether they thought they should follow any special rules
8 about dating.

9 The two groups gave different responses about dating
10 non-Koreans. Two of the older people said they should only
11 date Koreans; one person said dating other people is fine.
12 However, he said that for marriage, the young person
13 should choose a person with the same background. For young
14 people, the responses were the opposite. Two people thought
15 dating other people was no problem, but one person said
16 he would only date or marry Korean girls. The first two
17 also thought that marriage to a person of a different na-
18 tionality was all right. The next question I asked the
19 respondents was about their own children, whether they
20 thought they would date or marry someone with a differ-
21 ent background. All of them said no, because other peo-
22 ple don't understand Korean culture and this would cause
23 problems, especially if they marry. For example, usually
24 Korean children, especially the first son, have to serve
25 their parents after the parents grow old. People of other
26 nationalities may not understand this. Each of the three
27 younger people had a different idea. The first one said
28 when she becomes a parent, she will let her children de-
29 cide. The second one said he would only let his child marry
30 a non-Korean if the other person agreed to follow Korean
31 culture. The last one said he would never let his chil-
32 dren date or marry non-Korean people.

33 All of the respondents said they have special rules
34 about dating. One young respondent said she will only date

35 someone who has a good job with good pay. She wants to
36 marry someone who is rich, smart and Korean. If he is not,
37 she will not go out with him. I asked the respondents what
38 they would do if they didn't like their parents' rules.
39 All the older respondents and two of the younger ones said
40 they would follow them anyway. One of the younger people
41 said that if he didn't like them, he would break the rules
42 and do what he wanted. For example, if he liked an Amer-
43 ican girl and wanted to marry her but his parents didn't
44 like it, he would marry her anyway. He would do this even
45 if he had to leave his family.

46 From all of these responses, I can say that there is
47 a big difference between younger and older people. Usu-
48 ally old people don't want to make trouble so they fol-
49 low the old ways. Some young people will break with the
50 old style and follow their own way. Sometimes it is hard
51 to change from the old ways, but if it is a serious sit-
52 uation like love, it is important to follow your heart.

Esther

Student Essay 2

53 We learn about how to create and keep relationships
54 with other people from our parents. Every culture has a
55 different way of educating its children and the parents
56 seem to be an engine pushing their children to grow up
57 and become good members of society. The United States is
58 a country of many cultures and when people come from dif-
59 ferent places, sometimes ideas change and sometimes par-
60 ents and children do not agree about changes. I interviewed
61 six people from two generations about their relationships
62 with their friends, parents, and children. The generations
63 agree on some points and disagree on others.

64 The two generations gave me a lot of information
65 about how they communicate with their friends and neigh-

66 bors. Now we are living in the United States, where peo-
67 ple are always busy and running a race against time. Peo-
68 ple do not always have time to spend with their family,
69 friends and neighbors. The older people spend more time
70 visiting their neighbors and meeting them at church. Most
71 of them work, so they only have time to do this on week-
72 ends. One woman said she feels her life has more meaning
73 when she spends time with her neighbors and shares food
74 with them. She sometimes feels bored and lonely, espe-
75 cially at work. When she sees her friends, even if it is
76 for a little while, she feels that she is flying in the
77 sky because she can share her sadness and happiness. One
78 other person says she is lonely sometimes but she must
79 work hard at two jobs so she can save money to go back
80 to her country and visit relatives. She has no time for
81 friends and neighbors.

82   The younger people have a different idea from the
83 older generation. They have more opportunity to meet their

84 friends. One person said she usually goes out on week-
85 ends, for a party or a picnic. I was surprised that her
86 parents allowed her to go out freely. She said that in
87 her country her parents had not let her do this because
88 they did not trust her. They would not let her go out
89 alone or with friends. When she turned twenty, her par-
90 ents saw her confidence and self-esteem and they began to
91 change in the way they treated her. They trusted her and
92 knew that she would not dishonor the family. However, not
93 all young people have this freedom.

94   The two generations also have different ideas about
95 how they should treat their children. The older people
96 are much stricter. They told me many things about how they
97 were disciplined when they were children in their coun-
98 try. All three of the older respondents were women and
99 they all reported that when they were young, they were
100 not allowed to go to school. They studied only at home.
101 Their parents believed that nice girls should stay at
102 home, take care of babies, cook, and keep the house. One
103 woman said that each time she made a mistake, her father
104 became exceedingly mad at her and beat her with a stick.
105 Once, she feel asleep at the table while she was study-
106 ing and her father hit her with a metal cup until she
107 bled. Her life was not easy then. She said her life was
108 like a dark sky and she had no chance to see the sun's
109 light. She could not go anywhere or enjoy her life. She
110 had no opportunity to continue her education although her
111 dream was to become a useful person in society.

112   When this generation came to the United States, many
113 things changed. Americans have different ideas about dis-
114 cipline and many young people started to change to Amer-
115 ican ideas. One of them said that her father's ideas have
116 changed too. As children, they were spanked when they mis-
117 behaved but now they are allowed to make phone calls and
118 go out with friends and sometimes come home late from par-
119 ties. One girl told me she feels closer to her parents
120 than before because she can talk about important things.

121 However, another person told me that nothing has changed.

122 She is not allowed to go anywhere but school. She is for-

123 bidden to talk on the phone except in emergencies. Her

124 parents expect so many things from her. It upset her even

125 to talk about it with me. She told me that one day her

126 friend came to invite her to go skating. Even though her

127 father knew nothing about her friend, he started yelling

128 at the friend. She was so embarrassed that she cried all

129 day. Of course, he did not allow her to go skating. Now

130 she is ashamed to talk to her friend.

131   Every culture and every family has a different view

132 of relationships and different way of treating children.

133 It depends on one's culture and experience. Often, younger

134 and older generations have different ideas. All parents

135 want their children to be successful and to bring happi-

136 ness to the family. Sometimes it is very hard for immi-

137 grant families. Some families try to do this by keeping

138 their own culture; some keep some things and adapt some

139 things from the new culture. It seems that the second way

140 works better. If they think only their culture is the best

141 way to educate their children, their minds will be like

142 a box and never broaden. The girl who was not allowed to

143 skate will not benefit from her father's bondage, even

144 though he wants a good future for her. The younger gen-

145 eration will change even if the older one does not. If

146 that happens, it will be very difficult for families to

147 communicate with each other.

Pang

Throughout this book, you have had guidance in responding to sample es-says or to your peers' papers, either in Response Sheets or simply with a set of questions. By now, you could probably write your own questions about Es-ther's and Pang's drafts. In fact, that is precisely what you will do now.

Activity 5.7

A. *Think back over the responding activities you have done in this book, and then think about this assignment in particular. What are the most important elements of a good paper? Go through the two sample essays step by step—the introduction, body,* *and conclusion. Think about what claims the writers make and what support they offer.*

1. Write about eight questions.

2. Leave blank spaces after each question.

3. Make at least two copies of this Response Sheet.

B. *Exchange your Response Sheet with your partner. What do you think of the questions? Discuss your views with your partner.*

- Did your partner write useful questions?

- Did he or she ask about important things?

- Did he or she omit important issues?

C. *Based on your discussion with your partner and any new ideas you have, make any necessary revisions in your Response Sheet. Make three copies. You will use the first two in Activity 5.8. Save the third for later.*

Activity 5.8   *Use the Response Sheet you developed in Activity 5.7 to respond to Esther's and Pang's drafts.*

❧ WRITING FOCUS: TAKING RISKS

Think again about the two essays to which you have just responded. Is one better? Why did you choose one over the other? Think about how you felt as you read each one. Did one make you feel differently than the other?

As you probably noted on your Response Sheets, both essays have an introduction that tells where the information came from and that gives a main point. Both also have body paragraphs with clear points and enough evidence to support those points. Pang states in her conclusion what she thinks this information means. Esther's conclusion, however, simply summarizes the information in the body rather than evaluating it in any way. This is a major difference between the essays for two reasons. First, Pang's essay fulfills this part of the assignment, but Esther's does not. Second, the evaluation in Pang's essay makes it more interesting because it answers that familiar question—**"So what?"**—and gives readers more than just the findings from the survey. Aside from the conclusion, which Esther needs to revise, the two essays both have all the elements you worked on in Units One through Four.

What else sets them apart? Pang's paper not only has all the basic elements, but also has a lot of detail that makes the essay richer and more complete. In the first body paragraph, for example, she describes in lines 72–75 how one woman feels about her life. First she writes:

```
One woman says she feels her life has more meaning when she
spends time with her neighbors and shares her food with
them. She sometimes feels bored and lonely, especially at
work.
```

Pang could stop there and it would be sufficient, but she goes on.

```
When she sees her friends, even if it is for a little
while, she feels that she is flying in the sky because she
can share her sadness and happiness.
```

Adding this kind of detail is the difference between writing an adequate, acceptable paper and taking a risk to include richer material. Pang's essay is not perfect. In fact, there are parts of the paper that need some clarification, as you probably noted earlier in your Response Sheet. The point is that she has gone beyond the basics of fulfilling the assignment and made a creative effort to interest her readers.

Esther's paper demonstrates a more conservative approach. This does not mean that Esther's paper is bad; there are many things that she has done well. Again, the paper has most of the basic elements and is clearly written. In this respect, it is stronger than Pang's, but it lacks the richness of detail that Pang's essay has.

EVALUATING YOUR OWN WORK

Activity 5.9

As in the last unit, you will be responding to your own first draft and trying to come up with ideas to improve it for the second draft. This time, instead of using guidelines in the book, you will use the Response Sheet that you developed for Esther's and Pang's first drafts to guide your revisions. You should still have an extra blank copy.

Now leave your paper and do something else for a while. You will be able to look at it with "new eyes" when you come back to it later. This may not seem so important to you but, in fact, you do a lot of thinking and revising when you don't actually have the paper in front of you. You may get ideas about the paper when you are doing other things. This is one of the reasons it is important to leave enough time to write your paper and not wait until the last minute to do it.

Activity 5.10

Read over your Response Sheet. Do you wish to make any changes to your draft? Use these lines to make a revision plan.

_____

_____

_____

_____

_____

_____

_____

_____

_____

_____

_____
_____
_____
_____
_____
_____
_____
_____
_____
_____
_____
_____

WRITING YOUR SECOND DRAFT

Now write your second draft, using the ideas you have developed here.

4. EDITING

Editing Practice

#5 Present and past tense

Choosing the right tense is a difficult part of writing. It is important that the tense you choose reflect the time in which the event is taking place. Sometimes this is difficult because you may be writing about both the past and the present. One of the most common problems for second language writers is not marking tense at all.

Read through the writing samples and then look at the guidelines.

Sample 1

1   When I live in Hong Kong, I had a best friend. She
2 lived in China all her life so when she come to Hong Kong
3 she didn't speak Cantonese very much. She never studied
4 Cantonese either. Cantonese is the major language of Hong
5 Kong. She was a nice girl and she was very friendly to
6 me. We became friends very quickly and soon we are doing
7 everything together.

8   When we were in school, she have a big language bar-
9 rier and she have a lot of problems with her studies. She
10 only understands the teacher a little bit, so I tried to
11 explain what the teacher is saying to her. We always did
12 our homework together. She helped me too because she study
13 more math than me back in China so she is able to help
14 me with that. We help each other. However, because she
15 had the language barrier, she have to study harder on
16 her own.

17   One thing she try to do to improve her Cantonese is
18 watch the TV programs. Most TV programs in Hong Kong were
19 in Cantonese. Although she only understand a little bit
20 in the beginning, she kept watching every day and soon
21 her Cantonese begin to improve. She listened to the ra-
22 dio too. She say this was very helpful to her. Because
23 of her experience, now I think radio and TV are good ways
24 to learn a new language. So sometimes I listen to the ra-
25 dio and TV in English to improve my language.

26   My friend still lives in Hong Kong, but now I live
27 in the United States. Last week I received a letter from
28 her. She likes Hong Kong very much now. She told me that
29 now she had many friends and there is no more language
30 barrier with her friends. She could speak Cantonese very
31 well now. She still missed me a lot when she thinks about
32 the time we are in school together. She is very glad that
33 I am going to college and now she is going to college
34 next year too. I am very happy for her. I hope someday

35 she can visit me in Chicago or maybe I can visit her in
36 Hong Kong.

Sample 2

37 Arab parents in the U.S. like their sons and daughters to
38 marry other Arabs. They think if their children marry for-
39 eign people, they will have difficulty communicating and
40 have different daily routines. In order to marry other
41 Arabs, the parents have taught their children to meet more
42 Arab friends. The parents still accept foreign friends,
43 but not the ones that their daughter or son wants to
44 marry.

45   One of my best friends, Ali, had this problem. He met
46 an Irish lady named Carmen and they date for about one
47 year. His parents didn't know it. One day, Ali came home
48 to tell his parents that he wants to marry Carmen. His
49 parents opposed it. His mother says she have a hard time
50 communicating with his girlfriend. She doesn't understand
51 what Carmen said. Also, she said she spoke Arabic and Car-
52 men spoke English. So they cannot communicate with each
53 other.

54   Ali's mother also said they have different daily rou-
55 tines. Arab daughters-in-law have to wake up early in the
56 morning to clean up the house and to cook the breakfast.
57 In the afternoon, they have to wash the clothes and cook
58 lunch. Arab daughters-in-law have to do all housework.
59 Then, his mother said Carmen knows nothing about it. Af-
60 ter an hour arguing about this problem, his parents said
61 they do not accept her as their daughter-in-law. Ali said
62 he wants to marry Carmen no matter what they say because
63 he really loves Carmen. Then his father said he will not
64 give any money to him. So this was the big problem for
65 Ali and Carmen. But Ali still wanted to marry Carmen.

66   After they argue, Ali started to find some more
67 money. He worked three jobs a day. He worked in the auto

68 repair company in the morning. In the afternoon he helps
69 people fix air conditioners and he worked in a restaurant
70 at night. Still they need more money because it's not
71 enough. Their wedding party is two weeks away. Then he
72 comes up with the idea to sell his boat. He really likes
73 this boat. However, he also really loves Carmen, so he
74 sold it. Then their wedding party was on time. His fa-
75 ther did not come to the wedding because he didn't want
76 Ali to marry Carmen. Ali's mother did come to the wed-
77 ding because she really loves Ali and also because Ali
78 was the eldest son in the family. In Arab eyes, the el-
79 dest son was very important because the other brothers
80 and sisters have to listen and follow what the eldest
81 brother did.

82   After they married, Carmen lived together with Ali's
83 parents. Carmen didn't go to work. She stays home to do
84 the housework for her mother-in-law. Her mother-in-law was
85 a very kind person. She is not angry that Ali married Car-
86 men. After a month of living together, she began to love
87 Carmen because she think Carmen was a very helpful daugh-
88 ter-in-law. So, she began to speak with Carmen. She try
89 to speak as much as she can with Carmen. Carmen is a very
90 smart person and she can understand most of the words. If
91 she can't understand it, she told her mother-in-law and
92 her mother-in-law point out something to help her under-
93 stand it. Otherwise she asked her son to translate.

94   Now Ali and Carmen have a son. He looks American, but
95 he can speak Arabic. Ali's father loves his grandson. He
96 always played with him. Now he accepted Carmen as his
97 daughter-in-law because of his grandson and Carmen is a
98 very nice daughter-in-law. She also helps him out with
99 everything like reading letters because he can speak En-
100 glish but he can't read English.

The guidelines that follow contain examples of correct and incorrect usage from the writing samples and show you how to signal present and past events correctly.

A. The very first thing to remember is that all main verbs in English (except for modal verbs, such as *can, should, must, might*) show tense. It may seem as if the verb *like* in the next sentence has no tense, but it does.

*Arab parents in the U.S. **like** their sons and daughters to marry to other Arabs.*

Although the verb has no ending, it is in the present tense (see Editing Practice #7). Only the third person singular has an ending, *s*, in the present tense. All other subjects take a verb with no ending in the present tense. If you use a verb with no ending, readers will assume that either:

■ it is in the present tense

*Still they **need** more money because it is not enough.* **or**

■ if it has a third person singular subject, it is ungrammatical,

*She **try** to speak as much as she can to Carmen.*

> Remember: You can never use a bare verb for an action in the past. As you go through the guidelines, pay special attention to your use of bare verbs.

B. Next, ask the question:
Is this state or event from the past or is it from the present?

Example:

INCORRECT: *She only **understands** the teacher a little bit.*

If you look at the paragraph, it is clear that this took place in the past.

CORRECT: *She only **understood** the teacher a little bit.*

Sometimes, when there are many verbs in one sentence, it is not as obvious that you must use a **past** tense. Look at the rest of the sentence.

Example:

INCORRECT: *She only **understands** the teacher a little bit, so I **tried** to explain what the teacher **is saying** to her.*
CORRECT: *She only **understood** the teacher a little bit, so I **tried** to explain what the teacher **was saying** to her.*

As you can see in this example, some verbs are in the simple past and one is in the past continuous. This is fine. Both tenses are used to express actions that took place in the past.

C. Sometimes, you need to write a sentence about **present** time right in the middle of several sentences about **past** time.

> Remember: It's fine to write about both the present and past, but make sure your tenses reflect what you mean. Make sure your tenses switch only when your time frame switches.

It may help you to think of events and states on a **time line**. Anything that occurred in the past should appear on the left side of the time line; anything that is happening in the present or is true today should appear on the right side. The verbs in this time line are taken from the example that follows.

past	present
	loves
	plays
accepted	
	is
	helps

Example:

CORRECT: *Ali's father **loves** his grandson. He always **plays** with him. He **accepted** Carmen because of his grandson and because Carmen **is** a very nice daughter-in-law. She also **helps** him out with everything like reading letters.*

Ali's father accepted Carmen *in the past*, but he plays with and loves his grandson *now*. Carmen continues to be a nice daughter-in-law and to help him with reading. Because the writer has changed time frames, he or she can and should change tense as well. Here is another example:

Example:

INCORRECT: *One thing she **try** to do to improve her Cantonese **is** watch the TV programs. Most TV programs in Hong Kong **were** in Cantonese.*

The first sentence is about an action in the **past**, but most TV programs in Hong Kong are still in Cantonese, so this sentence should be in the **present**. This may be easier to see on the time line.

past	present
tried	
was	
	are

CORRECT: *One thing she **tried** to do to improve her Cantonese **was** watch the TV programs. Most TV programs in Hong Kong **are** in Cantonese.*

Above all, **be consistent**. Sometimes you have a choice; both present and past are possible. However, you shouldn't switch back and forth unless there is a reason to do so.

Example:

INCORRECT: *His father **did not come** because he **didn't want** Ali to marry Car-
              men. Ali's mother **did come** to the wedding because she really **loves**
              Ali and also because Ali **was** the eldest son in the family.*

Switching to the present is fine here, because she **still** loves Ali now, but
he is also **still** the eldest son, so the last verb should also be in the present tense.

past	present
did not come	
didn't want	
did come	
	loves
	is

CORRECT: *His father **did not come** because he **didn't want** Ali to marry Car-
            men. Ali's mother **did come** to the wedding because she really **loves**
            Ali and also because Ali **is** the eldest son in the family.*

This is not the only choice. If the author wanted to stress that all of this
took place in the past, he could keep everything in the past.

CORRECT: *His father did not come because he **didn't want** Ali to marry Carmen.
            Ali's mother **did come** to the wedding because she really **loved** Ali and
            also because Ali **was** the eldest son in the family.*

past	present
did not come	
didn't want	
did come	
loved	
was	

Activity 5.11

Follow these steps to check for tense errors in Samples I and II:

1. Go through each sample and underline all the non-modal verbs.

2. For each verb, check: When does the action or event that is described take place?
   a. If the action or event in the present, check for a present tense verb.
   If the verb is not in the present tense, change it.

   b. If the action or event in the past, check for a past tense verb.
   If the verb is not in a past tense, change it.

   c. Move to the next verb. Has the time frame changed?
      i. If so, you must change tense to reflect the new time frame.

ii. If not, you must keep the same tense. If the time frame has not changed, make sure the tense has not either.

3. If you are unsure of your tense choices, complete the time line in Activity 5.12.

4. Are there any bare main verbs? Are they appropriate? Bare verbs signal present tense for most subjects.

5. Don't forget to check for agreement too! Consult Editing Practice #7 for more information on this topic.

> In future drafts, you may see the abbreviation **vt**. This means there is an error in verb tense, and you need to repair it.

Activity 5.12

The time line that follows is for Sample I at the beginning of this Editing Practice. It has been started for you. As you reread the essay, fill in the rest of the verbs in the correct part of the time line.

past	present and future
lived	
had	
lived	
came	
did not speak	
studied	
	is
was	

EDITING YOUR OWN WORK: THE FINAL DRAFT

Activity 5.13

A. *Check your draft to see if the tenses you have chosen accurately reflect the meaning you wish to convey. You may find it helpful to write out a time line for your own work as you did in Activity 5.12. Correct any errors that you find in preparation for your final draft. You should also identify and correct any other grammatical errors you find. In particular, check for -ing and -ed adjectives, comma splices, run-on sentences, and fragments. If you are unsure of the meaning or form of any of the words you have used, look them up in a learner dictionary.*

B. *This is also the right time to review the strategies you wrote in your Learning Log. Use these strategies in preparing your final draft. Once you have finished editing, you are ready to turn in your final draft.*

 LEARNING FROM YOUR FINAL DRAFT

Activity 5.14

Look over your final draft from this unit. You may also want to review your other final drafts. Are there some new grammar problems that you think you should start working on?

- Choose at least one new entry for your Learning Log.
- Decide on the strategy you are going to use to try to improve.
- Include an Editing Practice if there is one. If there is no Editing Practice, consult with your instructor on a step-by-step strategy for improving your performance and write it down in your Learning Log.

EDITING PRACTICE

In this section, you will have an opportunity to practice more editing. The last Editing Practice was found in Unit Five and, therefore, we begin here with Editing Practice #6.

- 6. Working with sentence and clause boundaries
- 7. Agreement
- 8. Present perfect versus past tense
- 9. Embedded questions
- 10. Word form
- 11. Noncount nouns
- 12. *Must* and *should*
- Editing Abbreviation Chart

Practice Exercises
- Sentence boundaries
- Common grammatical problems
- Combined errors

Editing Practice

#6 Working with sentence and clause boundaries

When you edit your own work, you need to be able to identify sentences and clauses. The following guidelines will help you.

What makes a sentence or a clause?

All **sentences** and **clauses** must have two things:

1. a subject
2. a verb

1. Subjects can be short or long. A subject could be a **noun** such as *people, Ruth,* or *technology;* a **pronoun** such as *he, it,* or *there*; or a **noun phrase** such as *my brother, the last time I saw her, the houses across the street,* or *cats and dogs.* Other things may look like subjects, but they are not. For instance, a prepositional phrase cannot be a subject because it is not a noun phrase.

Example:

INCORRECT: *In the middle of the night was a terrible crash.*

This has no subject and therefore is not an acceptable sentence.

CORRECT: *In the middle of the night, **we** heard a terrible crash.*

This sentence does have a subject: "we."

2. The verb must be a modal, such as *must, can,* or *will,* or else one that has tense, such as *goes, liked,* or *do.*

Therefore, your first step is to make sure that all your sentences have a subject and a verb.

Activity 6.1

A. *Look through Sample 1. Check every sentence and clause and underline the ones without a subject. Mark the places where you think the subjects should be, as in the example.*

Example:

The second half of the sentence has no subject.

INCORRECT: *There is an Indian town a few blocks down, **and** ⌃ **are grocery stores and restaurants.***
CORRECT: *There is an Indian town a few blocks down, and **there** are grocery stores and restaurants.*

B. *Read the sample again, and this time underline any sentences and clauses without a verb. Mark the places where you think the verbs should be, as in the example.*

Example:

INCORRECT: *Sometimes kids ⌃ **beaten up for no reason.***
CORRECT: *Sometimes kids **are** beaten up for no reason.*

Sample 1

1   In the area I live around, most people are preju-
2   diced against people who are from India. This prejudice
3   has been here for a long time. Where I live, there are
4   close to one thousand Indian people. There is an Indian
5   town a few blocks down, and are grocery stores and restau-
6   rants. Around the area live different kinds of people too.
7   They all call the Indians names and sometimes beat them.

8   Prejudice means when you hate a person for his color

9   of skin or religion. Most people hate Indian people be-

10   cause of their religion. Call them Hindus and Gandhi. Some

11   times kids beaten up for no reason. About two months ago

12   a lady was robbed right on the street. The people who

13   robbed her took all of the gold she was wearing.

14   This prejudice around the area because of the way In-

15   dian ladies dress. Sometimes people do not like Indians

16   because they very rich and they have a good life. These

17   people jealous of Indian people. One other reason is most

18   of the Indian kids go to school and get a good education.

19   The people who hate Indians think, "These foreigners

20   should not do better than us." This our country and they

21   are getting too powerful. Sometimes people just don't like

22   Indians because of the way they look or the way they

23   dress, but it should not matter how a person looks or

24   dresses. The one major reason for prejudice against In-

25   dian people is they are not Americans. Can't speak good

26   English.

27   There are many reasons for the unfair prejudice

28   against the Indian community in the area that I live in.

29   Is unfair to hate a person just because he is from a dif-

30   ferent country and has a different religion. Most Ameri-

31   cans are not Americans; they are all from Europe or some

32   other country. I think everybody should be treated equally.

33   Then the world would be a very safe place to live in. You

34   should not hate a person from looking at him; you should

35   always get to know him then you may have a reason to

36   hate him.

Now that you have reviewed the essential elements of sentences and clauses, it is time to look at different kinds of clauses.

What is the difference between a sentence and a clause?

In some cases, there is no difference, but in other cases, there is. **Independent clauses** are the same as sentences, but **dependent clauses** are not.

What is the difference between a dependent and an independent clause?

Some books will tell you that the important thing about sentences and independent clauses is that they contain a complete thought, but dependent clauses do not. Other books say the important thing is that independent clauses can stand alone, but dependent clauses cannot. These observations are both true, but they are not very helpful if you have a hard time figuring out what can or cannot stand alone in the first place. Until you develop an intuition about "standing alone," the easiest way to be sure is to check the **connectors** that are attached to clauses and sentences. Here are some examples.

This is a simple sentence (and an independent clause as well). It has a subject and a verb.

```
1. The hostages remained face down on the floor.
```

The difficulty comes when you try to make connections between clauses. There are several types of **connectors**. What if you wanted to connect the previous sentence with each of the following sentences?

```
2. The bank robber was waving the gun wildly.

3. The bank robber was quickly taken away by the police.
```

There are a number of possibilities.

```
4. The bank robber was waving the gun wildly; the hostages
   remained face down on the floor.

5. The bank robber was waving the gun wildly, and the
   hostages remained face down on the floor.

6. The bank robber was quickly taken away by the police,
   but the hostages remained face down on the floor.
```

In the first example (4), two independent clauses are simply connected with a semicolon (;). This is a good way of connecting two clauses, but it is not used as frequently as some of the other ways. Your reader will probably assume that the semicolon means pretty much the same thing as *and*. In examples (5) and (6), two independent clauses are connected with *and* and *but*. In this text, these are called **but-type connectors**. *And, but*, and *or* are used to *connect* two independent clauses. They may not be used to *introduce* them; that is, you cannot start a sentence with them.

INCORRECT: *The bank robber was quickly taken away by the police.* **But** *the hostages remained face down on the floor.*

This is simply a grammatical rule; it has nothing to do with the meaning of these words. In fact, there are other words, with much the same meaning, that can introduce sentences. For instance, *but* and *however* are quite similar in meaning, but they behave differently. *However* can both introduce *and* connect independent clauses.

```
7. The bank robber was quickly taken away by the police.
   However, the hostages remained face down on the floor.

8. The bank robber was quickly taken away by the police;
   however, the hostages remained face down on the floor.
```

In (7), **however** begins a new sentence. In (8), it links the two clauses. Both are fine. Notice that in (8), a semicolon precedes **however** and a comma follows it. In this text, these are called **however-type connectors**.

So far, this explanation has been limited to linking independent clauses. What about dependent clauses?

What makes a clause dependent anyway?

The answer is quite simple: The thing that makes it dependent is the presence of a **dependent clause connector**. The rest of the dependent and independent clause may have exactly the same words; the connecting markers are simply different. Here is an example:

9. Independent: **However**, the hostages remained face down on the floor.

10. Dependent: **while** the hostages remained face down on the floor.

The only words that are different are the connectors. **However** marks a clause as independent, as in (9); **while** marks a clause as dependent, as in (10). Because they are dependent, those clauses containing connectors like **while** must be joined to an independent clause.

11. **While** the hostages remained face down on the floor, the bank robber was waving the gun wildly.

In this text, these are called **while-type connectors**.

The final thing you need to know about these **while-type connectors** concerns the order of the clauses and punctuation.

■ If the dependent clause comes first, a comma must separate the two clauses.

12. **While the hostages remained face down on the floor,** the bank robber was waving the gun wildly.

■ If the independent clause comes first, no comma is necessary.

13. The bank robber was waving the gun wildly **while the hostages remained face down on the floor.**

It is important to emphasize that these are grammatical rules: you simply have to learn and remember if the connector you are using is a **but, however,** or **while**-type. The type of connector you use depends on the kinds of clauses you have in your sentence. It has little to do with meaning. For instance, the meaning of **but, however,** and **although** is very similar, but they are used with different kinds of clauses. There are a huge number of possible connectors; it is not important that you learn them all now. On the next page you will find a brief list of connectors that fall into the three types described here.

You will notice that the **however**-type connectors often have to do with logical relations, such as contrast and cause and effect, but this is also true of other types of connectors. **While-**type connectors often mark conditions and time relations. However, there is a lot of overlap, and you cannot use mean-

• Table EP.1 •

CONNECTOR FUNCTIONS

Connector Type:	BUT[1] and or so	HOWEVER furthermore in addition therefore as a result consequently in other words on the other hand	WHILE although even though because since when after before as soon as if until

[1]You may have seen other names for these connectors. **But-type connectors** are sometimes called coordinating conjunctions, **however-type connectors** are sometimes called conjunctive adverbs, and **while-type connectors** may be called subordinating conjunctions. The important thing to remember is that the **while-type connectors** make the clause dependent but the others do not.

ing to distinguish one type of connector from another. The differences among them are purely grammatical. Remember that a sentence or clause becomes dependent only when you add a **while-type** connector.

Activity 6.2

A. *Read through Sample II. Draw a single line under **but-type** connectors, draw a double line under **however-type** connectors, and circle **while-type** connectors.*

B. *Above each clause, write IC or DC to mark independent or dependent clauses.*

_____

Sample 2

1   Systems of nonverbal communication differ throughout

2   the world because every culture has its own way of es-

3   tablishing communication by nonverbal means. Western and

4   eastern cultures are different and so is their nonverbal

5   communication or body language. There are big differences

6   in how much physical contact and affection is allowed, and

7   there are also differences in social behavior in general.

8   In China, for instance, people are careful to main-

9   tain physical distance among themselves while in America,

10   people hug their friends and family in greeting. Chinese

11   do not accept embracing as a way to show friendship or

12   kissing as a way to show their love. A daughter-in-law is

13   not allowed to hug her father-in-law, and a brother-in-

14   law and sister-in-law are also not allowed to hug. Hus-

15   band and wife only hold hands to show their affection in

16   public; on the other hand, parents kiss and hug their ba-

17   bies all the time. With their elders, all young people

18   must bow in greeting to show respect.

19   Social behavior in public is different too. Most

20   Americans feel free to say "hi" or smile at strangers,

21   but they are not comfortable looking at them for very

22   long. However, in China, people do not say "hello" or

23   smile at strangers although they are allowed to look at

24   them. When people are happy, they don't laugh or allow

25 their faces to express how they really feel. They only

26 smile a little bit.

27 These examples might suggest that the social behav-

28 ior in the United States allows closer contact than in

29 China, but this is not necessarily true. For instance, I

s30 was surprised by the fact that Americans close or lock

31 their doors even though they are home. Furthermore, many

32 Americans do not know their neighbors even though they

33 live next door. In contrast, in China, everyone leaves the

34 doors and windows open all day. Neighbors can walk in any

35 time they like. If you see any house that is not open, it

36 means that there is no one at home. As you can see, dif-

37 ferences in nonverbal communication can be very complex.

You may need to review the information in this Editing Practice when you edit your own work. Use this summary to help you remember the important points.

Summary: Connecting clauses

Remember that the only requirements for a clause are a subject and a verb. Your choice of connector type determines whether the clause is dependent or independent.

1. Clause + ; + clause

 The bank robber was waving the gun wildly; the hostages re-
 mained face down on the floor.

2. Clause + **but-type connector** + clause

 The bank robber was waving the gun wildly, **and** *the hostages*
 remained face down on the floor.

3. Clause + ; + **however-type connector,** + clause

```
The bank robber was quickly taken away by the police; how-

ever, the hostages remained face down on the floor.
```

4. Clause + . + **however-type connector,** + clause (second clause begins a new sentence)

```
The bank robber was quickly taken away by the police. How-

ever, the hostages remained face down on the floor.
```

5. Clause + **while-type connector** + clause

```
The bank robber was waving the gun wildly while the

hostages remained face down on the floor.
```

6. **While-type connector** + clause + , + clause

```
While the hostages remained face down on the floor, the

bank robber was waving the gun wildly.
```

Editing Practice

#7 Agreement

Agreement errors are common but easy to correct. The form of the verb depends on the subject. This is called **agreement**: The verb must *agree* with the subject. For instance, in the present tense, the verb *to be* has several forms: *am, are*, and *is*. The verb *to have* has two forms: *has* for third person singular and *have* for everything else. For most verbs in the present tense, though, there is only one very important but very simple rule: **Add s to the verb for any third person singular subject, that is, he, she, or it.** Although it is an easy rule, many writers forget to add *s* when they write.

In the past tense, the only verb that requires agreement is the verb *to be*. *Was* is used for the first and third person singular, and *were* is used for everything else.

■ Don't forget the exception to this rule: Modal verbs, such as *can, should, could, would, might, may*, and *will*, never take an *s*.

Read through the sample and then look at the guidelines that follow.

Sample

```
1      In the past, in Chinese culture, males and females

2   were raised differently than they are today. Traditionally,

3   men are valued more than women. Men has more freedom than

4   women. Today most women is valued as much as men. Most
```

5   of the things men does women can do too. They are raised
6   similarly in terms of social life, education and respect
7   for the elderly.

8   One of the similarities in how men and women are
9   raised in China are their social life. People believes
10 men and women are equal. The government strongly support
11 the idea that women should contribute to the family in-
12 come and participate in social and political activities.
13 Every woman do some sort of work outside the home. Their
14 work are very similar. They share the housework, shop-
15 ping, cleaning, and caring for the children. In the past,
16 in some families, the parents was very strict with their
17 children and limited their social lives. There was some
18 parents who did not want their children to have boyfriends
19 or girlfriends in school. They could not go out late and
20 they had to listen to their parents and obey what they
21 said. Today, each person do what they want to do. One of
22 the most important changes are in education. Today, all
23 children's education are considered important. However, in
24 my grandmother's generation, girls never attended school.
25 Only boys went to school because only the boys were ex-
26 pected to support their parents when they got old. Men
27 held all the responsible positions in society. Today, ed-
28 ucation is very important for boys and girls. Every boy
29 and girl attend school. One of the government's aims are
30 to give every child an education as a key to reaching
31 their political, social, and economic goals. There is laws
32 that require children to stay in school for at least six
33 years. Boys and girls go to the same schools and study
34 in the same classes. Each child have the same opportu-
35 nity. If they want to get higher learning, they must pass
36 an entrance exam. Then it is up to the parents to decide
37 if their children can attend school. Of course, every par-
38 ent want their children to have the best education, so in
39 the future they can have a better job to support their
40 family.

41   Finally, both men and women are raised to give re-
42 spect to their elders in Chinese culture. They are taught
43 to respect their teachers, bosses, parents, and older rel-
44 atives. They do not speak badly to elderly people. Peo-
45 ple takes good care of their parents when they get old
46 and give them respect.
47   Today all men and women are raised similarly in
48 China. Males and females is equal and have the same kind
49 of opportunity. I like the way we are raised in my cul-
50 ture. I think this is the right way and the best.

The guidelines that follow contain examples of correct and incorrect usage from the writing sample and show you how to correct the **agreement** errors.

Activity 7.1

Some agreement rules can be tricky. It can be hard to tell if a subject is **singular** *or* **plural**. *Some subjects are particularly difficult.*
Follow these steps to check for agreement errors in the sample:

A. *The words on this list can be confusing. These words* **can** *function as subjects.*

each

every

one of the

one kind/type of

These words function as subjects. They are all singular and thus need a singular verb. *Find all the sentences in the sample that contain any of these words in the subject and draw an arrow from each of these words to the verb, like this.*

Examples:

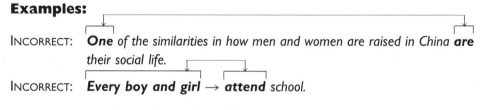

INCORRECT: **One** *of the similarities in how men and women are raised in China* **are** *their social life.*

INCORRECT: **Every boy and girl** → **attend** *school.*

These subjects are **singular**. Are the verbs **singular** too?
Because they are not, they need to be changed.

CORRECT: *One of the similarities in how men and women are raised in China* **is** *their social life.*

CORRECT: *Every boy and girl* **attends** *school.*

Now review all the sentences you have just marked with arrows. Change any that contain errors.

B. *Another word that can cause agreement problems is* people. **People** *is* **plural** *and needs a plural verb.*

Find all the sentences that have with the word **people** *in the sample and draw an arrow from* people *to the verb, like this.*

Example:

INCORRECT: ***People*** → ***believes*** men and women are equal.

Is the verb **plural***?*

> *Because it is not, it needs to be changed.*

CORRECT: People ***believe*** men and women are equal.

Now review all the sentences you have just marked with arrows. Change any that contain errors.

C. *Collective nouns are another source of agreement errors. These nouns are grammatically singular even though they refer to more than one thing or person. Here are some examples of collective nouns:*

family	*class*	*committee*
government	*society*	
group	*team*	

They are singular and require a singular verb.

> *Find all the sentences in the sample that have* **collective nouns** *in the subject and draw an arrow from the subject to the verb, like this:*

Example:

INCORRECT: The ***government*** strongly ***support*** the idea that women should contribute to the family income and participate in social and political activities.

Is the verb **singular***?*

> *Because it is not, it needs to be changed.*

CORRECT: The *government* strongly ***supports*** the idea that women should contribute to the family income and participate in social and political activities.

Now review all the sentences you have just marked with arrows. Change any that contain errors.

D. *Noncount nouns can also be difficult. Noncount nouns are singular and require a singular verb. If you are unsure about this concept, check Editing Practice #11 on the topic. Here are some examples of noncount nouns that often confuse learners.*

information	*luggage*	*clothing*
equipment	*pollution*	*jewelry*
work	*physics*	*power*
help	*advice*	*speed*
furniture	*stuff*	

Check the subject of each sentence in the sample to see if it contains a **noncount** *noun and draw an arrow from the subject to the verb, as in the example on the next page.*

Example:

INCORRECT: ***Their work are*** very similar.

*Is the verb **singular**?*

> *Because it is not, it needs to be changed.*

CORRECT: Their work **is** very similar.

Now review all the sentences you have just marked with arrows. Change any that contain errors.

Activity 7.2

Now that you have corrected the more difficult problems, go through the rest of the sample and make sure that all of the other verbs agree with their subjects.

> In future drafts, you may see the abbreviation **agr**. This means there is an agreement error, and you need to repair it.

Activity 7.3

Use the guidelines in Activity 7.1 to help you find and correct errors in your own writing.

Editing Practice

#8 Present perfect versus past tense

Choosing the right tense is a difficult part of writing. In Editing Practice #5, you worked on making sure the tense of the verb matches the time in which an action takes place.

What happens when the choice is not so clear? Sometimes the **present perfect** is one of your choices. In this Editing Practice, you are going to work on choosing between the present perfect and the simple past tense.

Read through the writing sample and then look at the guidelines that follow.

Sample

1   Drawing has been one of my hobbies since my early

2   childhood. I remember I had an inclination to draw as a

3   kid, but I always did it for myself. I never showed it to

4   anyone because I felt fear that someone would laugh. I was

5   afraid that someone would say, "What's the big deal? I can

6   do a better one," and it might make me look kind of stupid.

7   That spirit of thinking made me keep all my pictures to

8   myself until the day I learned to trust my talent.

9   I have liked to draw for years. Even before I

10   have gone to school, I drew basic pictures like houses,

11 flowers, and trees with neat shapes and textures. When I
12 was older, I started to draw figures I saw in cartoons.
13 I had a secret book and never showed those drawings to
14 anyone. Sometimes my mother snooped in my room and showed
15 pictures that she found to her friends. This made me re-
16 ally upset because I never thought my drawings were any-
17 thing special. My mother tried to persuade me that I had
18 some talent but I didn't believe her.

19 Finally, two years ago, I met a woman named Sally.
20 She was an artist before she got a disease that para-
21 lyzed her and she hasn't been able to paint or draw
22 since then. At first, I didn't tell her I drew because
23 I was afraid she wouldn't see anything special in my
24 pictures. I didn't want to tell her I could draw and
25 then disappoint her when she saw my work. Again, my
26 mother did me the favor of telling her. She has always
27 spoken up when she thinks something is important. Sally
28 was really happy to hear that and even gave me some
29 sketch paper and charcoal. She has asked me to draw a
30 face. I didn't know where to start. I had no artistic
31 methods, but it was the beginning of a new phase for
32 me. Sally began to teach me the method that helped me
33 draw a face.

34 Since then I have asked Sally for advice many times.
35 Every time I have gone to her for help, she asks me to
36 draw for her and gives me instruction while I work. She
37 was an important teacher for me. Her belief in me has
38 helped me begin to change my attitude about my drawing.
39 I know that to be really good I need to put in a lot of
40 work and practice, but now it seems possible to me.

41 I recently found out that my mother has kept all the
42 drawings I made when I was a kid. She was the greatest
43 help of all ever since I was little. If not for her, my
44 drawings might still be a secret deep inside me.

The guidelines that follow contain examples of correct and incorrect usage from the writing sample and show you how to correct **tense** errors. Concentrate on present perfect and past tense.

Present Perfect Tense

There are a number of functions of the present perfect tense. One of the most common is to describe an event that began in the past and continues into the present.

```
past                      present
x————————————————————x
```

Examples:

1. Drawing **has been** one of my hobbies since my early childhood.

2. She was an artist before she got a disease that paralyzed her and she **hasn't been** able to paint or draw since then.

3. Since then, I **have asked** Sally for advice many times.

Look at sentence (1) and ask yourself:

When did the action begin?
—It began in early childhood.

When did the action end?
—It hasn't ended. Drawing continues to be one of the writer's hobbies.

What about sentence (2)? When did the action begin?
—It began when she got the disease that paralyzed her.

When did it end?
—It hasn't ended. She still cannot paint or draw.

What about sentence (3)? When did the action begin? When did it end?

_____

_____

_____

Grammar Tip

Note that in these examples, the word *since* is used. When you are choosing between the simple past and the present perfect tense, the word *since* is often a clue that the present perfect must be used. It signals the beginning of a period of time during which something has been happening.

Past Tense

So far, you have seen sentences that require the present perfect tense. How are sentences that require a past tense different? If a specific time is given in the sentence and that time is in the past, a past tense must be used. The present perfect tense is incorrect in these instances.

Examples:

INCORRECT: _I remember I **have had** an inclination to draw as a kid._
INCORRECT: _Finally two years ago, I **have met** a woman named Sally._

CORRECT: *I remember I **had** an inclination to draw as a kid.*

CORRECT: *Finally two years ago, I **met** a woman named Sally.*

Ask yourself again: When did the action begin and end?

In these examples, there are specific times given that are in the past. The phrases *as a kid* and *finally two years ago* indicate that the action began and ended during a specific period in the past. Therefore, a past tense is required.

Meaning Changes with Present Perfect and Past Tense

There isn't always a clear signal like a specific time period or the word *since* that requires you to use one tense or the other. Sometimes using either one will result in a **grammatical** sentence. However, your choice of tense can completely change the **meaning** of a sentence.

Examples:

*a. I **have liked** to draw for years.*

*b. She **has always spoken up** when she thinks something is important.*

*c. Every time I **have gone** to her for help, she asks me to draw for her and gives me instruction while I work.*

In these examples, the present perfect tense leaves the action open-ended. It may continue in the present and future. Again, it is a good idea to ask the questions:

When did the action begin?

When did it end?

In example (a), the word *for* is an important time marker that can help answer this question. In this case, the phrase *for years*, used with the present perfect tense, means the writer started years ago and she still likes to draw.

In example (b), she continues to speak up. She began speaking up in the past and she still does. There is no indication that she plans to stop doing this.

In example (c), she began going for help in the past and continues to do so. Again, there is no indication that she plans to stop.

What if the writer used the simple past tense? In the examples that follow, the sentences are still all grammatically correct, but they mean very different things now that the tense has changed.

Examples:

*d. I **liked** to draw for years.*

*e. She always **spoke up** when she **thought** something was important.*

*f. Every time I **went** to her for help, she **asked** me to draw for her and **gave** me instruction while I **worked**.*

What's the difference between (a, b, c) and (d, e, f)?

When did the actions begin and end?

In all three sentences in the second set, the action is completed. In example (d), the phrase *for years* is used again, but this time the verb is in the past tense. The sentence now means the writer drew for years but **doesn't draw anymore**.

In example (e), she **no longer** speaks up, and in example (f), she **no longer** goes for help.

■ **Note that when the first verb is changed to simple past tense, the other verbs in the sentence also change to past tense.**

Activity 8.1

Now follow these steps to check for tense errors in the sample.

1. *Go through the sample and underline all the non-modal verbs.*

2. *For each verb, check:*
When does the action or event that is described take place?
a. If the action or event is in the past, check for past tense.
If the verb isn't in the past tense, change it to the past.
b. If the action or event is started in the past and continues to the present, check for present perfect tense.
If the verb isn't in the present perfect, change it to the present perfect.

■ Remember to check for the signal *since*. This is often a clue that present perfect must be used.

In future drafts, you may see the abbreviation **vt**. This means there is an error in verb tense, and you need to repair it.

Activity 8.2

Use these guidelines to find and correct errors in your own writing.

Editing Practice

#9 Embedded Questions

Embedded questions are questions that are inside other questions or statements. The most important thing to remember about embedded questions is that their word order is different from the word order in normal questions.

As you probably know, there are basically two kinds of questions: yes/no questions (1a) and WH questions (2a and 3a).

1a. Did they wait for the other students?
2a. What did you get on the test?
3a. Where is the post office?

As you probably also know, these questions require (i) the auxiliary verb *do* if they have a verb other than *be* or a modal and (ii) subject-verb inversion. Compare them to the statements with the same information; these have no *do*, and they have regular subject-verb order.

1b. They waited for the other students.
2b. I got an A on the test.
3b. The post office is around the corner.

When you write, especially when you write a narrative, sometimes you want to report what people say. For instance, sometimes people ask questions and you want to report them. What would happen if you wanted to include questions 1a, 2a, and 3a in your narrative by simply adding them to a main clause?

1c. Camille asked + 1a.
2c. Camille asked + 2a.
3c. Camille asked + 3a.

In fact, they all become ungrammatical, as you can see here.

INCORRECT: *Camille asked **did they wait for the other students**?*
INCORRECT: *Camille asked **what did I get on the test**.*
INCORRECT: *Camille asked **where is the post office**.*

The correct form of these embedded questions actually ends up looking more like 1b, 2b, and 3b because

(i) they have no auxiliary *do*, and
(ii) they keep subject-verb order.

CORRECT: *Camille asked **if they waited for the other students**?*
CORRECT: *Camille asked **what I got on the test**.*
CORRECT: *Camille asked **where the post office is**.*

Notice that the yes/no questions require an *if* to introduce the embedded question. The most common error with embedded questions is keeping the *do* and putting the subject and verb in the wrong order. If you try to remember to use the **statement order** for embedded questions instead of normal question order, you can avoid mistakes.

There are other problems, such as tense shifting, that sometimes come up in using embedded questions. You may wish to consult the Drafting Tip in Unit Five, *Tense use in reporting interview data* p. 201–202, for more information on this topic. The most important point to remember, however, is to use the statement form in embedded questions.

Activity 9.1

Find and correct the errors in the embedded questions in the following sample.

Sample

1   Last week, my class took a field trip to the aquar-
2   ium. The visit was fine, but getting there was a disaster.
3   The driver wasn't sure which way should he go and he had
4   to ask at three different gas stations where was the aquar-
5   ium. When we finally got there, my friends and I went
6   straight to the dolphin show. We started to sit in the front

7 row but then a guard asked us did we want to get wet. He

8 said the dolphins usually splash up to the first five rows.

9 We moved back to the sixth row so we could still get a good

10 view. The dolphins were amazing. One of the trainers was

11 riding on the dolphin's back and then the dolphin jumped

12 high into the air. It dove down into the water with the

13 trainer still on its back. They were down there for so long

14 that I wasn't sure were they ever going to come back up.

15 After the show, there was a question-and-answer period. I

16 have wondered for a long time about dolphin communication.

17 I asked the trainer can dolphins talk to each other and can

18 they communicate with people. She told us all about their

19 specialized system of communication.

20   After the dolphin show, there wasn't much time left

21 but we wanted to see the sea lions before going. My friend

22 Stefanie found out what time was the feeding hour and for-

23 tunately it was in a few minutes! We rushed over just in

24 time. A man with a pail of fish asked would I like to

25 feed them. I held out the fish and the sea lion jumped

26 out of the water to catch it.

27   We had a great time at the aquarium but on the way

28 back, the bus driver had to ask our teacher what was the

29 way back to the school!

In future drafts, you may see the abbreviation **emb-Q**. This means there is an error in an embedded question, and you need to repair it.

Activity 9.2

Use these guidelines to find and correct errors in your own writing.

Editing Practice

#10 Word form

Choosing the correct form of a word can cause problems for second language writers. For instance, is *I am confidence* correct or is it *I am confident*? This Editing Practice will help you make those decisions.

Activity 10.1

Look at the following paragraph written by a student about her experiences as a new student in her university. Notice the words in bold. In particular, pay attention to the

*form of each one. Are they **nouns**, which **name** someone or something? Or are they **adjectives**, which **describe** someone or something? Make a list of each.*

Sample

1   Like most new students, I had difficulty with many
2 things on campus before I learned how to manage. At first
3 I was really **nervous** about everything. The biggest chal-
4 lenge for me after I actually found all my classes was
5 learning how to get the most I could from lectures. I
6 had to learn how to take good notes in lecture classes.
7 This skill is **important** because many of my classes are
8 in large lecture halls where the professor doesn't al-
9 ways take questions. I have to take good notes and re-
10 member my questions to ask in the study session with the
11 TA in order to be **successful**. There is a big **difference**
12 between these classes and the ones I had in high school.
13 It was hard to adjust, and at first, I was very **uneasy**.
14 Then I went to the tutoring center and got some help
15 with lecture note-taking. Along with the skills they
16 taught me, I found I also need **patience**. By continuing
17 to practice, I have improved my skills and my grades a
18 lot. My attitude is **different** now. The higher grades I
19 receive boost my **confidence** every time I enter the lec-
20 ture hall.

Compare your list of adjectives and nouns to this list.

Nouns	Adjectives
difference	nervous
patience	important
confidence	successful
	uneasy
	different

How did you decide which words were which? Some frequent pairs, such as *confident/confidence*, *important/importance*, and *different/difference*, offer clues in their endings (*-ce* for nouns and *-t* for adjectives). In other cases, it is not so easy to tell.

So how do you know which form to use?

1. Look at the sentence and decide if a noun or an adjective is required.

2. If you are not sure of the correct form for the word you want to use, look it up in the dictionary.

For instance, in the preceding sample, the student writes:

> My attitude is **different** now.

In this sentence, *different* describes her attitude. When the writer uses words to describe something or someone, she needs the adjective form. If she isn't sure about which form is correct, she should look it up in the dictionary. She will find entries like these from the *Newbury House Dictionary of American English.*

> **difference** *n* [U] **1** a way of being different, (*syn*) a dissimilarity: *What is the difference between the new model and the old one?* **2** the amount by which two numbers differ: *The difference between 7 and 9 is 2.*

> **different** *adj* **1** unlike, not the same: *The new and old models are different from each other.* **2** varied, several: *This model comes in different colors; which one would you like?*

Notice that the words are identified as a noun with an *n* or as an adjective with *adj*.

Look at some more examples from the paragraph you just read.

> The higher grades I receive boost my **confidence** every time
>
> I enter the lecture hall.
>
> There is a big **difference** between these classes and the
>
> ones I had in high school.

Why use *confidence* and *difference* and not *confident* and *different*? In the first sentence, *confidence* is the name of something, a quality the writer has. This is clearly a noun, so the writer used the noun form. In the second sentence, although *difference* is not the name of a quality, it is still a noun. There are several clues to help you identify it.

1. There is the article *a* in front of the word.

2. There is the adjective *big* in front of the word.

3. There is the prepositional phrase *between these classes* after the word.

All these things signal the need for a noun.

What about these sentences from the same paragraph?

> At first, I was really **nervous** about everything.
>
> It was hard to adjust, and at first, I was not **confident**
>
> about my abilities at all.
>
> My attitude is **different** now.

In the first sentence, *nervous* describes the writer's feeling at the time. In the second sentence, *confident* describes the kind of person the writer was. She could have chosen other adjectives to describe herself, such as *happy, sad, noisy,* or *quiet.* In this case, however, *confident* and *nervous* are the words that fit. In the third sentence, *different* describes the kind of attitude the writer has. In these three instances where she is using words to describe something or someone, the writer needs the **adjective** form.

Activity 10.2

*Now look at another paragraph the writer has written on the same topic. Decide whether the writer needs an **adjective** or a **noun** and choose from the list of nouns and adjectives that follows to fill in the blanks with the correct form of the word. If you need help, consult a dictionary.*

confident	difference	impossible	nervousness
confidence	excellent	impossibility	patient
courage	excellence	important	patience
courageous	happy	importance	
different	happiness	nervous	

1   Another thing I had difficulty with was the finan-
2   cial aid office. When I went there to get an application,
3   I had to take a number and wait. I waited a long time
4   and it was hard to be _____. Once I had the forms,
5   I was very _____ because these forms were very
6   _____. All my _____ left me as I looked at
7   pages of forms I had to fill out. I didn't understand all
8   the instructions and this was just the initial applica-
9   tion. I knew I would have more forms to fill out after
10   I sent in the first one. I decided to ask for help and
11   I called my cousin who had also applied for financial aid
12   as a new student. She was a big help. The advice she gave
13   me was _____. With her help, I filled out the forms
14   and sent them in. After I was finished, I noticed a big
15   _____ in the way I felt. I was much more _____
16   that I could find my way through the university bureau-
17   cracy.

In future drafts, you may see the abbreviation **wf**. This means there is a word form error, and you need to repair it.

Activity 10.3

Do you ever wonder which form is correct? How do you decide between words like difference and different or success and successful? Look through one of your own essays. Check over your use of nouns and adjectives. Have you used the correct form? If you are not sure which form to use, don't just guess. Use these guidelines to help you.

- Decide if you need a **noun** or an **adjective**. Ask yourself if you are naming something (such as the quality of *patience*) or describing something (such as what kind of person someone is—*patient*). Remember to look for clues such as articles (*a, the*), adjectives (*big, small*), and prepositional phrases (*around the corner*).

- Look the word up in the dictionary to make sure you have used the correct form.

Editing Practice

#11 Noncount nouns

Noncount nouns refer to things or ideas that cannot easily be counted or divided. They do not have a plural form and they cannot occur with the indefinite article *a(n)*. You have probably studied examples of noncount nouns, such as *rice*, *coffee*, and *air*. These words don't usually cause problems for second language writers, but there are others that do cause difficulty. This Editing Practice concentrates on the problematic ones.

The noncount nouns that often prove troublesome are generally of just two types. A few examples of each type are given here.

- abstract nouns: *information, hope, help, work, knowledge, luck, advice, success, art, business, homework, life, trust, power, recreation,* etc.
- general category names: *furniture, machinery, equipment, fruit, clothing, money, luggage, food, medicine,* etc.

Problems can arise when writers mistakenly use noncount nouns as if they were count nouns. Noncount nouns are grammatically singular. This means:

- they cannot take a plural *s*,
- they must take an appropriate quantifier, and
- they need a singular verb.

(a) Noncount nouns are never plural.

Example:

INCORRECT: I sent the university registrar's office all of my **informations**, but they claim they have not received **them**.

CORRECT: I sent the university registrar's office all of my **information**, but they claim they have not received **it**.

(b) Quantifiers are words that express amounts or "how much/many." Choosing the correct quantifier can be a difficult task because there are many to choose from. Just a few are listed here. Some can be used only with count nouns, some can be used only with noncount nouns, and others can be used with both.

Quantifiers

count only	noncount only	both
many	a little	lots of
few	a few	a lot of
a few	much[2]	some
		most

Example:

INCORRECT: *The teacher gave us so **many homeworks** over the weekend.*
CORRECT: *The teacher gave us **a lot of/so much homework** over the weekend.*

(c) If you are using a noncount noun as a subject, you must also use a singular verb.

Example:

INCORRECT: *All the **equipment** on the playground **were** broken so the children had to play inside.*
CORRECT: *All the **equipment** on the playground **was** broken so the children had to play inside.*

Refer to Editing Practice #7 on agreement for more information on this topic.

So far, you have looked at fairly clear examples of noncount nouns. Sometimes, however, nouns can be *both* count and noncount. Usually, the two uses mean something slightly different. In most cases, a noun that is typically noncount can be used as a count noun if it means *an example* or *type of*. Following are some examples; the (a) sentences contain noncount nouns and the (b) sentences contain count nouns.

a. **Hope** was an important element of the patient's recovery.
b. She thought about all the **hopes** and dreams she had when she graduated.

a. Many people emigrated in search of greater **liberty**.
b. The organization was established to protect citizens' civil **liberties**.

a. Politicians who are running for election always talk about street **crime**.
b. The FBI announced that there has been a drop in the number of violent **crimes**.

If you use one of these words, consider whether you mean the count or noncount noun. If you are not sure, check a learner dictionary. Only learner dictionaries contain information on the count/noncount distinction; you will not find this information in a regular native speaker's dictionary. Some learner dictionaries use the term *mass* or *uncountable* instead of noncount. They may use an abbreviation, such as *m, u,* or *c.* Here is an example of an entry for a noncount noun, *information*, from a learner dictionary, the *Newbury House Dictionary of American English.*

---

[2]*Much* usually appears in questions and negative statements or statements containing *too* or *so*: *I didn't get much help. He drank too much beer.*

information *n* [U] knowledge, news, facts: *Newspapers carry useful information about current events.*

This dictionary uses the symbol U for "uncountable." You can also see from the example that there is no indefinite article and no plural *s*. A learner dictionary can also tell you if the noun you have chosen is the kind of noun that can be both count and noncount. For example, look at the entry for *spirit* in the *Newbury House Dictionary of American English*.

spirit *n* **1** [C; U] the nonphysical part of a person, made up of thoughts, emotions, etc., the soul: *My aunt feels the spirit of my uncle, even many years after his death.* **2** [C] a being who is not of this world, a ghost: *People think that old house is full of spirits that come out at night.* **3** [U] a feeling or mood: *The spirit of the Civil War lives on in many southern states.*

As you can see, this entry shows that *spirit* can be both a count and a noncount noun and gives examples of each. This is just one of the many important uses of a learner dictionary. You may wish to refer to Editing Practice #3: Using a Learner Dictionary.

In future drafts, you may see the abbreviation **ncn**. This means you have made an error in the use of a noncount noun, and you need to repair it.

Activity 11.1

Read through one of your own essays.

1. *Identify all the nouns that you think are noncount.*

- Does the noun refer to things or ideas that cannot easily be divided? If so, underline it.
- Does the noun refer to things that are abstract? (Refer to the examples on p. 240.) If so, underline it.
- Does the noun name a general category? (Refer to the examples on p. 240.) If so, underline it.

If you are still not sure if the noun you have used is count or noncount, consult a learner dictionary.

- Remember that some nouns like *hope* and *crime* can be both count and noncount. If the noun you have used can be both, check a learner dictionary to make sure that you have used the correct form.

2. *Review each underlined noun.*
a. If it is in the plural, change it to singular.
b. If it has a quantifier, is it an appropriate one? Check the list on p. 240 and make any necessary changes.

3. *Go back and find all the underlined nouns in the subject position and then look at the verbs that follow them. If a verb is in the plural, change it to singular.*

#12 *Must* and *Should*

Choosing correctly between **must** and **should** can be difficult. The two words mean different things, but that's not all. The choice can also depend on the relationship the writer has with the person or group he or she is writing about.

Giving Advice

Read the following examples. As you read, think about what each one means. What is the difference between #1 and #2?

1. *My friend's sister Nina has been in the U.S. for six months. She studied English for several years before she came here and she lived in London for a while. Although she can understand almost everything, sometimes the American accent and vocabulary confuse her. She wants to study here and get her degree. I keep telling her if she wants to get into college, she* **must** *take English classes first to prepare herself.*

2. *My friend's sister Nina has been in the U.S. for six months. She studied English for several years before she came here and she lived in London for a while. Although she can understand almost everything, sometimes the American accent and vocabulary confuse her. She wants to study here and get her degree. I keep telling her if she wants to get into college, she* **should** *take English classes first to prepare herself.*

There are a couple of things to consider when you think about what the two examples mean. In example #1, the writer uses **must**, which means that she thinks Nina doesn't have a choice; it is absolutely necessary for her to take classes.

In #2, she uses **should**, which means that she thinks it would be a good idea for Nina to take classes but not absolutely necessary. Clearly, **must** is stronger than **should**. *When giving advice,* **must** *is used when the writer believes something is a requirement or necessity.* **Should** *is used when the writer believes something is a good idea.*

There is, however, more involved than just the literal meaning of the words. The relationship the writer has with Nina also plays an important part in the choice between **must** and **should**. Having a close personal relationship can allow the writer to make strong statements. In example #1, the writer uses **must**. This probably means that she knows Nina very well, so she feels she can make a strong statement without causing offense.

There may be other reasons to choose **must**. In order to tell someone what his or her obligation is, writers have to have some sort of **authority**, either:

a) by having a superior position of power that allows them to make strong statements,

   or

b) by having some kind of expertise in a particular area.

Sometimes both may be involved. For instance, if Nina's academic advisor told her she **must** take English classes to prepare to enter the university, this would be appropriate. Her academic advisor not only has expertise, but is also in a position of power because he or she is the person with whom Nina is required to discuss her plans.

In example #2, two things could be happening. The first one you have seen already: The writer thinks it's a good idea for Nina to take classes, but not necessary. The second is that the writer doesn't know Nina well enough to tell her what she is obliged to do. That is, **must** is too strong a word to use based on their personal relationship, and so she softens what she says by using **should**.

It is important to note that all of the examples you have just looked at are correct. They simply mean different things.

Now look at one more example. How is this version of the story different from the previous two?

*My friend's sister Nina has been in the U.S. for six months. She studied English for several years before she came here and she worked in London for a while. Although she can understand almost everything, sometimes the American accent and vocabulary confuse her. She wants to study here and get her degree. We talked about her plans and I suggested that she **could** take some English classes before she begins regular classes or she **could** work with a tutor and start her classes right away.*

In this case, the writer is no longer giving advice. Instead, by using **could**, she is suggesting possibilities; taking English classes or working with a tutor are simply options Nina has.

Expressing an Opinion

Besides giving advice, there are other functions of **must** and **should**. An important one is expressing an opinion. Read the following examples written by a student on the subject of pollution. What's the difference between them?

1. *Pollution has become a huge problem all over the world. There are big polluters like factories that dump chemicals in the rivers and release toxic fumes in the air but there are also individuals who pollute. I think this is where change **must** begin. People **must** clean up their own mess before they tell other people what to do. If*

individuals stop throwing their garbage on the ground and using pesticides in their yards, and start recycling their paper, bottles, and cans, then they would be in a better position to take on the big polluters.

2. *Pollution has become a huge problem all over the world. There are big polluters like factories that dump chemicals in the rivers and release toxic fumes in the air but there are also individuals who pollute. I think this is where change should begin. People should clean up their own mess before they tell other people what to do. If individuals stop throwing their garbage on the ground and using pesticides in their yards, and start recycling their paper, bottles, and cans, then they would be in a better position to take on the big polluters.*

3. *Pollution has become a huge problem all over the world. There are big polluters like factories that dump chemicals in the rivers and release toxic fumes in the air but there are also individuals who pollute. I think this is where change could begin. People could clean up their own mess before they tell other people what to do. If individuals stop throwing their garbage on the ground and using pesticides in their yards, and start recycling their paper, bottles, and cans, then they would be in a better position to take on the big polluters.*

To determine what these examples mean, think about what the writer is trying to express (is it a requirement or a good idea?) and to whom the writer is saying it (does the writer have the authority to make the statement?). In #1, the writer uses **must**, which, as you know, means that people are required to pick up their garbage and recycle. However, there is an important question to ask.

Does the writer have the authority to make this statement?

Probably not. The writer is a student expressing a personal opinion about what he considers to be the best course of action. It is likely that he does not have the expertise or the superior position of power to make such a judgment. **Must** is probably too strong a word to use in this case. **Should** is what the writer means. Therefore, example #2 is the best. **Should** is the right choice for the student writer expressing an opinion on a world issue.

What about example #3? Is it strong enough to express an opinion? Not really. Again, **could** expresses possibility rather than an opinion and is therefore not strong enough.

Drawing Conclusions

So far, you have seen several examples where **must** is too strong and **should** is more appropriate. However, sometimes the opposite is true. Sometimes, **must** is the better choice. Look at the next examples.

1. The Catcher in the Rye *is one of my favorite books. I have lent it to lots of my friends since it is such a great book. My father gave me the book, which makes it really special, so everyone has always been careful to return it afterwards. The last time I wanted to lend it to someone, I went to the shelf to get it, but it wasn't there. I looked everywhere for it but still couldn't find it. I called everyone I remembered lending it to, but no one had it. I thought it* **must** *be lost, but I wasn't certain. I was very upset. Finally, I remembered that I had lent it to my friend Ben, who is always slow to return things. I called him up and he still had it. He brought it right over. What a relief!*

2. The Catcher in the Rye *is one of my favorite books. I have lent it to lots of my friends since it is such a great book. My father gave me the book, which makes it really special, so everyone has always been careful to return it afterwards. The last time I wanted to lend it to someone, I went to the shelf to get it, but it wasn't there. I looked everywhere for it but still couldn't find it. I called everyone I remembered lending it to, but no one had it. I thought it* **should** *be lost but I wasn't certain. I was very upset. Finally, I remembered that I had lent it to my friend Ben, who is always slow to return things. I called him up and he still had it. He brought it right over. What a relief!*

3. The Catcher in the Rye *is one of my favorite books. I have lent it to lots of my friends since it is such a great book. My father gave me the book, which makes it really special, so everyone has always been careful to return it afterwards. The last time I wanted to lend it to someone, I went to the shelf to get it, but it wasn't there. I looked everywhere for it but still couldn't find it. I called everyone I remembered lending it to, but no*

one had it. I thought it **could** be lost but I wasn't certain. I was very upset. Finally, I remembered that I had
lent it to my friend Ben, who is always slow to return
things. I called him up and he still had it. He brought it
right over. What a relief!

In these examples, **must** has a different function than it did in the first set of examples. This time, the writer is making an inference, that is, coming to a conclusion based on the information available at the time. The relationships between the writer and others don't play a part here because making an inference is about logic rather than positions of power or expertise. In this case, **must** is the best choice because the writer has strong evidence to infer that the book was lost. **Could** makes sense but means something a little different: The writer is not as sure that this is what happened. It is possible, but the writer is still not convinced. **Should**, however, simply doesn't make sense in the example. In fact, **should** is not used to make inferences of this type. The writer has two options, **must** and **could**, depending on what she wants to say.

Activity 12.1	*When you are choosing between **must** and **should**, it is very important to think about what you are trying to say and to whom you are saying it.*

Read through one of your papers and follow these steps to check your papers for ***must*** *and* ***should***.

1. Underline every **must** and **should** in your paper.
2. Are you making an inference? Is there strong evidence to support it? If so, have you used **must**? If not, change **should** to **must**.
3. Are you giving advice or expressing an opinion? If so, have you chosen a word that is the right strength in terms of meaning (i.e., **must** for requirement, **should** for a good idea) and one that is right in terms of the relationship between you and your reader? If not, change the word.

• **Table EP.2** •

EDITING ABBREVIATION CHART

agr	agreement
cs	comma splice
emb-Q	embedded question
frag-d.c.	fragment—dependent clause
frag-noV	fragment—no verb
ncn	noncount noun
ro	run-on
v-adj	verbal adjective
vt	verb tense
wf	word form

PRACTICE EXERCISES

Sentence Boundaries

Read through the following sample, which contains a variety of errors that are addressed in Editing Practice sections #1, #2, and #6. You may wish to look back over some of the guidelines. Then find and correct all **fragments, run-ons**, and **comma splices**.

Sample

1   My family and I immigrated to the United States four
2   years ago. As a foreigner I have a problem with my En-
3   glish. When I first came to the United States. I could
4   not speak or write English. I also found I was so unfa-
5   miliar with the American people.

6   As newcomers, we did not have enough money to begin
7   a new life in Chicago. Our living was based on welfare.
8   And the help of the Vietnamese association. After a month
9   I went to school. I had to walk two miles to school. Be-
10   cause I didn't have enough money to pay the bus fare. I
11   had to face the weather when it was winter and it was cold
12   and I didn't have a warm jacket or boots. I had to walk
13   through the snow and on the slippery sidewalk to arrive
14   at school on time. Since I was an immigrant. I had to try
15   hard to overcome my problems. I was going to find a part-
16   time job after school, I worked three hours a day. I was
17   paid four dollars and twenty-five cents an hour. The min-
18   imum wage. I used this money for school supplies and bus
19   fare, so I didn't have to walk to school every day.

20   I remember the first day I came to school, I didn't
21   understand what the teachers said and I didn't answer
22   their questions. It was hard for me to pass classes. The
23   assignments that were given to me by the teachers. They
24   were very difficult for me. I had to look up every word
25   in the Vietnamese dictionary. I was always behind my
26   classmates. They laughed at me, they made fun of me. I
27   was very angry, I wanted to take revenge. But I didn't
28   know how to say anything to them. I just ignored them
29   when they made fun of me.

30   A week later, I wanted to quit school but my parents

31   did not agree with my decision. They wanted me to con-

32   tinue learning. Because they were old, they depended on

33   me for everything. If I didn't know how to speak. How

34   could we make a better life? Because of that, I didn't

35   ask my parents again if I could quit school.

36   The first year passed, I got low grades, but I was

37   not so sad. I took an E.S.L. course. I got a part-time

38   job. I learned many new words there. At home, I also had

39   a new friend, he was very nice. Every time we went out

40   together, he taught me new words in English. Two months

41   later, my second year of school started. I was more con-

42   fident. And I was not so sad. I got better grades and my

43   English improved and I wasn't scared when someone asked

44   me a question.

45   In my last year of high school, I was chosen for the

46   National Honor Society. I was so proud, my parents were

47   too. My English was getting better. I still didn't un-

48   derstand all the words but I understood the main point.

49   Now I feel my life is more colorful. The thing that helped

50   me succeed. It was my E.S.L. class.

Common Grammatical Problems

Read through the following sample, which contains a variety of errors that are addressed in Editing Practice sections #5, #7, #8, and #9. You may wish to look back over some of the guidelines. Then find and correct all the **tense, agreement, word order**, and **embedded question** errors.

Sample

1   A lot of people from other countries has a strange

2   impression of the United States. In my country, people

3   think that if you have a chance to come to the United

4   States, you were very lucky. So, a lot of people try any-

5   thing they can to come to the United States. Therefore,

6   when people in my neighborhood have found out that I was

7   going to come to America, they all looked at me and my

8   family with jealousy. People who already knew me started

9   to treat me differently. They wondered am I going to get

10   rich and have a lot of money to send back to them. At

11   first, I was happy because I was going to a place that

12   everyone dream about. After a while, I didn't feel so

13   happy anymore when they look at me that way. It made me

14   feel that I didn't belong anymore.

15   After two years in America, I decided to go back to

16   my country to visit my grandmother in Poland. When I got

17   there, I have suddenly felt like I was home again, but I

18   also have felt that many things were different. One big

19   difference was how teenagers dressed. Next to them, I

20   looked like a very old-fashioned person. Now I dress like

21   an American, in faded blue jeans and a T-shirt, but peo-

22   ple in my country looks at me like I was someone from

23   outer space. Some people thought I dressed like that to

24   trick them and make them think I had no money. I heard

25   them complain and say that my family were very cheap be-

26   cause we did not bring them enough money. One uncle asked

27   why didn't I bring him a television. It made me very sad.

28   I was in the United States for five years now. I

29   think I have a more realistic picture of my old country

30   and my new country. I hope that one day, the rest of my

31   family will share these pictures with me.

Combined Errors

Read through the following samples, which contain a variety of errors that are addressed in all of the Editing Practice sections. You may wish to look back over some of the guidelines. Then find and correct the errors.

Sample 1

1   People of all ages makes mistakes during their life-

2   time. Some realize that they have made a mistake and they

3   try not to do it again, but others just let it go on. A

4   long time ago I made a mistake and I always remembered

5   it since then. When I was growing up in the Ukraine. I

6   always had a bad attitude about people from the big city,

7   especially people from Moscow. I was from a small town,

8   people from the big city always act as if they were bet-

9   ter than us: they dress better than us, they have all the

10   modern fashions and they always find out the latest news

11   faster than us. They even made fun of our accent when we

12   spoke Russian. I despised them and always looked for a

13   reason to put them down or insult them. So when I finally

14   met a girl from Moscow, I assumed that she was as pride

15   as all the others and that she would look down on me.

16   It all happened long ago and it made me change the

17   way I looked at people even today. I try not to judge

18   people by the way they look or where they come from, or

19   because they are difference from me. It was June of 1988

20   and I was twelve years old. I left home for the first

21   time and went to summer camp. It was in another city and

22   I had to take a train to get there. I met a lot of new

23   people there, most of them from around the Ukraine. The

24   camp was very big and nice, I loved it from the first

25   minute and I was sure it would be the best summer of my

26   life. I shared a big room with eight other girls. Soon

27   we all became good friends with the exception of one girl.

28   This girl was from Moscow, all the other girls were

29   Ukrainian. We were happiness that we were a majority be-

30   cause for once we had more power than someone from Moscow.

31   This girl was also very beautiful, with beautiful clothes

32   and shoes and that made me hate her even more. All the

33   boys were attracted to her and so none of the girls would

34   speak to her. Of course, we were jealous. We would not

35   make friends with her or even speak to her. She was com-

36   pletely alone. When we had parties in our room. She would

37   sit on her bed and try not to cry. We didn't care.

38   One day, one of the Ukrainian girls, who I consid-

39   ered one of my best friends, could not find her money.

40   She said her money were in her drawer when she left the

41   room but when she came back it was gone. I knew that none

42   of the girls from the other room had taken it because no

43 one else had a key to our room. All of us immediately
44 thought that it should be the girl from Moscow. When we
45 asked her did she steal it, she cried and swore she never
46 touched it. But no one would listen to her. We told ev-
47 eryone in the camp that she was a thief. The camp lead-
48 ers, who had been nice to her in the beginning, started
49 to ignore her when they have found out about the wallet.

50 A few days later, my friend found her money among her
51 things. Later, we found out that she hid her wallet and
52 then forgot where she put it. I don't know about the other
53 girls, but I was ashamed. I went up to the girl from Moscow
54 and told her that I was very, very sorry. She smile and
55 said, "It's OK. Everyone makes mistakes." Her kind words
56 made me so embarrassing that my face turned red. I real-
57 ized that this beautiful, shy girl was a better person than
58 any of us. We became good friends and after camp was fin-
59 ished, we wrote each other letters. I value her friendship
60 but most of all, I value the lesson I learned. Now I try
61 not to judge people before I get to know them.

Sample 2

1 As we all know, the population of the world is in-
2 creasing. In some parts of the world, the population is
3 growing so fast that it is difficult to feed everyone. In
4 some countries, the government are encouraging people to
5 have smaller families, in China, for instance, the gov-
6 ernment have a one-child policy.

7 There are both advantages and disadvantages to limit-
8 ing married couples to just one child. It has important for
9 society because eventually the population will decrease and
10 there will be more resourceful for everyone. It may also
11 be an advantage for each couple because they do not have
12 to pay the expenses for a second child. There are a lot of
13 expensive in raising a child, such as food, clothings and

14 education. If they have only one child, the couple may be

15 able to buy more luxuries and securities for themselves.

16   On the other hand, it may be lonely for the single

17 child because he will have no one to play with at home.

18 I cannot imagine being the only child in my family. Even

19 in my family of five, I sometimes felt lonely because I

20 am the only son. Sometimes I listen to my sisters laugh-

21 ing and joking. I am jealousy because I don't have a buddy

22 for "guy talk." But at least I have my sisters to talk

23 to. Another concern is if there is an accident or an ill-

24 ness and the first child dies. The parents would be very

25 lonely and sad. Also, many people has always wanted a son

26 and if their only child is a girl, they are very disap-

27 point. Probably that girl will not have an easy life be-

28 cause she is not the son that her parents wanted. But if

29 everyone had a son, then there would not be enough girls

30 for the sons to marry and there would be trouble because

31 everyone would fight over a small number of girls.

32   In agriculture countries, there are also economic

33 disadvantages to just one child. In these countries, there

34 is not many technology so the farmers have to rely on

35 their families to work hard. If they have only one child,

36 it is very difficult for them to continue their farm life.

37 Since the beginning of this Chinese government policy, the

38 biggest problems were in the countryside. Even in the

39 cities, there may be problems. In twenty or thirty years,

40 when everyone who are working now retire, there will not

41 be enough people to run the factories and offices. Who

42 will take care of all the retired people? I don't think

43 the Chinese government has thought about what will they

44 do in fifty years when there are so many old people and

45 not so many young people.

46   Although there are both advantages and disadvantages

47 to a one-child policy, I believe that there are more dis-

48 advantages. I feel sorry for the parents who have to fol-

49 low it and for their only children. I think China must

50 reconsider this policy.

Sample 3

1 When I have read the title of this course "English
2 Composition for Foreign Students" on the first day of
3 class, I didn't notice anything that was very annoyed.
4 Now the situation has changed. Now, when I think about
5 this title, it bother me very much. Just because we are
6 not native English-speaking students. We do not deserve
7 to be called foreign students. It may not seem like a big
8 deal to a lot of people, but I strongly believe that the
9 title of this course is offense and should be changed.

10 When people refer to me as a foreign student, I feel
11 very left out and also a little bit offending. My under-
12 standing is that foreign students are people who comes to
13 this country for a short time. They come here with only
14 one purpose: to study. Then they return to their coun-
15 tries after they finish their studies. This is not true
16 of most of my classmates and me, we are here for the rest
17 of our lives. Because this is our home now. We will get
18 jobs here, pay taxes, and serve in the United States mil-
19 itary if there is a war. I don't understand why do peo-
20 ple think we should be called foreign students. Even
21 though I don't write or speak English as well as other
22 American students. I am doing pretty much the same thing
23 as the rest of the students at this university. In fact,
24 I recently became an American citizen and since then, I
25 was really frustrating every time anyone assume that I am
26 a foreigner. I know more about the history of the United
27 States than the history of Iran, the country where I was
28 born. I can write English better than I can write Farsi.
29 I am not a foreigner any longer.

30 I believe that it is time for the university to show
31 respect for this large population of students. There are
32 many other students just like me, from many countries
33 around the world. We might expect people on the street
34 to call us names. But we don't expect it from our
35 university.

ADDITIONAL READINGS

In this section, you will find a selection of additional readings that are related to the topics in the rest of the book. Some explore a somewhat new direction; others pursue the same topic in greater depth. You may wish to read some of the selections before you begin writing your draft.

READINGS FOR UNIT ONE

The United States has always been a country of immigrants. At the same time, there has always been some degree of anti-immigrant feeling, usually directed against the most recent and numerous immigrant groups. All immigrants will decide how much they want or are able to maintain their own cultural identity and how much they want or need to adapt to mainstream culture. Part of that decision involves language and what role English and the immigrant language will play in their lives and their community. Some Americans say that it is essential that English be everyone's language. This article explores the arguments for and against English Only.

English Spoken Here
Karen N. Peart

In many communities across America, immigrants can live their entire lives without ever having to learn English. Street signs in some Miami neighborhoods are printed in both English and Spanish. Immigrants in California can vote in six different languages. In New York City, driver's license tests are given in 21 languages and schools are taught in 115 languages. For Russian kids who want to study math or Cubans who want to drive legally, multilingual services allow them to go on with their lives in their new country.

(continued on next page)

(continued from previous page)

But to a growing number of Americans, multilingualism is just plain un-American. The English language, they say, is part of what unites this country and makes America, America. "Without English as a common language, there is no [American] civilization," writes [former] House Speaker Newt Gingrich in his book, *To Renew America*. While the U.S. has never had an official language, a growing movement is sweeping the country to have one. Twenty-one states have already enacted laws making English the official language. And several bills now before Congress would make English the country's official language.

These laws tend to be more symbolic than practical. Most of them only require that all government business be conducted in English. Still, Arizona's law has been challenged in the courts as a violation of the free speech of government employees. The Supreme Court is expected to rule on the case this fall.

But English-only advocates want to go a step further, banning government services in any language other than English. They propose laws that would outlaw such government programs as bilingual education, election ballots and driver's license tests. So far, only the state of Alabama has gone as far as to offer driver's license tests in English only.

These multilingual programs cost the government billions of dollars every year. But more important, critics say, they threaten American culture and slow the **assimilation** of immigrants.

assimilation absorption; incorporation

The largest and most controversial of these programs is multilingual education, which costs the federal government an estimated $206 million a year. Multilingual education began as an effort to allow students to temporarily continue their academic studies in a language they understand while they learn English. But critics say the program has been **exploited** to allow non-English-speaking students to get by without ever learning English.

exploited taken advantage of

"Promoting English is not an act of hostility, but a welcoming act of inclusion," says former U.S. Senator Bob Dole. "Thousands of children are failing to learn the language that is the ticket to the American dream."

Supporters say that bilingual education programs work. They point to studies showing the success of such instruction, and say it is the best way to teach new immigrants. English-only laws, they say, amount to thinly **veiled** racial and ethnic prejudice. According to education writer James Crawford, the message to immigrants is that they are not welcome until they have completely given up their own cultural identity. He says you don't have to speak English exclusively to be an American. "The agenda of English only is hard-core anti-immigrant," he says. "It is certainly more respectable to discriminate by language than by race."

veiled disguised

Experts say the conflict is a result of changing characteristics of immigrants to the U.S. Earlier in this century, most immigrants came from Europe. Even though they spoke a variety of languages, they soon felt at home in America, whose cultural roots were in Europe. Greater language diversity among early immigrant groups forced them to learn English to understand one another as well as the natives.

(continued on next page)

(continued from previous page)

But today, the majority of immigrants come from Spanish-speaking countries. Many have settled in tightly knit communities that keep their language alive. Some 17 million U.S. residents speak Spanish as their first language, an increase of 50 percent since 1980. Spanish is the second-most-common language spoken in the U.S.

Gerda Bikales, executive director of U.S. English, a group promoting laws to establish English as the official language, sees that as a threat. "A group that speaks a separate language is all too likely to start regarding itself as a separate culture," she says. She points to the French-speaking province of Quebec that tried to **secede** from the rest of English-speaking Canada.

secede formally withdraw

A recent study by Michigan State and Johns Hopkins universities suggests that Bikales' fears may be **unfounded**. Virtually all of the 5,000 children of immigrants studied were found to be passionately committed to speaking English fluently, and 81 percent of those born in the U.S. said they would rather speak English than their parents' native tongue.

unfounded not justified

Francis Fukuyama, a researcher at the Rand Corporation, says it is unfair to blame the lack of cultural identity on immigrants. "Even if the rate of new immigration fell to zero tomorrow, and the most recent 5 million immigrants were sent home," he says, "we would still have an enormous problem in this country with the breakdown of a core culture."

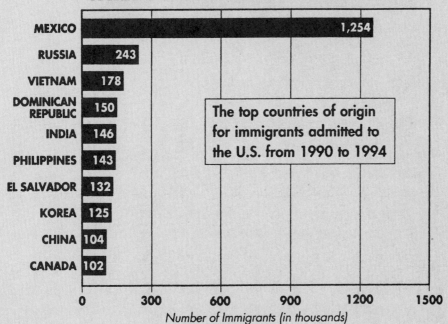

WHERE IMMIGRANTS COME FROM

	Number of Immigrants (in thousands)
MEXICO	1,254
RUSSIA	243
VIETNAM	178
DOMINICAN REPUBLIC	150
INDIA	146
PHILIPPINES	143
EL SALVADOR	132
KOREA	125
CHINA	104
CANADA	102

The top countries of origin for immigrants admitted to the U.S. from 1990 to 1994

Source: U.S. Bureau of the Census, *Current Population Survey, 1994*

Discussion Questions

What is your view on these issues?

1. Should English be the national language? Why or why not? Should the use of other languages be allowed in government services? Explain your answer.

2. Should the government provide bilingual education? Explain your answer.

3. Will maintenance of immigrant languages lead to separatism? Why or why not?

— • — ▬ — • — ▬ — • — ▬ — • — ▬ — • — ▬ — • — ▬ — • —

Stereotyping is not limited to ethnic, racial, and religious groups. Some of the most powerful stereotypes are based on gender. Girls and boys learn very early in their lives how they are expected to behave. This article describes a new way that they may absorb stereotypes about gender: through computer games.

Sexism and Kids' Software

Bronwyn Fryer

Six-year-old Caitlin Baird and her brother, 2-year-old Dylan, of Los Angeles, are pretty mean with a mouse. When playing *Aladdin: Disney's Activity Center*, one of their favorite CD-ROMs, they can **maneuver** with the best of them. Click: There's a bare-chested Aladdin, zooming around on his magic carpet. Click: There's **buxom** Princess Jasmine being forced into marriage. And while Caitlin and Dylan learn to work with a computer, they're also learning a thing or two about gender roles.

maneuver get around

buxom full-figured

Disney Software's Aladdin is only one of a host of programs targeted at kids. The good news is that children's software is being **touted** by educators as the most exciting learning tool to come along in years. The bad news is that choosing the right software can be difficult and confusing.

touted publicized; praised

Worse, even the most popular **"edutainment"** software can teach kids a lesson parents hadn't counted on: sexism. That's because in most programs the male characters **embark on** exciting adventures, while the females merely watch, await and support them. In fact, of the 344 edutainment titles reviews last year by the Ypsilanti, Michigan newsletter, *Children's Software Review*, only 28 featured an active female lead.

edutainment education+entertainment

embark on begin; set out on (*usually a trip or adventure*)

Even products starring animal characters can **typecast**. "Many manufacturers like to call software with animals 'gender neutral,'" notes Susan Haugland, Ph.D., a child psychologist who directs the Kids Interacting with Developmental Software research project at Southeast Missouri State University in Cape Girardeau. "But

typecast give a role to play based on a stereotype

(continued on next page)

(continued from previous page)

that's a **copout**. Take Stickybear ABC's by Optimum Resource. Any child can tell you that Stickybear is a boy. And the only time a female character appeals is when a girl bear who is in the segment on the letter 'K' kisses him." To some parents, however, the sex of Stickybear—or any other software character—is a minor consideration. "I don't see this sexual stereotyping as a big deal," says Caitlin and Dylan's mom, Deirdre, a 37-year-old property manager. "Playing with software has helped my daughter gain confidence at school. The benefits definitely outweigh the problems."

Still, experts insist that the gender stereotypes these games depict may have far-reaching effects. "Children identify with the characters in the program and absorb that this is how girls and boys are supposed to behave," says Judith Brown, a child psychologist in Fremont, California, "and what kids are learning is girls are expected to be passive, decorative and quiet, and boys are expected to be active, aggressive and smart." In this politically correct era, how could sexism in software even exist? Software companies claim they're simply following the time-honored tradition of the children's book, television, movie and toy industries. "There are two ways to develop content," says Heidi Roizen, president and CEO of T/Maker, a Mountain View, California multimedia firm. "You either create characters **from scratch** or you license known winners from books, films or television. And unfortunately," she adds, "very few known winners are female."

copout failure to admit or take responsibility for the true situation

from scratch from an original idea

Discussion Questions

1. Some of the people quoted in the article think that these games have a significant effect on the development of children's self-images. Do you think this is true? Why or why not?

2. One mother thinks that the benefits that children get from playing computer games far outweigh any possible problems. Do you agree? Explain.

3. Do you find greater stereotyping in the computer games you have played? Explain.

READINGS FOR UNIT TWO

For some people, the Internet has opened up a whole new social life. Unfortunately, some of those people substitute a cyber social life for a real one. This article looks at several instances of people who found new relationships online. Some worked out; others did not.

Intimate Strangers

When she first joined ECHO, an East Coast electronic community, Marcia Bowe **dubbed** herself "Miss Outer Buro 1991," a **handle** that **facetiously** implied beauty-queen like poise, glamour, **congeniality**. And soon enough, Bowe was enjoying the adulation of fellow "ECHOIDS" who posted messages praising her wit, candor and smarts. Such celebrity was **heady** stuff for Bowe, a freelance writer who describes herself in real life as shy and wary of emotional encounters. "I became addicted to this constant stream of approval," she says. "It was like a big **co-dependency** machine."

As Bowe began spending up to 100 hours a month online, however, her life began to take on the burdens of celebrity. "Some people were envious of me," she says. "They accused me of snobbery and elitism." More disturbing, Bowe began to realize that her own hyperactivity was masking an underlying unhappiness with her life. So she dropped out of ECHO **cold turkey**. "I had forgotten that the real world was so complex and fascinating."

She's back in cyberspace now, this time in a paid position at ECHO overseeing its 54 conferences, but she has learned to navigate online **with** greater perspective and **a thicker skin**. That doesn't mean she's become **detached** though. "This is an emotional place, not just a communications device," she says. All this may sound strangely **overwrought** to those who have yet to venture online. The Internet, after all, has been **touted** largely as an unwalled **repository** of raw data, not of raw emotions. But the truth is that the vast majority of people who **troll** the Internet's byways are there in search of social interaction, not just sterile information. An estimated 80% of all users are looking for contact and commonality, companionship and community—all the **conjugations** implied by E. M. Forster's famous injunction: "Only connect!"

Relationships can be complicated in cyberspace because the very technology that draws most people together also keeps them apart. Over time, the safe sense of distance that initially seems so liberating to newcomers on the Net can become an obstacle to deepening the bonds of friendship, romance and community. At some point, most networkers find, the only real way to move a relationship forward is to risk personal contact—and then hope the **phantom** bond will hold up in a 3-D world. "You can't lead a total life online," says Dave Hughes, founder of the Old Colorado City Electronic Cottage, a cybersettlement. "But if it's done right, online communication can lead *to* face-to-face communication, not *away* from it."

At its best, the sprawling Internet brings together people with mutual interests who, for reasons ranging from geography to social and income **disparity**, would otherwise never have met. These virtual friendships can lead to physical encounters that may cement lifelong relationships. "The cybercommunity is not separate from your community of friends; it's just not geographically local," says Carolyn Ybarra, an anthropology Ph.D. candidate at Stanford University.

When Ybarra moved west from Minneapolis, her online quilting group threw her an in-person farewell party. Since then, she has become good friends with two

(continued on next page)

dubbed named

handle computer nickname

facetiously falsely

congeniality agreeable and friendly temperament

heady intoxicating; producing feelings that are strong enough to affect the sense of balance

co-dependency unhealthy and destructive interdependent relationship

cold turkey the sudden and complete withdrawal from anything on which one is dependent; this expression is usually used in reference to drug addiction or smoking

with a thicker skin without being so sensitive

detached unemotional

overwrought overemotional

touted advertised

repository storage place

troll surf

conjugation joining together

phantom imagined

disparity difference

(continued from previous page)

of her fellow quilters, keeping in constant touch online. "I feel just as close to these women as I do to my college friends," she says. "I tell them more up-to-date details of my personal life, more often, because the response is so quick."

Ybarra was fortunate to encounter women who, in person, were much the same as they were online. That is often not the case. The disembodied voices that whisper through cyberspace can often be manufactured identities that can disguise or **distort** or amplify aspects of a user's personality. Fortunately, only a relative few—Lotharios, who **woo** indiscriminately, for instance, or **pederasts**, who prey on vulnerable children—have devious and potentially dangerous intent.

distort twist out of shape

woo seek affection

pederast adult who prefers sex with children

Most Net users are more likely to project aspects of the person they wish they could be. Pauline Borsook, author of *Love over the Wires,* calls this "selective lying by omission"; psychologist Kenneth Gergen, author of *Saturated Self,* more charitably regards it as "playing out our other selves."

Either way, even unintended distortions can prove bruising. When Christine Rance, 28, struck up a Net relationship with a man she knew as "MyPalJoey," she says, "I told him things I had never told anyone in my life. I was really able to be more open. He was too." After more than three months of furious messaging, the couple had their first F2F (face-to-face) encounter. About six months later, Rance secured a job transfer from Chicago to San Francisco, anticipating a **trip to the altar**. But after six weeks, the couple broke up, crushed by conflicting schedules and personalities. "He's a very selfish person, more than I ever thought," says a chastened Rance. "He didn't want to give up anything. He wanted me to give up everything."

trip to the altar wedding

Dan Marsh, by contrast, knew within five minutes of his first F2F with Audrey that their four years of online messaging between the West Coast and Pennsylvania had been time well invested. "I don't react well to meeting people in person," says Marsh. "I'm very reserved." But the relative safety of cyberspace had enabled him to be more trusting and vulnerable. "Even though I'm the most private person you ever want to meet, I let my guard down right away," he says of their online courtship. In 1993, two years after meeting, the couple married.

Discussion Questions

1. Does the percentage of people who are using the Internet to look for social interaction surprise you? Why or why not?

2. Why do you think people establish relationships on the Internet?

3. What are the benefits and problems with these relationships?

4. Have you or someone you know ever met anyone on the Internet? What happened?

As more and more people communicate by e-mail, they have realized how easy it is to be misunderstood. It is a very different form of communicating than talking on the phone or speaking to someone in person, or even writing a letter. There are some basic rules to follow, which are discussed in this article.

E-mail Smiles and Other Basic Netiquette

David Clark

netiquette rules of behavior on the Internet

The trouble with e-mail is that you can't see the other person's body language. Plain text can be confusing or misinterpreted; you may say something **ironic**, and your recipient may take it as deadly serious. Before you know it, you've got some **disgruntled psycho** looking you up in the student directory and hunting you down with a chainsaw (well, just hope that it doesn't come to that). At any rate, remembering the limitations of plain text is important.

ironic having a meaning opposite of what the words actually say

disgruntled psycho a mentally ill person who is unhappy (in this case, about what was said in the e-mail)

Smileys

One way of expressing yourself in a text-only world is through the use of something called *smileys* (also known as *emoticons*). Smileys are textual representations of the human face in a variety of different poses. Your basic smiley looks like this: :-) This symbol may look like so much garbage until you look at it sideways and see the smile. You can use a smile to tell the reader that you are happy about what you just said, as in the following example:

I'm coming home for the holidays. :-)

You can also use a smile when you don't want to be taken too seriously, as follows:

Don't wait up for me; I'll be coming down the chimney with Santa. :-)

Either way, the smile tells the reader how you feel about what you have said. Contrast the following statement with the one shown earlier in this section:

I'm coming home for the holidays: :-(

The writer of this message is telling you that he or she would rather be on a ski trip or hanging out on campus.

Other smiles you may want to use include ;-) (used when you make a sarcastic remark) :-o (wow) and :-x (a kiss).

You can make up your own smiles or check out the ones at the following Web site: **http://www.stcom.co.at/atcom/smileys.htm**

You can find a smile for every occasion at this Web site, including ones for a buck-toothed vampire, the Pope, a person who wears glasses (although what difference it makes, I don't know; I don't make these things up; I just write about them).

Some other conventions

conventions standard rules of behavior

Here are a couple of other recognized text based conventions for giving meaning to your e-mail message.

(continued on next page)

(continued from previous page)

If you want to put emphasis on a certain piece of text, such as in:

I didn't mean *that* boyfriend!

place asterisks around the piece of text to give extra meaning to that word or phrase.

Place an underscore before and after a piece of text that would normally be underlined, such as book title; for example, _Moby Dick_.

Don't shout and other courtesies

IF YOU WANT TO SHOUT AT SOMEBODY, TYPE YOUR MESSAGE IN CAPITAL LETTERS; OTHERWISE, AVOID DOING THIS. CAPITAL LETTERS ARE VERY ANNOYING AND DIFFICULT TO READ, AND SOME PEOPLE FIND THEM OFFENSIVE.

There—glad I got that out of my system.

Following are a few other suggestions that can make your e-mail messages more **palatable** to the person at the other end.

palatable acceptable

concise using few words

- Be clear and **concise**.
- Always include your name and e-mail address at the end of your message.
- Check your spelling and grammar.
- Don't waste computing power. Limit your attachments to those that are really necessary.

Don't spam. *Spamming* is a rather annoying habit a few people have acquired; they feel the entire planet needs to hear what they have to say. Consequently, they send messages out to every list and e-mail address they can get their hands on. This wastes a lot of computing power and disk space on machines all over the world.

Flame **judiciously**. A *flame* is a message that puts another person in their place (according to your standards, of course), sometimes quite nastily. I'm not going to say never flame; there are people who deserve it. But do it rarely and only when absolutely called for.

judiciously wisely

- Use basic common sense and courtesy. You have real people at the other end of your communication.

Follow these rules and you'll be off to a great start in communicating on the information superhighway.

Discussion Questions

1. Have you ever received spam? If so, how did you react?

2. Why do you think someone would flame another person? Have you ever flamed someone? What happened?

3. Can you think of any other conventions that would improve e-mail communication?

READINGS FOR UNIT THREE

*Advertisements are not always as straightforward as: "Buy Zippy Potato Chips. They taste best." Often, they use more indirect ways of trying to convince you that this particular product is better than others. Sometimes what is said in advertisements is not even completely honest. In fact, advertisers may not just try to **convince** you, they may try to **fool** you. In this excerpt, you will read about how some advertisements can be deceptive.*

Mediaspeak

Donna Woolfolk Cross

By now the falsity—either direct or **inferential**—of most television commercials is a matter of well-documented fact. Most people accept that ads are not true and yet, because they do not understand the methods by which they are influenced, are still taken in. Can *you* detect the deception behind the following statements?

inferential implied

■ *"Ford's LTD is over 700% quieter."*

The clear **implication** is that the LTD is quieter than cars of comparable size and price. What is really meant is that the *inside* of the car is 700% quieter than the *outside*—a great advantage for those who prefer not to ride on the hood.

implication a conclusion that is not stated directly

■ *"All aspirin is not alike. In tests for quality, Bayer proved superior."*

Most people assume this means that Bayer aspirin has been shown to relieve pain better than other aspirin. In fact the "tests for quality," which were conducted by Bayer and not an independent testing agency, showed Bayer was superior, in its own manufacturer's opinion, because the tablets were whiter and less breakable than other aspirins tested. Nevertheless, this claim is so effective that a recent FTC survey revealed that forty percent of consumers believe Bayer is the most effective aspirin.

■ *"Sominex makes you **drowsy** so you can sleep."*

drowsy sleepy

Time and again the advertising agencies peddling over-the-counter **remedies** for **insomnia** have been **rebuked** for stating or implying that these products insure a good night's sleep.

remedy cure
insomnia sleeplessness
rebuke scold

Undaunted, the nimble admen simply found a new way of making the same claim: The remedies still do not insure a good night's sleep, but they **purport** to make us drowsy so we *can* sleep. Reading a dull book or watching an uninteresting TV show would probably have the same effect. It is even possible that ads for insomnia cures can put you to sleep sooner than their product will.

undaunted not discouraged
purport claim

(continued on next page)

(continued from previous page)

■ *"Lots of things have changed, but Hershey's goodness hasn't."*

The logical conclusion to draw from this would be that through the years Hershey's hasn't changed its recipe for making chocolate. But it has; it's the "goodness" that has remained the same. And "goodness" is so **subjective** a word as to be almost meaningless. As G. K. Chesterton said, "A man who shoots his grandmother at 500 yards may be a good shot but not necessarily a good man."

subjective interpretable in many ways

■ *"Count Chocula is part of your child's nutritious breakfast."*

True enough. But then your child's napkin and spoon could be said to be "part" of her nutritious breakfast. The ad doesn't say that the cereal *itself* is particularly nutritious. Indeed, many of the sugared cereals pitched at the kid's market are almost worthless nutritionally except for the added vitamins and minerals (which you can get just as effectively from a vitamin pill). One study conducted by the University of Georgia in the late 60s showed that if kids ripped up their cardboard cereal boxes and ate them they'd be getting as much nutrition as they did from the cereal itself!

Many advertising claims are so vague and **illusive** that it's impossible to tell what is really meant:

illusive not real; deceptive

■ *"Harley-Davidson motorcycles: more than a machine."*

(Maybe there's a little person inside who cooks you chicken soup when you're on the road?)

■ *"I can practically set my clock by Senokot [a laxative]."*

Scene: Family gathered in a cozy living room. Suddenly:

Mom: Oh-oh! (dashes out)

Son: Must be 8:30, Dad—Mom's going to the bathroom again!

■ *"Gallo: because the wine remembers."*

If true, this should **put a crimp in** dinnertime conversations: "Hush dear, not in front of the **Hearty Burgundy**."

put a crimp in block; disrupt
Hearty Burgundy a kind of wine produced by Gallo winery

Discussion Questions

1. Are you surprised that these kinds of advertisements are permitted? Do you think they should be?

2. In what way is the following advertisement deceptive?

"La Beauté Silken Skin Cream reduces the appearance of wrinkles in just ten days and helps you to look and feel younger."

3. Have you ever bought anything based on ads like these? What happened?

■—·—■—·—■—·—■—·—■—·—■—·—■—·—■—·—■—·—■—·—■—·—■

Wearing clothes with a designer label has always been a status symbol, but starting in the 1970s, it became possible for people other than the very rich to buy clothes with a designer's name on them. Since then, there has been an explosion of designer labels on everything from perfume to underwear. It is always only a matter of time before children start imitating their parents. This article explores the growth of the market in designer clothes for children.

"Sunday Best" Becoming More of A Daily Ritual

Adrienne Ward Fawcett

When it comes to clothing, children are a **paradox**. They want to conform, but individuality is **of the essence**. This need to forge their identity through their **wardrobes** has opened doors for designers of children's clothing.

The notion of an 8-year-old in a $180 DKNY pea coat may seem **preposterous** in these **allegedly** scaled-down times, especially since kids are far more likely to outgrow than outwear. But according to children's market researchers, it's not such a **farfetched** idea to clothing designers or the children and the parents they target.

Most designers won't release sales figures, but it's apparent that their playtogs have appeal: Sales at Baby Guess stores reportedly have doubled each year for the past three years and more designers are entering the $20 billion kids' apparel market.

Witness such names as Ralph Lauren, Tommy Hilfiger, Adrienne Vittadini, DKNY, and Marithe & François Girbaud. And Alexander Julian plans to come out with a kids' line too.

According to James McNeal, a marketing professor at Texas A&M University and author of "Kids As Customers," children aged 4 to 12 annually spend about $11.2 billion of their combined income of $15 billion on their own wants and needs. "They have learned admirably [from their parents] and then spend it on **high-ticket** items, which is often designer-brand clothing, shoes and apparel," he says. Many kids marketing and research experts agree kids are drawn to designer brands because it makes them feel grown up. Today's fast-paced world, the thinking goes, leaves little room for childhood. "One of the things children learn very quickly, by first grade, is they can buy and or wear designer brands similar in name to those of adult brands and obtain some level of distinction, enough to drive self-image to that of adulthood," Mr. McNeal says.

"If there's ever any meaning to the phrase 'fashion statement,' this is it. It's an identity," he adds. Mr. McNeal remembers one focus group in which a 9-year-old girl drew a picture of herself shopping. In the illustration, she spells the Esprit brand name correctly but misspells shirts, pants and skirts.

paradox puzzle
of the essence of the greatest importance
wardrobe collection of clothing
preposterous outrageous; unthinkable
allegedly supposedly
farfetched crazy; outrageous

high-ticket expensive

(continued on next page)

(continued from previous page)

Many children will **succumb** to peer pressure and demand designer togs, whether or not their parents encourage them, market researchers say. The peer pressure on kids is such that parents will "buy the **house brand** for themselves and designer brands for their children because they want the child to start with an even playing field," says Marian Salzman, president of consultancy BKG Youth. The power of peer pressure on a child's clothing wants is something Vickie Lee Katy, Texas mother of three girls, ages 11, 13, and 14, knows well. "Advertising and TV shows don't make them interested in any type of clothing," she says. "It has the most to do with seeing the object at school, or I'm wearing it." Recently, Danielle, Ms. Lee's eldest daughter, saw classmates wearing Girbaud jeans, a name the mother had never known, and wanted a pair for herself. But once Danielle learned the price, she decided against the jeans. That's a trait Ms. Lee says her daughters have acquired after years of discussing each potential purchase with their mother. "I think that's what a parent is for," she says. But unlike Ms. Lee, some parents play a negative role in developing kids' shopping patterns. "It's a guilt market," Ms. Salzman says. "Parents who are buying this fashion [for their kids] are parents who use department stores as a source of entertainment." According to a survey by BKG Youth of children, parents, and grandparents for the trade publication *Kids Fashion,* 64% of parents say it is important for their kids to wear status brands.

Of the children polled, 77% agreed. Parents who dress a child in designer clothing can set a dangerous precedent. It can inspire **materialism** and make kids more judgmental of others, experts say. "The whole sense of needing to actually consume your garments is missing from this group [of parents,]" says Mary Ann McGrath, an associate professor of marketing at Loyola University in Chicago.

Apparel makers, predictably, don't feel their wares promote improper values and say they're fulfilling a product need. In fact, they do very little advertising to children directly. "It's not opulent clothing," says a spokesman for DKNY, when asked why a consumer would be drawn to a $100 cotton-jersey bomber jacket, size 6X. "It's clothes you want to wear. It's oversized so they grow into it. It's comfortable, no taffeta-ribboned trimmed dresses. They're real clothes." DKNY has only one ad for its kids' clothing line, which ran in *Men's Journal.*

"Good design has economic value to customers," says Richard Hauser, VP-children's at Bloomingdale's. "If not, we would all wear Mao jackets and drawstring pants."

succumb give in

house brand store brand; a label manufactured for a department store, such as **the Hunt Club label for JCPenney**

materialism a love of possessions or anything that can be bought

Discussion Questions

1. What do you think when you see children wearing expensive designer clothing?

2. How would you answer the vice president at Bloomingdale's who says that "Good design has economic value . . . otherwise we would all wear Mao jackets and drawstring pants"?

READINGS FOR UNIT FOUR

The college experience has changed a great deal in the past forty years. Costs have gone up dramatically, and approaches to both teaching and learning have changed as well. The selection that follows is a transcript of a radio interview with a journalism professor named Anne Matthews, who recently wrote a book about this topic. The interviewer's name is Terry Gross.

Terry Gross, Host: The cost of going to a private college is **staggering.** Is the product worth the price? That's one of the issues Anne Matthews explores in her book, "*Bright College Years: Inside the American Campus Today.*" Matthews is a journalist who has spent most of her life on or around college campuses. Her father was a professor and she now teaches at New York University's Graduate School of Journalism. She reports that college tuition has tripled in the past fifteen years.

staggering astonishing

Anne Matthews, Instructor, Graduate School of Journalism, NYU; Author, *Bright College Years: Inside the American Campus Today:* It used to be that you could get a perfectly good education at a public school for about $200 a semester, and at a private college for roughly twice that. For most of the twentieth century, it was perfectly possible to work all summer, and earn enough tuition to get you through the next year—books, expenses, room and board, and tuition itself.

And in the last ten years, all of that has fallen away, and now at your average public institution—Berkeley, say, or Illinois or Michigan, any of the **flagship** campuses, the so-called "public **ivies**"—tuitions are hovering at about $10,000 a year.

flagship main; major

"ivies" this is a reference to the *Ivy League,* a group of expensive, elite, private universities and colleges, such as Harvard and Yale.

And at private campuses, regardless of ranking—a Harvard or a Reed, a St. John's or Middlebury—families are now obliged to go into extraordinary debt; $30,000 a year is not unknown, and some of the largest Northeast campuses will break that, probably within the next twenty-four months.

Gross: What's behind those soaring prices?

Matthews: Well, a lot of things—none of them terribly pretty. One is the fact that colleges are now run like luxury resorts, and students—the student services empire grew enormously in the '70s and in the '80s—and now there's so many extras and frills expected as part of the college experience.

Gross: Like what?

Matthews: Oh, for instance, students expect state-of-the-art computing. They expect state-of-the-art radio and television studios. They expect state-of-the-art printing facilities for student papers. They expect excellent music facilities.

They expect student unions, which are full of retail operations. It's very rare these days to find a student union or campus that does not have a say, a Reebok

(continued on next page)

(continued from previous page)

outlet or a McDonald's or Burger King on campus. And the commercialization of the campus has, in a strange way, raised costs tremendously.

Gross: Some college people call this price tag the "**Chivas Regal** effect."

Matthews: Yes.

Gross: What does that mean?

Matthews: I think it means that people will pay more for a fancy college label. And if one can go out into the world with Oberlin stamped on your forehead or Harvard or Berkeley, people consider it an adequate investment—more than adequate, worth taking out a third mortgage on your house; worth taking on college loans so extraordinary that they may not be paid off 'til the 18-year-old's own 18-year-old heads off to college in the year 2030.

Gross: So you're saying that often what people are paying for is the **pedigree** of their degree rather than the quality of the education they're getting?

Matthews: Yes, very much so. College has become extremely brand conscious.

Gross: Do you have any idea what percentage of money is actually going toward education, and what are—where's the rest of the money going?

Matthews: Part of it to the student services empire. Part of it to the administrative empire. The number of administrators has grown 48 percent in the last two decades on college campuses, and that means that salaries for faculty get squeezed out and that financial aid gets squeezed out.

So, a great deal of money on the campuses is migrating to the **periphery**, rather than the core. And faculty salaries are not rising nearly as fast as they might. Time spent with students by individual faculty is actually going down. The number of contact hours goes down, and the amount of work that students are expected to do also falls.

Gross: You say in your book that about half of all students are walking away from college with huge debts now. That's a lot.

Matthews: Yes, they are, and people are willing to risk everything because the price of not going to college means a life of poverty and no chance of advancement. The degree has become absolutely necessary.

Gross: You say there's a **two-tiered** system at the universities now. The top colleges could sell every seat many times over, and the other 95 percent of the colleges can't afford to be selective. Describe more what this two-tiered system is like now.

Matthews: The name-brand campuses are very much in charge these days, and a two-tier universe is clearly forming: 50 or so extremely rich schools, and then everybody else—the other 1,500 American campuses—campuses of permanent abundance and campuses of grinding scarcity is increasingly the norm. Very little middle ground for everybody else. I mean, we're still the world's higher education superpower, and the U.S. is still the great location of **second or third or seventh-chance learning**. You never know when somebody will take to higher education or how or why.

(continued on next page)

Chivas Regal a well-known and very expensive brand of Scotch

pedigree an impressive line of ancestors; usually refers to animals such as racehorses and show dogs

periphery edge

two-tiered having two levels

second-, third-, seventh-chance learning opportunities for education outside the traditional direct high-school-to-college path

(continued from previous page)

And the campus population reflects that these days. Only one in five under-graduates in America now fits the traditional profile of being under twenty-two, living full-time on campus, attending full-time. The American campus population is increasingly female, adult, part-time, and in debt.

Gross: Can you give us a sense of the range of policies you found at colleges on admissions policies for minority students?

Matthews: Colleges are desperate to have minority students, and they're thrilled when minority students apply.

Gross: What do you mean, they're desperate to have minority students?

Matthews: Because the number of minorities applying to higher education is actually falling, and with the **affirmative action** crisis, it's falling faster. So colleges want, passionately want, middle-class black kids, middle-class Hispanic kids, middle-class Asian kids—someone with the mixed-race student or the mixed-background student is **the rage** now.

If they can pay their way, that's perfect. That's the ideal student. You get into real trouble when you have smart kids with no family assets applying, because financial aid is getting very tight. It used to be that colleges would invest in poor smart kids, and try to get them through, because in the end, they more than repaid the investment. But now, increasingly, it's pay your own way.

Gross: You say that colleges really prize students who have mixed ethnic background. Is that because the colleges believe in multiculturalism? Or is there something else on the agenda here?

Matthews: Oh, couple of reasons. One is that colleges can get far more federal money if they admit minorities. A minority student is an excellent business proposition. You can get three to five dollars back in federal funds without ever touching your endowment if you admit one or if you admit 200.

Gross: Is this only if you are a state school?

Matthews: Yes, yeah, administrators like that. Another reason to admit minority students is that colleges do have quite a sincere commitment these days to diversity. They've seen that it works in their endowment portfolios, and they're coming 'round to the idea that it works in their student bodies as well.

Gross: A lot of people are complaining that academic standards have declined on the campus. Did you find that to be true?

Matthews: The debate over what an educated person should know is fascinating, but it's also a little off-topic, because what's really declining is the number of hours that students put into classwork.

In the earliest—quite a striking drop—in the early '60s, the average student spent about sixty hours a week in class and doing class assignments. These days, it hovers around twenty-nine hours, leaving a great deal of time to either get into trouble or work like mad to pay their tuition bills. But for both faculty and under-graduates, college is increasingly a part-time operation, and that's led to enormous changes on the campus.

affirmative action programs designed to improve educational and employment opportunities to groups that have traditionally been excluded, such as African-Americans, Latinos, and women

the rage popular

(continued on next page)

(continued from previous page)

Gross: Are you teaching on the university level now?

Matthews: I teach in the graduate program at New York University in the Department of Journalism and Mass Communication, and I find that the students are very cautious, very worried about careers, very worried about survival. They've taken on enormous debt. It's a risk as great as any immigrant getting on a ship and coming to America in the nineteenth century. They've staked everything they own—all their future earnings—on a $40,000 or $50,000 investment in higher education because many of them are from families that can't help very much.

And so, yes, they could ask their parents to take out a third mortgage on the home, but they're often not willing to. And so, students are facing the world at twenty-five or twenty-eight, with debts that they know they won't pay off 'til they're fifty.

Gross: Does that put extra responsibility on your shoulders, as their teacher?

Matthews: Yes, it does, and it's interesting because they're getting increasingly harder to teach. I find—I've been teaching for almost fifteen years now, and I find that the effect of television is genuine, especially in the departments where I've taught: history, American studies, English, journalism.

The students are bright. They're ambitious, and they know the world almost entirely from the screen instead of the page. And so, when students aren't from a print culture anymore, it changes the way the university thinks about itself and what it teaches.

It's interesting: If you want a shock, you should ask any student at any college just to read a page of nineteenth-century prose. If you want another shock, give them one fragment from any episode of **"Gilligan's Island,"** and they will identify it perfectly, explain the context, explain the characterization, and explain how it fits into the entire flow of the series and the significance of the director.

Gilligan's Island a television comedy series popular in the late 1960s; it can still be seen in syndication on many television stations today

They're completely visually oriented and it makes articulation very, very difficult for them. On the other hand, students understand and love computing in ways that the faculty often don't. Except for very, very young, or very, very innovative faculty, most college professors are terrified of machinery and they're terrified of change. They often have to have media services come to their lectures to push "play" on the video.

And so, you have two cultures—student and faculty—moving apart from each other at much greater speed than anytime in the last 500 years.

Gross: Anne Matthews, thank you very much for talking with us.

Discussion Questions

1. What does Gross mean by the "pedigree" of a degree? How important do you think this is?

2. How many hours a week do you spend on schoolwork? Do you have a job that takes time away from your schoolwork? Do you think financial pressures affect your academic performance?

Many students have difficulty adjusting to university life. Lecture classes in huge auditoriums often present problems. The following is a description of how some students might feel on the first day in this kind of class.

Lives on the Boundary [excerpt]
Mike Rose

The students are taking their seats in a large auditorium, moving in two streams down the aisles, entering from a side exit to capture seats in the front. You're a few minutes late and find a seat somewhere in the middle. There are a couple of hundred students around you and in front of you, a hundred or so behind. A youngish man walks onto the stage and lays a folder and a book on the **podium**. There are track lights above him, and in back of him, there's a system of huge blackboards that rise and descend on rollers in the wall. The man begins talking. He raises his voice and taps the podium and sweeps his hand through the air. Occasionally, he'll turn to the moving boards and write out a phrase or someone's name or a reference to a section of the textbook. You begin writing these things down. He has a beard and smiles now and then and seems wrapped up in what he's talking about.

This is Introductory Sociology. It's one of the courses students can elect to fulfill their general education requirements. The catalogue said that Introductory Sociology would deal with "the characteristics of social life" and "the processes of social interaction." It also said that the course would cover the "tools of sociological investigation," but that came last and was kind of general and didn't seem too important. You're curious about what makes people tick and curious, as well, about the causes of social problems, so a course on social interaction sounded interesting. You filled Sociology 1 in on some cards and sent them out and eventually got other cards back that told you were enrolled. "These are social facts that are reflected in the interpretations we make of them," says the man on the stage and then extends his open hand toward the audience. "Now this is not the place to rehearse the arguments between **Kantian idealists and Lockean realists**, but . . ." You're still writing down, ". . . reflected in the interpretations we make of them . . ." and he continues, "But let us stop for a moment and consider what it means when we say 'social fact.' What is a fact? And in considering this question, we are drawn into **hermeneutics**." He turns to write that last word on the board, and as he writes, you copy it down in your notes. He refers the class to the textbook, to a "controlling **metaphor**" and to "**microanalyses**"—and as you're writing this down, you hear him stressing "**constructivist** interpretations" and reading a quotation from somebody and concluding that "in the **ambiguity** lies the richness."

People are taking notes and you are taking notes. You are taking notes on a lecture you don't understand. You get a phrase, a sentence, then the next loses

podium stand used to support a speaker's book or notes

Kantian idealists and Lockean realists two groups of philosophers with opposing views

hermeneutics the branch of knowledge that deals with theories of interpretation

metaphor a thing considered as representative of some other thing, for example, *the stars in her eyes*

microanalyses examination of very small samples or very small areas of an object

constructivism a philosophical viewpoint

ambiguity ability to be understood in more than one way

(continued on next page)

(continued from previous page)

you. It's as though you're hearing a conversation in a crowd or from another room—out of phase, muted. The man on the stage concludes his lecture and everyone **rustles** and you close your notebook and prepare to leave. You feel a little strange. Maybe tomorrow this stuff will clear up. Maybe by tomorrow, this will be easier. But by the time you're in the hallway, you don't think it will be easier at all.

rustle make series of small sounds, typically used to describe things such as leaves or papers

Discussion Questions

1. What kind of problems is the student having while listening to the lecture?
2. Have you ever had this kind of experience? If so, how did you handle it?

READINGS FOR UNIT FIVE

This excerpt comes from **How the García girls lost their accents**, *a novel about a family named García de la Torre, who moves from the Dominican Republic to New York in the 1960s. The story is told from the perspective of the four daughters, who are children when they immigrate. This particular excerpt describes their lives after they have been in the United States for a number of years, especially their experiences in high school and college.*

A Regular Revolution
Julia Alvarez

For three-going-on-four years Mami and Papi were on green cards, and the four of us shifted from foot to foot, waiting to go home. Then Papi went down for a trial visit, and a revolution broke out, a minor one, but still.

He came back to New York reciting the Pledge of Allegiance, and saying, "I am given up, Mami! It is no hope for the Island. I will become *un dominican-york*." So, Papi raised his right hand and swore to defend the Constitution of the United States and we were here to stay.

dominican-york a combined reference to Dominican and New York

You can believe we sisters wailed and paled, whining to go home. We didn't feel we had the best the United States had to offer. We had only second-hand stuff, rental houses in one **red-neck** Catholic neighborhood after another, clothes at

red-neck *(slang)* an insult referring to unsophisticated, white farm laborers

(continued on next page)

(continued from previous page)

Round Robin, a black and white TV **afflicted** with wavy lines. **Cooped up** in those little suburban houses, the rules were as strict as for Island girls, but there was no island to make up the difference. Then a few weird things happened. Carla met a **pervert**. At school, epithets ("spic," "greaseballs") were hurled our way. Some girlfriend of Sandi's got her to try a Tampax and Mami found out. Stuff like that, and soon she was writing away to preparatory schools (all-girl ones) where we would meet and mix with the "right kind" of Americans. We ended up at school with the **cream of the** American **crop**, the **Hoover** girl and the **Hanes** twins and the **Scott** girls and the **Reese** kid who got incredible **care packages** once a week. You wouldn't be as **gauche** as to ask, "hey are you related to the guy who makes vacuum cleaners?" (You could see all those attachments just by the way Madeline Hoover turned her nose up at you.) Anyhow, we met the right kind of Americans all right, but they didn't exactly mix with us.

We had our own kind of fame, mostly on the rich girls' supposition and our own silence. Garcia de la Torre didn't mean a thing to them, but those brand-named beauties simply assumed that, like all third world foreign students in boarding schools, we were filthy rich and related to some dictator or other. Our privilege **smacked of** evil and mystery whereas theirs came in recognizable panty hose packages and candy wrappers and vacuum cleaner bags and Kleenex boxes.

But hey, we might be fish out of water but at least we had **escaped the horns of our dilemma to a silver lining**, as Mami might say. It was a long train ride up to our prep school in Boston, and there *were* guys on that train. We learned to **forge** Mami's **signature** and went just about everywhere, to dance weekends and football weekends and snow sculpture weekends. We could kiss and not get pregnant. We could smoke and no great aunt would smell us and **croak**. We began to develop a taste for the American teenage good life, and soon, Island was **old hat**, man. Island was the hair-and-nails crowd, chaperones, and icky boys with all their **macho** strutting and unbuttoned shifts and hairy chests with gold chains and teensy gold crucifixes. By the end of a couple of years away from home, we had more than adjusted.

And of course, as soon as we had, Mami and Papi got all worried they were going to lose their girls to America. Things had calmed down on the Island and Papi had started making real money in his office up in the Bronx. The next decision was obvious: we four girls would be sent summers to the Island so we wouldn't lose touch with *la familia*. The **hidden agenda** was marriage to homeland boys, since everyone knew that once a girl married an America, those grandbabies came out jabbering in English and thinking of the Island as a place to go get a suntan.

The summer plans met with annual resistance from all four of us. We didn't mind a couple of weeks, but a *whole* summer? "Have you got anything better to do?" Mami questioned. Like yes, like *yes* we did, if she and Papi would only let us do it. But working was **off-limits**. (A boss hiring a young girl was after one thing only. Never mind if his name was Hoover.) Summer time was family time. Big time

(continued on next page)

---

afflicted troubled
cooped up trapped

pervert a person who engages in strange sexual behavior

cream of the crop the best
Hoover, Hanes, Scott, Reese names of rich American families, whose companies manufacture panty-hose, vacuum cleaners, paper products, and candy
care packages gifts sent from home to children staying at school or camp, usually containing sweets
gauche awkward; tactless

smacked of suggested

escaped the horns of our dilemma to a silver lining *the girls' mother, whose English is not the best, mixes up two English expressions; what she means is that the girls went from a bad situation to a better one*
forge a signature copy it dishonestly
croak *(slang)* die
old hat *(slang)* old, familiar and, therefore, of little interest
macho *(slang) from Spanish machismo, which means* male pride

hidden agenda real purpose

off-limits forbidden

(continued from previous page)

family time, a whole island of family, here a cousin, there a cousin, everywhere we turned a kissing cousin was **puckering up** at us.

Winters whenever one of us got **out of line**, Mami and Papi would march out the old "Maybe what you need *right now* is some time back home to help set you straight." We'd shape up pretty quick, or pretend to. Sometimes the parents **upped the ante**. It wouldn't be just the bad daughter who'd be shipped back, but *all four girls.*

By the time the three oldest were in college—we all started out at the same all-girls one, of course—we had devised as sophisticated and complicated a code and **underground** system as Papi had when he and his group plotted against the dictator. The parents' habit was to call on Friday or Saturday nights around ten right before the **switchboard** closed. We took turns "on duty" to catch those calls. But Mami and Papi were like *psychics.* They *always* directed the first call to the missing daughter, and when she wasn't in, they'd ask to talk to another missing daughter. The third, on-duty daughter would get the third call, in which the first question would be, "Where are your sisters?" At the library studying or in so-and-so's room getting tutored on her calculus. We kept most things from the old people, but sometimes they **caught on** and then we rotated the **hot seat**.

Fifi was on for smoking in the bathroom. (She always ran the shower as if smoking were a noisy activity whose hullabaloo she had to drown out.)

Carla was on for experimenting with hair removal cream. (Mami threw a fit, saying that once you get started on that road, there was no stopping—the hairs would grow back thicker and uglier each time. She made it sound like drinking or drugs.)

Yoyo was on for bringing a book into the house, *Our Bodies, Our Selves.* (Mami couldn't quite **put her finger on** what it was that bothered her about the book. I mean, there were no men in it. The pictures all celebrated women and their bodies, so it wasn't technically about sex as she had understood it up to then. But there were women "exploring what their bodies were all about" and a whole unit on lesbians. Things, Mami said, examining the pictures, to be ashamed of.)

Sandi was on when a visiting aunt and uncle dropped in for a visit at college early Sunday morning. (She wasn't back yet from her Saturday night calculus tutorial.)

It was a regular revolution: constant **skirmishes**. Until the time we took open aim and won, and our summers—if not our lives—became our own.

puckering up preparing to kiss
out of line behaving badly

upped the ante *this term comes from poker; it means they increased the possible penalty*

underground hidden

switchboard an old method of connecting a telephone call to individual rooms at a hotel, school, office, etc.

caught on figured (it) out
(on the) hot seat an uncomfortable position of responsibility

put (her) finger on say specifically

skirmish small battle

Discussion Questions

1. In the beginning of the excerpt, the girls were begging to return to the Dominican Republic. By the end, they viewed going back as a punishment. Why did they change their minds?

2. How did the parents' views change during this period?

At one time or another, most people find that their ideas differ from their parents' ideas. This is especially true when the parents have grown up in one culture and their children in another, and misunderstandings often result. This reading consists of several letters from Asian-American high school and college students asking for advice about problems they are having with their parents.

Dear Diane: I'm 17 and have two brothers, one 19, the other 15. My parents let the two of them do whatever they want. They can stay out after school and go out in the evenings. They can even have girlfriends.

With me, it's totally the opposite. Whenever I go out (which isn't too often), **I get the third degree.** My parents ask me about my friends, especially the guys, about where I've been, and where I'm going.

This double standard stinks. It's so unfair. What do you think?

get the third degree be asked lots of questions as if you were a criminal

Double Standard Victim

Dear Double Standard Victim: The double standard—one for guys, and a different one for girls—is definitely unfair, but it would probably be easier to change your sex than change your parents' attitudes about it. This has gone on for centuries and your parents are just two of the millions of Asians who believe in and **perpetuate** this practice. They all believe(d) that girls had to be protected in social situations so that their purity would remain intact. That would make them acceptable in marriage. After all, they argue, girls can get pregnant, but guys can't. And if a girl becomes pregnant, who's going to want to marry her?

perpetuate continue

On a more serious note, however, you can take a few steps to try to convince your folks to relax their hold on you. Show them that you are a responsible person and can make sound decisions about your friends and activities.

For instance, bring your friends—guys and girls—home so your parents can meet and get acquainted with them. If you go out with people they know personally, they'll feel less anxious. Give your folks a detailed schedule of your plans for the evening, and tell them who else will be there. Phone in to inform them if you're going to come home late—which hopefully won't be too often.

If you can, enlist your brothers' help. Perhaps you can go out in groups of which your brothers are also a part. Or have them talk with your parents.

The mountain you've chosen to move is an exceptionally large one, but it can be moved with a lot of work. So be patient: it takes time to retrain parents.

Dear Diane: After living at home for the first year of college, my folks finally agreed to let me move to a dormitory. As part of the bargain though, they made me promise to come home every weekend and on holidays. I'm trying my best to **live up to this promise,** but sometimes it's hard.

live up to this promise keep this promise

There are times when I would prefer to just stay in the dorm with my friends. If I have to keep going home every week, I'm still just a kid who hasn't left home.

(continued on next page)

(continued from previous page)

My friends are more independent and only go home on special occasions. How can I convince them to loosen the ties?

Fed Up

Dear Fed Up: The original agreement involved their promise to let you live away from home and your promise to come home and visit. Thus, unless both of you agree to change the terms, you're stuck with parents who miss you so much that they want to see you as often as they can; and they're stuck with a daughter who wants independence from home. As is true with most agreements, you can **mutually** change terms, and maybe now is a good time. Since you have tried to live up to your promise in the past, they may be willing to listen to your request for a change now. Be prepared to offer them a specific alternative, including exactly how often you would visit. Maybe you can replace some of the weekly visits with a phone call to check in.

> **mutually** equally; one toward the other

Your parents don't want to lose you, so you're going to have to be patient with them as they slowly become accustomed to your lengthier absences from home. In your attempt to be more independent, don't go overboard and turn away your parents.

Remember, both of you need to agree to the changes—especially if you wish your parents to continue their support of your stay in the dorm.

Dear Diane: I'm a high school senior and, like with many of my friends, my main problem is my parents. They accept nothing except straight "A's" from me. Last report card I got a "B" in English and they immediately asked me why I only got a "B," and why couldn't I have gotten a higher grade. They're so critical of me. I can't remember a single time when they have told me they were proud of me or that I did a good job. I'm getting so discouraged. What can I do to get them to change?

Discouraged Student

Dear Discouraged: You have a problem in common with almost all the Asian students in America. Your parents demand a lot from you, but when you deliver it to them, they act as if it was nothing special and that you should have done it anyway.

It would be nice to have parents who can give you support and praise for your achievements. Many Asian parents, however, aren't used to acting like that. Their wanting you to be "perfect" is their way of showing their love and their concern for you. In some traditional Asian cultures, it was considered bad luck to give your child too much praise because you might draw attention and the **envy** of the gods, who would then steal your child or cause her to fail next time. Maybe your parents believe they are keeping you safe. Or, maybe they're hoping you won't become **conceited** and instead will keep trying to improve.

> **envy** jealousy

> **conceited** having too high an opinion of oneself

Whatever their reason, develop your own internal set of standards. If you know that you did your best, then whether or not you get "A's" and whether or not you get praise won't be as important.

(continued on next page)

(continued from previous page)

However, if you would still like your parents to recognize your achievements a little more, have a **frank** talk with them. Let them know how discouraged you're becoming because of their seeming lack of support. Explain to them that, if every once in a while they would say how proud they are of you, or if they would periodically **pat you on the back**, you'd be able to do more and feel better about doing it. They may not be aware of how their actions, or inaction, affect you.

Be patient with them, though; this is a whole new area for them, and they're going to have to learn some totally new behavior. While you're at it, when they do something nice, try giving them some encouragement, too. For instance, if they pat you on the back, give them a hug in appreciation.

Good luck.

frank direct; honest

pat you on the back express praise or satisfaction for something you have done

Discussion Questions

1. Summarize in a few words the issue presented by each letter.
2. Do you think the responses are helpful? Why or why not?

LITERARY CREDITS

Ali, Mohammed. "Blacks Can Be Racist, Too." by Mohammed N. Ali, from *Essence*, May 1994. Reprinted with the permission of Mohammed N. Ali.

Alvarez, Julia. "*A Regular Revolution*" from *How the Garcia Girls Lost Their Accents*. Copyright © 1991 by Julia Alvarez. Published by Plume, an imprint of Dutton Signet, a division of Penguin USA and originally in hardcover by Algonquin Books of Chapel Hill. Reprinted by permission of Susan Bergholz Literary Services, New York. All rights reserved.

Appleby, Drew. "Faculty and Student Perceptions of Irritating Behavior in the Classroom." Reprinted from *Journal of Staff, Program, and Organization Development*, v. 8, n. 1. 1990, New Forums Press.

Batstone, David. "Minefields: MiningCo.com Is Digging for Online Gems So That You Don't Have To." From the April, 1999 issue of *Business 2.0*. Reprinted with permission of Business 2.0.

Children's Britannica. "Advertising," an excerpt *from Children's Britannica*. © 1999 Encyclopaedia Britannica, Inc.

Clark, David. "E-mail Smiles and Other Basic Netiquette," from *Student's Guide to the Internet*, by David Clark. Copyright © 1995. Reprinted with the permission of Macmillan Computer Publishing USA, a division of Pearson Education.

Don Coleman Ad. Reprinted with permission from Tom Fox, Director of Community Relations for Don Coleman Advertising, Inc.

Colón, Jesus. "Little Things Are Big," from *A Puerto Rican in New York and Other Sketches*. 1961. Reprinted with permission from International Publishers Company.

Congressional Quarterly Researcher. "Black-Asian Tensions." Republished with permission of Congressional Quarterly, Inc., 1414 22nd St. NW, Washington, DC, 20037. "Black Asian Tensions," *Congressional Quarterly Researcher*, Dec. 13, 1991. Reproduced by permission of the publisher via Copyright Clearance Center, Inc.

———. "Hate Crimes." Republished with permission of Congressional Quarterly, Inc., 1414 22nd St. NW, Washington, DC, 20037. "Hate Crimes," *Congressional Quarterly Researcher*, Dec. 13, 1991. Reproduced by permission of the publisher via Copyright Clearance Center, Inc.

Cross, Donna Woolfolk. "Mediaspeak." From *Mediaspeak* by Donna Woolfolk Cross. Copyright © 1983 Donna Woolfolk Cross. Used by permission of Coward-McCann, Inc., a division of Penguin Putnam Inc.

Dugger, Celia. "For Many Immigrants, a Cultural Reluctance to Spare the Rod." Copyright ©1996 by the New York Times Co. Reprinted by permission.

Fawcett, Adrienne Ward. "Sunday Best" Becoming More of a Ritual. Reprinted with permission from the Feb. 14, 1994 issue of *Advertising Age*. Copyright, Crain Communications, Inc. 1994.

Fryer, Bronwyn. "Sexism and Kids' Software." From the December, 1995 issue of PC WORLD.
Reprinted with the permission of PC WORLD Communications, Inc.

"Intimate Strangers." From *Time*, special issue, Spring, 1995.
© 1995 Time Inc. Reprinted by permission.

JMCT Ad.
Reprinted with permission from JMCT Publicidad.

Lewis, Sydney. "A Totally Alien Life Form: Teenagers."
Copyright © 1996 "A Totally Alien Life Form: Teenagers" by Sydney Lewis. Reprinted by permission of The New Press.

Matthews, Anne.
Interview by Terry Gross, May 20, 1997. *Fresh Air*®. WHYY, Inc. and Fresh Air® with Terry Gross.

Mosaica Ad.
Reprinted with permission from Mosaica and Kang and Lee Advertising.

Neill, Michael and John Maier Jr. "Lotion Voyage." From the November 29, 1993 issue of *People* © 1993 Time Inc.

Thanks to *The Newbury House Dictionary of American English*, First Edition, for providing definitions for the following words: *advice, bathroom* (usage notes), *differences, different, information,* and *insist.*

Peart, Karen. "English Spoken Here."
From *Scholastic Update*, November 15, 1996 issue. Copyright © 1996 by Scholastic Inc. Reprinted by permission of Scholastic Inc.

————. "Hardship and Dreams."
From *Scholastic Update*, November 15, 1996 issue. Copyright © 1996 by Scholastic Inc. Reprinted by permission of Scholastic Inc.

Pollack, Andrew. "Japan's Newest Young Heartthrobs Are Sexy, Talented and Virtual."
Copyright ©1996 by the New York Times Co. Reprinted by permission.

Quittner, Joshua. "No Privacy on the Web."
From the June 2, 1997 issue of *Time*.
© 1997 Time Inc. Reprinted by permission.

Rose, Mike. *Lives on the Boundary* excerpted from *Lives on the Boundary: The Struggles and Achievements of America's Underprepared* by Mike Rose. Copyright © 1989 by Mike Rose.
Reprinted with the permission of The Free Press, a Division of Simon and Schuster, Inc.

University of Illinois at Chicago Financial Aid Application.
Permission granted by the Intellectual Property Office.

Excerpts from *Dear Diane: Letters from Our Daughters*, **Letters 1, 3, and 14.** 1983.
Reprinted with permission of Asian Women United of California.